ALCOHOL AND THE FAMILY

Alcohol and the Family

EDITED BY JIM ORFORD AND JUDITH HARWIN

CROOM HELM
London & Sydney

ST. MARTIN'S PRESS
New York

, ƽ

© 1982 Jim Orford and Judith Harwin
Croom Helm Ltd, Provident House, Burrell Row,
Beckenham, Kent BR3 1AT
Croom Helm Australia Pty Ltd, First Floor,
139 King Street, Sydney, NSW 2001, Australia
Reprinted 1984

British Library Cataloguing in Publication Data

Alcohol and the family.
 1. Alcoholism – Addresses, essays, lectures
 2. Family – Addresses, essays, lectures
 I. Orford, Jim II. Harwin, Judith
 362.2'92   HV5132
 ISBN 0-7099-0473-8

All rights reserved. For information, write:
St. Martin's Press, Inc., 175 Fifth Avenue, New York, NY 10010
First published in the United States of America in 1982

Library of Congress Cataloging in Publication Data
Main entry under title:

Alcohol and the family.

 Bibliography: p. 266.
 Includes indexes.
 1. Alcoholics – Family relationships – Addresses,
essays, lectures. I. Orford, Jim. II. Harwin, Judith.
HV5132.A43   362.8'2   82-50090
ISBN 0-312-01706-5   AACR2

Printed and bound in Great Britain by
Billing and Sons Limited, Worcester

CONTENTS

Preface

PREFACE

As long ago as 1804, Thomas Trotter included amongst his prescriptions for the treatment of alcohol addiction, the statement: 'The good sense and management of an amiable wife, we know, will often accomplish wonders.'

Trotter was perhaps more preoccupied with disease and disorder than we hope we have been in compiling this book. He also made the assumption, still mistakenly made to this day, that the excessive drinker is almost always the husband and the spouse the wife, but he was clearly aware of the danger of neglecting the family. We have ourselves researched and practised in the area of alcohol problems and the family and we were delighted to be approached by the Alcohol Education Centre (London) to edit this book. We feel its appearance at this time requires no special justification. We are persuaded that the family is amongst the principal settings in which the consumption of alcohol is both enjoyed and restrained, and that it constitutes the most important natural resource for the prevention and control of excessive consumption. As the family is our society's main source of social support, and alcohol its chief recreational drug, the field of overlap between the two is bound to be of the utmost practical and theoretical importance.

The bias of our own work has been towards the abnormal rather than the normal, and we have made a conscious effort to broaden the perspective in this book by including chapters on alcohol and the family in history, in literature, in everyday social life and in law. Some may question putting literature and history alongside apparently more rigorously scientific material from the behavioural and social sciences. We think, on the contrary, that most readers will agree with Ryle who in *The Concept of Mind* was firmly of the view that psychology was broader than the academic discipline of that name, and would agree with us that our understanding is strengthened by drawing on the insights of the arts and humanities.

Despite our efforts at breadth, we realise that there must be many potential aspects of this subject which we have neglected. We are aware, for example, that all our contributors are from Britain or the United States. Our understanding of alcohol and the family would undoubtedly be strengthened by knowing far more about countries in which our own assumptions about both the use of alcohol and the nature of the family may not hold.

We would like to acknowledge the following individuals who have given us great help in preparing the manuscript: Jill Darling, Christina Thomas, Diane Harding and Beryl Skinner. Also we should like to acknowledge the debt we owe to former and present colleagues at the Addiction Research Unit and Maudsley Alcohol Pilot Project, London, the Department of Social Science and Administration, London School of Economics, and Departments of Psychology at the University of Exeter and Exe Vale Hospital, Exeter, who have provided the stimulating work environments in which we developed an interest in this subject and were able to plan and organise this book. Finally we would like to pay special thanks to Mike Lewington for preparing the indexes.

Jim Orford, Exeter and Judith Harwin, London

1 ALCOHOL AND THE FAMILY IN HISTORY

Norman Longmate

If nouns in the English language were assigned genders, the word 'alcohol' would surely be masculine, as it is in French and German. Historically, drunkenness has been almost exclusively a male preserve. When alcoholism ravages a family the cause may, of course, be a lonely or harassed wife furtively seeking comfort from the hidden gin bottle, but it is far more likely to be the husband who regularly stops off for a drink, which speedily turns into half a dozen, on the way home.

Alcoholic women have no doubt always existed, but only as a rare phenomenon, perhaps because it has traditionally been their role on social occasions to bring in the bottles rather than help empty them. The physical difficulty faced by women, before the days of separate incomes and sexual equality, of obtaining drink has been reinforced by social attitudes. However unjustly, drunkenness among women has always been regarded with horror and disgust instead of tolerance. One of the earliest laws of ancient Rome authorised a husband to kill his wife if he caught her committing adultery or drinking wine — offences regarded as striking equally at the marriage bond. Among the first women alcoholics must be the Roman matron starved to death by her relations, apparently with impunity, after she had been driven to pick the lock of the chest containing the keys to the wine cellar. Even later, in somewhat more tolerant times, a Roman woman convicted of drinking more 'than was needful for the preservation of her health' was sentenced to lose part of her dowry. Such comparative leniency had its effect. In the first century AD Seneca complained that the laws against women drinking were everywhere ignored and that the sex gloried in 'vying with the men and, if they can, in overcoming them' (Morewood, 1824) but this seems to have been an exaggeration, the cry of an outraged chauvinist rather than the serious comment of a reliable observer.

As for alcohol-addicted children, now the not infrequent subject of alarmist press reports, they are barely referred to until the eighteenth century, and then appear only as the unwitting, and at first unwilling, victims of irresponsible parents. The great and overwhelming 'drink problem' which has affected the family through the ages has been that of the alcoholic father.

Today alcohol, although on balance it has clearly given humanity far more pleasure and innocent recreation than it has done harm, is recognised as a potential solvent of the normal family ties and affections if taken to excess, weakening and ultimately perhaps destroying them. Until at least the eighteenth century, however, with the exception of the countries where Islam had taken root, the effect of drinking on the family was not so much dismissed as never considered. Far from being regarded as a threat to family life, it was accepted without question as an indispensable part of a normal diet. It served, in addition, other functions. In classical society wine was the natural concomitant of hospitality, the visitor being offered a welcoming glass as a matter of course, and at banquets and other festivities where inhibitions were discharged, it flowed in profusion: who ever heard of a 'dry' orgy? Throughout biblical times alcohol was recognised as having an acceptable, even respectable, place in everyday life, to the great embarrassment of Victorian anti-drink propagandists, who devoted much effort to rewriting Holy Writ to try to discredit what they labelled 'the devil in solution'. The testimony of both the Old and New Testaments is, however, perfectly clear to all but the most blinkered bigot. The dangers of excess are by no means concealed; a favourite theme of the painters of murals in medieval churches, offering an agreeable change from more uplifting themes, was the text 'Noah drank of the wine and was drunken'. Most references to alcohol were, however, 'neutral' or positively approving. The medicinal value of alcohol was recognised by Saint Paul in a famous text when he urged his disciple Timothy to take a little wine for his stomach's sake, while Christ himself strikingly endorsed the innocence of moderate drinking on festive occasions by his very first miracle, when he turned water into wine at the marriage at Cana.

In the British Isles, for the 1,500 years following the arrival of the Romans, the accepted guardian of public morality, the church, did not regard alcohol as posing any threat to the souls of the laity or to the stability of the family. Drunkenness on the part of the clergy was indeed condemned, for disciplinary reasons, but even here the general attitude was only mildly disapproving. The gloomy chronicler Gildas complained about the year 540 that 'Not only the laity but Our Lord's own flock and its shepherds . . . slumbered away their time in drunkenness as if they had been dipped in wine', but the penalty he recommended was far from draconian: 'If any monk through drinking too freely gets thick of speech so that he cannot join in the psalms he is to be deprived of his supper.' An early church synod laid down that any priest who got drunk before a service must do three days' penance, raised on a second offence to forty (French, 1884). But drinking by clerics off duty was not disapproved of. In the Middle Ages the village tavern was often kept by the parish priest, fulfilling his Christian duty to provide shelter for strangers.

The arrival of the Normans and the foundation of monasteries all over the country had also led to a vast increase in the consumption of wine, the vineyard being regarded in most abbeys as an amenity as essential as the fishpond. In the villages where almost all the population lived, drinking was as much a part of everyday life as those other three basic occupations of medieval society — tilling the soil, bearing arms and praying. The villein drank home-brewed ale, the lord and his attendant knights wine, the parish and monastic clergy whatever they could obtain. No taint of any kind attached to moderate drinking and very little to immoderate. Indeed throughout the Middle Ages it was church festivals, the only holidays the average villager was permitted, which provided the chief occasion for festal, as distinct from routine, drinking. 'Church ales' where all the liquor drunk was brewed by the church wardens and sold in aid of parish funds were, by the fifteenth century, a popular institution, fulfiling the role of the modern fete or jumble sale. Also popular were 'bride-ales', at which a bride might offer drink she had brewed herself in exchange for gifts of money.

By this time, too, other drinking customs which still affect our attitude to alcohol, by conferring on its consumption the respectability of a long-standing ritual, were also well established. 'Toasting', for example, though not the name, which has other origins, had been introduced by the Danes, as a protection against treachery when entertaining visitors: the guest whose health was being drunk was required to raise his dagger into view, thus preventing any sudden, treacherous attack. The buying of rounds of drinks, a practice which must at some time have forced almost everyone to consume, or at least pay for, more alcohol than they wanted, probably had its origins in a measure designed to encourage moderation — 'pin-drinking'. This involved inserting pegs in a goblet at fixed points so one could keep a strict check on one's drinking. Instead, however, it became a matter of social duty to drink as deep as one's neighbour and to pay one's share accordingly, and when the pins vanished the convention, later known as treating, survived.

By the end of the Middle Ages, around 1500, the practice of public control of the drink trade had clearly come to stay, but all the attempts to impose it so far had been designed to further the interests of the consumer not, like most such regulations since, to protect the rest of society or the vested interests of the manufacturer. Drinking, in other words, was a right to be protected not a privilege to be restricted. The potential value of liquor taxation as a source of revenue had also been discovered. The pioneer was King John who, around 1200, claimed one tun (about 250 gallons) of every cargo of imported wine carried aft of the mast. Later monarchs levied similar imposts and some parishes also levied a tax on innkeepers. Such measures were designed, however, solely to raise revenue or to protect domestic industries, not to discourage demand.

By the sixteenth century, which was to prove, to use a perhaps inappropriate word, a watershed in drinking history, the general pattern of alcohol consumption, and of attitudes to it, was clearly distinguishable. Alcoholic drinks were regarded primarily as everyday beverages, more palatable than water, and as innocuous morally. To offer a drink was the regular symbol of hospitality, while any celebration called for drinking to the borders of excess, if not beyond them. Addiction, and its consequences, posed no problem because they were not recognised and the rigid structure of medieval society, overwhelmingly rural, with every man in close view of his master, left few loopholes through which the would-be drunkard could slip to avoid notice. The nature of the drinks available was limited. Those who could afford it drank wine, either what would now be called table wine, or fortified wines resembling sherry, such as sack and malmsey. The common people settled for mead, based on honey, but already going out of fashion; cider, in the apple-growing areas; and above all, ale brewed from barley, but often enlivened with spices such as pepper. Ale was the predominant English drink, 'English' here being the correct term since in Scotland and Ireland it was gradually being challenged by 'usquebagh', of which the word 'whisky' is a corruption, meaning 'water of life'. The name is significant. The process of distilling spirits was understood by this time but was practised mainly by alchemists, who tended to attribute magical properties to them and who supposed that they might even be a form of the 'elixir of life' for which they were perpetually searching. Even when this illusion had been discarded, the sharp distinction between spirits, which have to be produced by the chemistry and ingenuity of man, and wine and beer, produced by the normal processes of nature and hence, it was believed, a gift of God, remained. It was to have lasting consequences in attitudes to drink, as will shortly be seen.

During the sixteenth century the Englishman's favourite tipple changed its flavour, if not its character, with the introduction from the

Low Countries of a new and sharper-tasting variety of ale, more accurately known as beer, though the two names then, and since, have tended to be used interchangeably. A famous rhyme recorded that

Hops, Reformation, bays and beer
Came to England all in one year

presumably 1531, when Henry VIII proclaimed himself Supreme Head of the Church, and hops, which give beer its distinctive taste, were soon being grown everywhere, while the vines in the abandoned monasteries withered and rotted. Wine-drinking also fell into disfavour for other reasons, for it was the favoured beverage of those Roman Catholic countries from which England had broken away. When, in 1555, Philip of Spain married Mary I, he tried to demonstrate that he was now a true Englishman by drinking beer instead of wine at their wedding feast.

Just as beer was establishing itself as the national drink, drunkenness became, for the first time, a matter for governmental concern. Contemporaries put the blame for what was suddenly perceived to be a public nuisance on that favourite scapegoat, the foreigner. 'As the English returning from the wars in the Holy Land brought home the foul disease of leprosy, so . . . the English returning from service in the Netherlands brought with them the foul disease of drunkenness', explained one pamphleteer. The sin of 'superfluity of drink', formerly provoking contempt, had become tolerated 'ever since we mixed ourselves with the Low Countries' (Winskill, 1881). The first major Licensing Acts were passed in this period, in 1552 and 1554, and they marked for the first time the recognition that the consumption of liquor in public required supervision. No common pattern of control was laid down but the justices in each area were given power to impose almost any conditions they liked on 'tippling-houses', including, for example, a ban on Sunday opening, or dancing, and they had total freedom to regulate hours. The really vital change was that alcohol was now treated differently from all other commodities. Previously anyone could sell it until he or his premises had caused some form of trouble and attracted the justices' attention. Now everyone, however blameless, had to obtain a licence from the justices to sell beer or wine at all, a licence which had to be renewed each year and could be refused at the justices' discretion.

The Licensing Act of 1552 does not seem to have been prompted by concern for the victims of drunkenness; the authorities were probably more concerned about would-be traitors meeting in the ale-houses than about potential wife-beaters and child neglecters. Persistent intoxica-tion was not considered a disease but a voluntary offence for which the best answer was a good whipping or public ridicule. A blatant offender might be sentenced to parade the streets in the 'drunkard's cloak', a barrel with holes cut in the sides.

The next major landmark in the country's drinking history was the popular discovery of spirits, which was rapidly attributed, like Tudor drunkenness, to pernicious foreign influence. Dutch gin was allegedly introduced into England by William III in 1688 and a flourishing home industry was soon producing an English variety, very different from the original but no less potent. In 1690 the government, hoping to create a market for low-grade corn in the distilleries, removed all restrictions on the sale and manufacture of this new product, with disastrous results. Gin shops sprang up everywhere, proclaiming in the classic words later recorded by Smollett, that one could 'be drunk for . . . one penny . . . dead drunk for twopence and have straw for nothing' (Smollett, 1758). The urban poor — it was in the towns and above all in London that the results of the new policy were so strikingly visible — embraced with en-thusiasm this means of escape from their toilsome, uncomfortable lives. Not merely did they drink more, but the consequences of their drink-ing could no longer be ignored. Drunken men and women reeled about the streets or littered the pavements; abandoned babies and children imposed new burdens on the ratepayers; and the magistrates observed a sudden increase in drink-related crime. As a result of drinking parents, reported a committee appointed by the Middlesex Sessions in 1735, infants were 'forced to beg whilst they are children and as they grow up learn to pilfer and steal'. One unnatural mother had even removed her baby daughter from the workhouse and had murdered her for the sake of the new clothes she had been given, selling them for one and four-pence to buy gin. But even where actual crime did not result, gin struck savagely at the family, as the same bench of magistrates protested to Parliament:

Unhappy mothers habituate themselves to these distilled liquors whose children are born weak and sickly and often looked shrivelled and old as they have had numbered many years. Others again daily give it to their children and learn them . . . even before they can go (i.e. walk), to taste and approve this certain destroyer (George, 1966).

In London at the peak of the gin period three children out of four died before they were five years old, while the mortality of 'parish infants', unwanted or orphaned creatures loved by no one, was even worse, reaching in some parishes the murderous level of 99 per cent – no doubt the poor babies were farmed out to gin-drinking foster mothers.

Such comments and statistics highlighted for the first time the threat which alcohol posed to the whole family. Hitherto drunkenness had been regarded as a specifically male indulgence, which affected a man's wife and children only indirectly. If women drank wine to excess in the eighteenth, or even the nineteenth, century, there is remarkably little reference to it in the literature, either factual or fictional. Beer, too, as it still is today, was regarded as primarily, if not exclusively, a male drink. Gin, however, was considered from the first to be 'a woman's drink', though precisely why the female palate should have rejected the robust flavour of ale and responded to the subtler and more ferocious one of gin remains obscure. By about 1750, however, there were brands on the market with such names as *Ladies' Delight* – a companion presumably to *Cuckold's Comfort*, intended for male consumption. Attacks on the gin-drinking habit, in contrast to those on wine, made much of the fact that it afflicted women at least as much as men and women were frequent and welcome customers at the 'gin-palace' while they would have been unwelcome intruders in the ale-house. As early as the 1720s, the chairman of one metropolitan bench of magistrates had warned that the 'excessive drinking of gin and other pernicious spirits' was 'destructive of the lives, families and trades' of those addicted to it, one of the earliest references to the family, as distinct from the individual, as alcohol-victim.

Faced by a public outcry, Parliament sought to backtrack and passed a whole series of amending laws, which veered from imposing a totally prohibitive duty on gin-sellers, which simply drove them literally underground, to a purely nominal one. Propagandists like Hogarth weighed in with works such as *Gin Lane*, which contrasted the squalid debauchery of that thoroughfare with the healthy joys to be found in *Beer Street*. By the end of the eighteenth century the worst excesses caused by gin-drinking were within bounds. But henceforward, when practised by the poorer classes, drinking had lost its innocence and drunkenness was no longer regarded as a private matter between a man and his conscience, but as one involving the whole of society.

It was, however, only the working man whose drinking was censured; among the upper and middle classes in society over-indulgence in alcohol was expected. Lord Carteret's government in the 1740s had been nicknamed 'the drunken administration' and Macaulay wrote of its head that 'driven from office he retired laughing to his books and his bottle'. Dr Johnson recalled in 1773 a time 'when all the decent people in Lichfield got drunk and every night and was not thought the worse of' (French, 1884). The fact that Johnson's biographer, Boswell, had been found dead drunk in the gutter the night before was a subject for jokes in court the following day as late as 1782, although there were beginning to be signs of an increased respect for sobriety even in the highest reaches of society. The Prince Regent, who could barely stand at his wedding in 1795, was the last English monarch to indulge on such a scale. In any case, however, the distinction between the classes in relation to alcoholic excess, so unjust at first sight, rested in reality on sound pragmatic principles. The rich man could afford his excesses and leave his family barely affected by them; the wife and child of the proletarian drunkard were constantly vulnerable.

It was being realised, too, by the beginning of the nineteenth century, that a man's liability to become a drunkard was almost in inverse proportion to his income. It was not the solid artisan with a regular income who frequented the public house — or at least who regularly drank too much there — but the ill-paid out-worker, scraping a bare living in his own home, the pedlar and the beggar. Later temperance reformers liked to argue that it was drink which made such people poor, but the truth was really the reverse; it was poverty which made them drink. As was to be remarked by a Victorian observer, the quickest way out of Ancoats, a notorious Manchester slum, was through the public house door.

By 1830 working-class drunkenness was recognised as a major problem with which Parliament would ultimately need to deal. The immediate aim of the socially-concerned of all parties was to wean the working man away from his addiction to spirits, which he consumed to get drunk, back to what one leading politician described as 'a moral species of beverage', namely beer which, it was believed, he drank to quench his thirst and refresh himself. The result was the famous Beer Act of 1830, the effects of which were to be immortalised by the Reverend Sydney Smith a fortnight after it came into operation: 'The Sovereign people are in a beastly state. Everybody is drunk. Those who are not singing are sprawling' (Pearson, 1948). The Beer Act marked a reversal of the established principle of strictly controlling the right to sell alcohol, for it allowed anyone, irrespective of his premises or character, to sell beer on payment of a two-guinea fee. It was, if one believed that beer was as natural and harmless an article of diet as bread, a perfectly logical piece of legislation, but the result was to extend to this drink, too, the same associations of guilt which gin had already acquired. Some of the agitation against the beershops was exaggerated, a product of that desire to interfere with poorer people's pleasure so typical of Victorian England. But they undoubtedly made it easier to spend money on drink in preference to other articles, especially in rural areas where the nearest alehouse might be miles away, for the 'drier' the village the more attractive it was to the enterprising. In one Essex hamlet five out of fifty cottages obtained beerhouse licences, while one brewer boasted that the chain of beershops he had set up throughout Hampshire would introduce the joys of drinking to labourers who 'hardly know the taste of beer' until it became to them 'as it has to the inhabitants of towns, almost a necessary of life' (Long mate, 1968).

Just as with the Gin Act, Parliament soon had second thoughts and the freedom of the beerhouses was rapidly limited by a series of amending Acts, which left them almost as restricted as the ordinary public house. But their brief years of glory helped to draw attention to the effects of drink upon the family, especially outside the towns, where people had become accustomed to seeing half-starved children hanging about the public houses on Saturday nights or stepping over the recumbent figures of drunks as more sober citizens made their way to church on Sunday morning. It came to be widely believed that drink was a major cause of poverty, as indeed it was, or even that it was the sole cause, which it emphatically was not. The period from 1834, when the first reformed Parliament met, to 1915, when the first really effective measures of liquor control were introduced, is the time when virtually everyone accepted that something needed to be done to protect the family from the effects of drink and alcohol tended to be assumed to be guilty until proved innocent.

In 1834 a Parliamentary Select Committee on Drunkenness reported that 'the vice of intoxication has been for some years past on the decline in the higher and middle ranks of society, but has increased . . . among the labouring classes' (Report of the Select Committee on Drunkenness, 1834). It proposed the abolition of the gin shop and ultimately a ban on manufacturing spirits, and the tightening up of the licensing system, along with such related reforms as a reduction in the duties on tea, coffee and sugar. These suggestions, which could have formed the basis for a rational licensing policy, were laughed out of existence by the House of Commons and the 'Drunken Committee' became a national joke.

In fact public opinion was beginning to undergo a massive and decisive change, from acceptance of drunkenness to concern about its effects. Much of the credit for this achievement belongs to the temperance movement which, for practical purposes, was founded in Preston in 1832 by Joseph Livesey, a self-made cheesemonger who knew at first hand how the poor lived. He initially renounced alcohol because it made him 'feel queer', but rapidly convinced himself and a growing circle of supporters that drink was primarily, if not solely, responsible for most of the ills of mankind, including poverty, ill-health and crime. There had been earlier societies whose members had committed themselves to not drinking spirits or to moderation in the use of wine and beer. Livesey recognised, however, that for the habitual drunkard there could be no middle way. It must be all or nothing. The first drink, temperance dogma soon insisted, was the fatal one and 'signing the pledge' should mean renouncing all alcohol in all circumstances, even, though not everyone accepted this, as medicine. The teetotallers, as they became known, soon dominated the whole movement. The old 'moderation, botheration' pledge, as its critics called it, along with such escape clauses as one which permitted drinking 'in extreme necessity', was laughed into oblivion, to be retained only by such compromise-minded bodies as the Church of England Temperance Society. One by one the dissenting churches, which then often provided an outlet for the oratory and activity of the more articulate and ambitious working men, who still lacked a vote, were won over. By 1850 it would have been a brave Congregationalist or Methodist or Quaker who offered a visitor a drink and the dissenting chapels provided the temperance missionaries with their first meeting halls and a ready-made network of supporters. After 1867, when the urban male householder acquired the franchise, the movement became politically formidable, for its great strength lay in the industrial cities, especially in the north, which were now well represented in the House of Commons. The voice of the nonconformist conscience was something to be listened to, if not heeded, and by 1870 it was overwhelmingly anti-drink.

The nonconformist churches were also the great recruiting ground for the Band of Hope, founded in Leeds in 1847. This organisation provided for children the sort of innocent recreation offered later by the Scouts and Guides and it bred a whole generation pledged never to drink, and to campaign against the hated enemy. It soon numbered its adherents literally in their millions and though no doubt many later lapsed, it formed a formidable propagandist force, and, in the long

term, a valuable source of legacies, which still provide the few surviving
temperance organisations with a worthwhile income. Children who did
not belong to the Band of Hope were reached by temperance lect-
urers and temperance tracts, masquerading as health education sylla-
buses, which indulgent ministers, eager to buy off the anti-drink lobby
with minor concessions, allowed into the schools. The essential message
preached was no longer that excess of alcohol was harmful but that
drinking itself was wrong. Alcohol, it was argued, was a mere aberra-
tion of nature, the product of corruption – i.e. fermentation – which
served no useful purpose at all, though a few soft-liners grudgingly con-
ceded that 'it is useful . . . to painters for varnish and paint' or 'in
museums to preserve specimens' (Ridge, 1894).

The temperance activists attacked incessantly on all fronts. The rum
ration in the Navy, the prescribing of wine by doctors, the serving of ale
in workhouses or public schools –'Beer', warned the school physican
of Rugby in 1891, 'starts a vice which is as infectious as measles'
(Dukes, 1891) – all came under persistent fire, often with visible results.
A money allowance was offered to sailors in place of the rum ration,
for example, as early as 1847; the London Temperance Hospital, where
no alcohol was prescribed, was opened in 1873; while by 1885 the
drink bill in most workhouses was almost nil and, a little later, school-
boys were going beerless to bed. Some of the campaigners were guilty
of ludicrous exaggeration. One teetotal speaker (who in 1842 led a
secession from the chapel of a Wesleyan minster who had refused to
preach teetotalism) declared that since 'four pints of beer would make
a man drunk . . . a half pint would make him half a quarter drunk,
consequently they were all drunkards'. Two of the movement's
'scholars' devoted years to producing *The Temperance Bible Commentary*, published in 1868, which proved to their satisfaction that whenever the Old or New Testament referred to wine approvingly, it actually
meant non-alcoholic grape juice (Lees and Burns, 1894). Another en-
thusiast had already, in 1863, put such a product on the market, after
earlier versions (according to one lapsed teetotaller in 1849) had produced 'colic and diarrhoea' along with moral uplift.

Joseph Livesey and his first supporters had placed their faith in
'moral suasion', i.e. persuading one individual after another to sign the
pledge, either because he was himself at risk or to encourage his weaker
brother, until the drink trade withered away from lack of customers.
Once it became clear, however, that this process was taking an unaccountably long time, the demand arose for stricter control, and ultimately the closing down by law, of the whole licensed trade. In 1853

the United Kingdom Alliance for the Suppression of the Traffic in all Intoxicating Liquors was founded and thereafter the temperance movement constantly campaigned for total prohibition – indeed, although it prudently keeps quiet about it, this remains its aim today. A popular immediate panacea was 'local option', under which the electorate in every district could vote to close all, or some, of the public houses there, and in 1880 the House of Commons actually voted, by 229 to 203, in favour of the principle, though it was never implemented. Where they were supported by other groups, however, such as the increasingly active sabbatarian movement, the teetotallers were more successful. In 1845 Parliament voted to close all public houses in Scotland on Sunday and a similar restriction, with some exceptions, was extended to Ireland in 1878, and to Wales, with no exceptions at all except those devised by Celtic hypocrisy, in 1882. (The English succumbed to tyranny less readily. An attempt in 1854 drastically to limit Sunday opening hours led to such serious riots that the Act was repealed within a year, though some restrictions remained.)

The temperance movement's greatest achievement, however, was to bring the whole question of alcohol abuse into the forefront of British politics. By 1870 the 'drink question' was one which no parliamentary candidate could afford to ignore, though opinion was increasingly becoming polarised on party lines, with the Conservatives standing up for the brewers and licensed victuallers (and, they asserted, the ordinary drinker) against the attacks of the Liberals, the spokesmen of the temperance movement. The leading parliamentary advocate of prohibition,and one of the rare aristocratic teetotallers, was the Liberal MP, Sir Wilfrid Lawson, 'the high priest of the water pump', but he had many competitors, for every member now had his own remedy for the universally acknowledged evil. 'Everybody has now a Licensing Bill', Lawson remarked in 1883. 'A man is looked upon as rather an inferior sort of fellow if he has not a licensing scheme.' In 1890 alone 25 such Bills were introduced, 14 of them on a single day. Few ever got any further. Though successive Liberal governments found themselves forced to introduce *some* legislation to keep their supporters quiet, comparatively little was accomplished except to alienate many non-teetotallers and lose the party at least one general election.

Even those who voted against changes in the law professed concern about intemperance. What had prompted this reaction? One cause was the increasing complexity of daily life and the growing dependence of every citizen on new technology. A drunken carter, who endangered no one but himself, could be tolerated but a drunken train driver or machine-minder was a universal menace. Increased interest in social work, both on the part of professionals and, more commonly, by midde-class mothers who ran sewing classes or similar activities for working-class women, had made many people aware how often it was drink which caused a family to cross the line which separated the 'deserving' from the 'undeserving' poor and had given faces to what were formerly mere statistics. Drink was constantly, though often inaccurately, quoted as a factor in the spread of epidemic diseases, such as cholera. But principal motive for the desire to tackle the problem of the drunken breadwinner was compassion. What decent person could listen unmoved to the Bishop of London describing how on a tour of the East End he had seen three children playing at keeping house? One child, acting the part of the father, reeled back from the public house, to attack the mother, until pulled away by another boy, in the role of the policeman.

It would be an exaggeration to say that the Victorians invented the family, but they certainly gave it a new significance. At the start of the nineteenth century children tended to be regarded as mere appendages of their parents, lacking any rights of their own, as the slow progress of the campaign against child labour in the factories testified. The average wife was little better placed; the conception of the family as a small community in which all the members had rights, as well as duties, had hardly been formulated. By about 1845, however, it had become widely accepted and sentimental rituals such as those associated with Christmas were spreading from the middle-class to poorer households. The same impulse which led to the outlawing of child chimney sweeps and to the creation of Dr Barnardo's shelter for the destitute, helped to focus attention on cruelty to children in their own homes, and here drink was clearly the major factor. It was not the home *broken* by drink which troubled the Victorians; few mothers and children could, after all, afford to leave even the most brutal husband and father. What did concern the philanthropists and reformers was the extent to which alcohol dissolved the normal bonds of paternal affection on which the respectable classes set such high store. The title of one pamphlet published in 1860 told its own story: *Ragged Homes and How to Mend Them*. What caused the ragged homes was, of course, drink; what mended them was 'Education, Temperance and Sanitary Science'.

It was the plight of the children of drunken parents which really captured the public imagination. In 1872 it had at last been made illegal to sell spirits for 'on' drinking to children under 16, but they could still be sent to the public house to fetch drinks for their parents and publicans often rewarded such 'child messengers' with sweets. 'On a recent Sunday morning', a police court missionary wrote in the *Wigan Observer* in 1897, 'from 11.20 to one o'clock I saw 164 children ranging from eight down to three years of age, go in a licensed house and come out with beer and sweets. Some of these went round the corner, looked at the sweets and sipped some of the beer' (Turner, 1950). The teetotallers also made the most of reports of children knocked down while slowly crossing the road — they did not dare to hurry for fear of a thrashing for spilling from the jug they were carrying — and eventually in 1901 the 'Anti-Sipping Act' made it illegal to sell drink for 'off' consumption to anyone under 14 except in sealed vessels. Under the 'Children's Act', in 1908, it was made illegal for such juveniles to enter a bar at all and it also became illegal to give alcohol, except as medicine, to any child under five — the final end of the Gin Lane era.

But the real danger to children, as everyone realised, came in their own home. A popular theme in temperance pamphlets was the danger of 'overlaying', with a sleeping infant being suffocated by a drunken mother, perhaps lying on top of the baby. Even more evocative was the famous song in which a poor little waif begged the publican to sell no more drink to her father — 'It makes him so strange and so wild.' This, for all its sentimentality, reflected a very real truth. There *were* families where the children were herded together under the kitchen table every Saturday night to try and protect them from father's violence when he came home fighting drunk. A wife with a broken nose or black eye on a Sunday morning hardly prompted comment and to watch the drunks fighting or being thrown out was a recognised Saturday night amusement in many towns. In the poorest areas, the crowded bars, busy pawn shops and bare, cheerless homes bore silent witness to the consequences of drinking and in 1899 a massive report by an all party Royal Commission on Licensing acknowledged that 'a gigantic evil remains to be remedied'. Its members were divided on what needed to be done and only the minority favoured a drastic reduction in the number of public houses and much shorter hours, but it was their recommendations which, in 1908, inspired the Liberal government's major Licensing Bill, which went as far as any such measure could to meet the teetotallers' demands, short of total prohibition. In the event the Bill was thrown out by the House of Lords, who claimed, with some reason, that they were acting for the ordinary working man, although the response of temperance sympathisers was different. The Archbishop of Canterbury commented that among the 'simple people

who perseveringly work in the back streets of our great towns . . .
schoolmasters, schoolmistresses, the nurses, the rescue workers . . .
there will be heavy hearts and heavy disappointment today' (Hansard,
1908).

Seven years later, with barely a protest, the licensed trade accepted
far more rigid restrictions than even the most pessimistic publicans had
ever contemplated. The outbreak of war in 1914 was rapidly followed
by complaints about newly-rich munitions and shipyard workers reeling
drunkenly about their work-places or sprawling in pubs when they
should have been working to save the nation. What concern for the
drunkard's family had failed to achieve in a century of agitation,
anxiety about delay in turning out the means to kill fellow human beings
accomplished overnight. The United Kingdom Alliance managed to
defeat a plan for the nation to buy out the licensed trade, protesting
that under it all hopes of prohibition would have to be abandoned, for
the public house might become 'a safe place for the wife and child to
go as well as for the man himself'. Lloyd George, with a war to win,
gave in to these fanatics, although for £250 million all breweries and
public houses could have become the nation's property, a fantastic bargain, while the profits would have made possible a permanent reduction
in taxation. If drink has cost the nation dear, so too has temperance.
Instead of full-scale nationalisation in 1915, a Liquor Control Board
was set up with authority to impose any rules it chose: limiting hours,
banning the sale of spirits, insisting that drink only be served with food,
raising the standard of accommodation in bars, even closing down all
the licensed premises in an area or running them itself. At the same time
the price of alcohol was raised and the strength of beer reduced, while
'treating' was banned. The effect of these changes was dramatic. The
consumption of alcohol dropped by more than half during the war, the
number of cases of drunkenness by 85 per cent. From being an everyday sight in most towns the drunk became a rare one, even in the
roughest areas.

Although the strictest of the wartime regulations were relaxed after
the war, the basic principles of short hours, including an afternoon
break, and high prices have remained the basis of British licensing law
ever since. In the allegedly permissive 1980s a law-abiding citizen is
still denied a drink after a country walk at 6.30 on a summer Sunday
evening, because sixty-five years ago a few irresponsible factory hands
in Glasgow and Carlisle overindulged and neglected their work.

Once concern for the family prompted a demand for reform. Now it
is used to limit the freedom of the law-abiding citizen. In 1960, when

the Conservatives proposed to extend opening hours at Sunday lunch-time the rump of the temperance movement, joining forces with the licensed trade, successfully prevented the change, on the ground that it would threaten family life, by ruining a million Sunday dinners. (A similar campaign, to prevent the sale of liqueur chocolates in sweet-shops on the grounds that it would breed up a generation of child alcoholics, failed.) In 1972 the last major study of the whole subject appeared, the Errol Report, which aimed to make the public house a place of civilised resort for the whole family by encouraging the provision of drinks like coffee and of rooms where the children could sit comfortably with their parents instead of huddling miserably outside. So far, however, neither party has been brave enough even to attempt the Report's admirable recommendations, designed as they are for the benefit of the rational majority of drinkers.

But overall the signs are encouraging. Wine, so long the privilege of the rich, is now a familiar part of the diet of families of all classes, and beer can now be bought, along with the week's groceries, in nearly every major supermarket, emphasising that it is now a respectable part of a normal diet, with no more moral obloquy attaching to it than to beefburgers or fish fingers. No doubt alcohol is still a factor, though surely not the major, much less the only, one, in the break-up of some families and the neglect of some children, but the excesses which were commonplace a century ag, are now the infrequent exception, which attract attention when some tragedy results precisely because of their rarity. After all its vicissitudes, alcohol is at last coming to occupy its proper place in family life, as a valued companion and friend, albeit one which cannot be taken for granted.

2 ALCOHOL AND THE FAMILY IN LITERATURE

Carol Ghinger and Marcus Grant

Literature, like alcoholism, is open to a wide variety of interpretations. For the purpose of this chapter, however, the most relevant way to consider the literary works on which it is based is as descriptions or analyses of human interactions. This interpretation obviously neglects other important literary dimensions, particularly those which have to do with the relationship between language and expression, but it does focus upon the essential common denominator which will most readily assist an exploration of the theme of alcohol and the family.

In an attempt to concentrate upon a reasonably coherent, though richly varied, body of material, the authors have chosen to limit themselves to English and American novels and plays written during the last hundred years. Several reasons prompted this choice: the drinking practices referred to in these books are more likely to be comparable with contemporary drinking practices; the actual texts, from which, inevitably, only brief quotations can be given here, are reasonably accessible; and there are no linguistic or formal difficulties, as would have been the case had the selection included literature written at an earlier date, foreign language material or verse. Perhaps the most important reason for choosing this area was, however, the recognition by the authors of the sheer size of the task. What is included in this chapter is in no sense a comprehensive review. It is a partial, and therefore to an extent a personal, view of a number of salient themes.

It seems that there is a basic and important difference between the way in which alcohol problems are described in novels and in plays. An attempt will be made here, therefore, to contrast novels with plays in order to highlight this difference in approach. It is, of course, in the nature of the formal constraint imposed by choosing to write a novel or a play that differences in approach will be apparent in many themes, not just that of alcohol problems. Nevertheless, the difference in this area says a great deal about the way in which alcohol problems are perceived as well as about the relative strengths and limitations of two literary forms.

In most novels the alcoholic is seen as an essentially solitary figure, isolated from normal family connections, whilst in most plays the alcoholic is located more within a family context. There are, of course, exceptions to this rule, nor is the distinction always as neatly defined as suggested here, but in general terms the novels tend to explore the self-image of the alcoholic and to see all relationships, including family relationships, through the special and frequently distancing perception of that self-image. What is being developed in the novels tends to be a situation in which alcoholics are seen as being cut off (frequently cutting themselves off) from other people. Particularly when the alcoholic is the hero of the novel, a world is presented in which the alcoholic is not just the centre but, by virtue of his centrality, beyond the reach of the other characters.

Novels, of course, permit the readers to share in the thought processes of characters in a relatively direct way, to see human interactions from a particular and intense point of view. Plays, by contrast, present multiple views so that audiences observe human interactions with a greater objectivity, however sympathetic they may be to the plight of individual characters. Thus, in most plays which deal with alcohol problems, the alcoholic is seen as interacting actively with the other members of the family, rather than being the inviolable centre towards which others inevitably gravitate or away from which they choose to run. At its simplest, it would be possible to say that novels present the family from the alcoholic's point of view whilst plays present the alcoholic from the family's point of view. This is rather too schematic a description of the contrast and takes no account of the many subtle and complex layers of perception, irony and plot development which occur simultaneously within works of literature, but it does at least serve to highlight the difference in emphasis which is apparent in these two forms.

To illustrate this point, let us compare two major works which have alcohol problems as a recurring theme and which were both, as it happens, written by alcoholics. Malcolm Lowry's *Under the Volcano* (1947) has long been recognised as the most extraordinarily sustained portrayal of an alcoholic that has been written in the novel form, and Eugene O'Neill's *Long Day's Journey into Night* (1941), which has, like *Under the Volcano*, strong autobiographical elements, is a play which looks at a whole family for which communication has become possible only through alcohol, so that drinking emerges as both salvation and damnation.

One point which has to be made immediately about *Under the Volcano* has relevance for all the other works to be discussed here. Although we will be looking at them from the perspective of what they say about drinking, alcohol, alcohol problems and alcoholism, they are in no sense documentaries and only in a very crude sense fictionalised autobiographies. They make use of events, clusters of circumstances, even characters from the real life of the author only in so far as these events, circumstances and characters contribute to the integrity of the novel or play. Direct interpretation of the lives of authors based upon their fictional accounts of matters obviously similar to known facts about them, are likely to lead to all sorts of false assumptions about the relationship between the trigger and the target. The work of art, finally, has to stand by and for itself and supply its own internal dynamic without reference to more or less reliable data about the life of the artist. This is nowhere more relevant than when considering a novel like *Under the Volcano*, which has a narrative line closely connected with the major life events of Lowry (1909-57) and which certainly could never have been written had he not experienced that same omnipotence of alcohol that permeates the pages of his novel. As Stephen Spender (1967) notes in his introduction to the Jonathan Cape edition of the book: '*Under the Volcano* is no more *about* drinking than *King Lear* is *about* senility.' That being said, it is impossible to find any page in the whole book on which drink or drinking is not mentioned. The sheer quantity and variety of alcohol is impressive in itself.

The Consul dropped his eyes at last. How many bottles since then? In how many glasses, how many bottles had he hidden himself, since then alone? Suddenly he saw them, the bottles of aguardiente, of anis, of jerez, of Highland Queen, the glasses, a babel of glasses — towering, like the smoke from the train that day — built to the sky, then falling, the glasses toppling and crashing, falling downhill from the Generalife Gardens, the bottles breaking, bottles of Oporto, tinto, blanco, bottles of Pernod, Oxygenee, absinthe, bottles smashing, bottles cast aside, falling with a thud on the ground in parks, under benches, beds, cinema seats, hidden in drawers at Consulates, bottles of Calvados dropped and broken, or bursting into smithereens, tossed into garbage heaps, flung into the sea, the Mediterranean, the Caspian, the Caribbean, bottles floating in the ocean, dead Scotchmen on the Atlantic highlands — and how he saw them, smelt them, all, from the very beginning — bottles, bottles, bottles, and glasses, glasses, glasses, of bitter, of Dubonnet, of Falstaff, Rye, Jonny Walker, Vieux Whiskey blanc Canadian, the aperitifs, the digestifs, the demis, the dobles, the noch ein Herr Obers, the et glas Araks, the tusen taks, the bottles, the bottles, the beautiful bottles of tequila, and the   gourds, gourds, gourds, the millions of gourds of beautiful mescal . . . How indeed could he hope to find himself, to begin again when, somewhere, perhaps in one of those lost or broken bottles, in one of those glasses, lay, forever, the solitary clue to his identity? How could he go back and look now, scrabble among the broken glass, under the eternal bars, under the oceans?

But, despite appearances to the contrary, the focus of *Under the Volcano* is not alcohol, it is the Consul, Geoffrey Firmin, through whose eyes we participate in much of the action.

Under the Volcano describes the extraordinary life of the Consul (actually a British ex-consul), who has come to the end of his road in a remote Mexican town, where he is drinking himself to death. The action is communicated by means of extended flashbacks, sometimes flashbacks within flashbacks, and takes place during the course of a single day, the religious festival called the day of the dead. The Consul's ex-wife Yvonne has returned, it seems, prepared to try again to understand him and to save him from himself. She finds that his half-brother Hugh, an idealist keen to set off for the Civil War in Spain, is staying with him. Hugh, attracted to Yvonne, finds his position ambiguous. The Consul, torn between his love for Yvonne and his rapacious drinking, has doubts about his own identity, his recurrent feelings of guilt (based upon an incident during the First World War when he commanded a warship disguised as a merchantman which attacked German U-boats) and cannot bring himself to take decisive action. Hugh and Yvonne go off horseriding and then join the Consul for a trip to a bullthrowing in a neighbouring town. They are travelling there by bus when it has to stop because the injured body of a peasant, who has been attacked and robbed, is lying in the road. Under Mexican law, they are not able to help him because if they touched him they could be charged as accessories after the fact. Leaving him lying there, they travel on to the bullthrowing, where Hugh excels in the ring. The Consul starts off by himself into the night, followed by Yvonne and Hugh. In the closing pages of the novel, we see first Yvonne run down by the horse which originally belonged to the injured peasant and then the Consul shot dead by the fascist police who believe him to be a spy.

More than any other novel or play discussed in this chapter, *Under the Volcano* is a study of the isolation of the individual. The Consul's inability to accept human relationships cuts him off from the possibility of any growth which is not internal, which does not occur within the perpetually inebriated confines of his own consciousness. Yvonne has returned to him, something which he has, it seems, previously deeply desired but never believed would happen; yet, once she is there, he cannot bring himself to make the commitment to her that she needs and that he knows is required of him. The central dilemma of the novel is, in a sense, whether the Consul actually rejects love, which would be an active and participative step, or whether, as he believes, he simply fails to love, which implies an absence of action, even an inability to act. He recognises the dilemma himself and, near the end of the book, drunker even than he has been earlier in the day, and about to plunge off alone into the darkness, he explains to Hugh what it is that determines the quality of action:

> But there was a slight mistake. The Consul was not talking. Apparently not. The Consul had not uttered a single word. It was all an illusion, a whirling cerebral chaos, out of which, at last, at long last, at this very instant, emerged, rounded and complete, order:
>
> 'The act of a madman or a drunkard, old bean', he said, 'or of a man labouring under violent excitement seems less free and more inevitable to the one who knows the mental condition of the man who performed the action, and more free and less inevitable to the one who does not know it.'

Like Lillian Hellman's *The Little Foxes* (1939) and like the novels of Jean Rhys, which are discussed later in this chapter, *Under the Volcano* is about the breakdown of traditional values. There was a time, it is clear, when relationships were possible, when the Consul and Yvonne were happy together. We see glimpses of that possibility still in the episode when she goes horseriding with Hugh, although the premonitions of catastrophe are peripherally apparent even during that supremely lyrical section of the narrative. For the Consul, certainly, freedom to choose has become an illusion, not just because addiction removes the possibility in a simple and direct sense, but because valid choices are no longer available to him. Throughout the novel, there is the sense of a massive world conflict going on across the world in Europe. Within the microcosm of the Consul's consciousness, that conflict has already been resolved and the resolution leads to the total isolation of the individual.

It is possible to see glimpses of the old order specifically in terms of alcohol and the family. Jacques Laruelle remembers how he visited the Consul when as a young adolescent, he was spending the summer with an English family called Taskerson:

But indeed the whole family drank inordinately. Old Taskerson, a kindly sharp man, had lost the only one of his sons who'd inherited any degree of literary talent; every night he sat brooding in his study with the door open, drinking hour after hour, his cats on his lap, his evening newspaper crackling distant disapproval of the other sons, who for their part sat drinking hour after hour in the dining room. Mrs Taskerson, a different woman at home, where she perhaps felt less necessity of making a good impression, sat with her sons, her pretty face flushed, half disapproving too, but nevertheless cheerfully drinking everyone else under the table. It was true the boys usually had a head start — not that they were the sort ever to be seen staggering about outside in the street. It was a point of honour with them that, the drunker they became, the more sober they should appear. As a rule they walked fabulously upright, shoulders thrown back, eyes front, like guardsmen on duty, only towards the end of the day, very very slowly, with the same 'erect manly carriage,' in short, that had so impressed M. Laruelle's father. Even so it was by no means an unusual occurrence in the morning to discover the entire household sleeping on the dining-room floor. Yet no one seemed to feel any the worse for it.

Not only is it interesting to compare that view of family drinking with what happens in O'Neill's *Long Day's Journey into Night*, which is discussed next in this chapter, but for the Consul it clearly represents an unattainable model of family relationships. Drinking, for him, is fundamentally a solitary activity. He may press drinks upon others, invite them to share drinks with him, accept drinks from them or comment upon the slow pace of their drinking, but what interests him is how much he himself has to drink, where his next drink is coming from and what his current blood alcohol level seems to be. Although, from time to time, as a result of his drinking, he becomes talkative, it is generally as a spur to an argument or to forcing a crisis rather than a process of socialisation. Drinking, for the Consul, is self-directed, *his* passionate obsession. The aim of his drinking, and in particular of his use of mescal, is to achieve that fullest state of consciousness which is otherwise inaccessible to him.

Perversely, it is in such a state of heightened consciousness that he recognises the overwhelming need he has for Yvonne and yet finds himself still unable to do anything to express his love for her. *Under the Volcano* contains religious and mystical references to the Cabbala, Dante's *Divine Comedy* and to the Catholicism of Mexico, and these recurrent images form intricate patterns of meaning behind the action of the plot. The intensity of the Consul's real feelings for Yvonne, rooted irrevocably in his feelings about himself, are revealed when, after the bullthrowing, they are all three drinking together in a cantina when the owner, Senor Cervantes, beckons him into another part of the building:

> One small room occupied by a hugh brass bedstead. Rusty rifles in a rack on the wall. In one corner, before a tiny porcelain Virgin, burned a little lamp . . . Mescal tears came to the Consul's eyes, and he remembered sometime during last night's debauch going with Dr Vigil to a church in Quauhnahuac he didn't know, with sombre tapestries, and strange votive pictures, a compassionate Virgin floating in the gloom, to whom he prayed, with muddily beating heart, he might have Yvonne again. Dark figures, tragic and isolated, stood about the church, or were kneeling — only the bereaved and lonely went there. 'She is the Virgin for those who have nobody with', the doctor told him, inclining his head toward the image . . . Now the Consul made this Virgin the other who had answered his prayer and as they stood in silence before her, prayed again. 'Nothing is altered and in spite of God's mercy I am still alone. Though my suffering seems senseless I am still in agony. There is no explanation of my life.' Indeed there was not, nor was this what he'd meant to convey. 'Please let Yvonne have her dream — dream? — of a new life with me — please let me believe that all that is not an abominable self-deception', he tried . . . 'Please let me make her happy, deliver me from this dreadful tyranny of self. I have sunk low. Let me sink lower still, that I may know the truth. Teach me to love again, to love life.' That wouldn't do either . . . 'Where is love? Let me truly suffer. Give me back my purity, the knowledge of the Mysteries, that I have betrayed and lost. Let me be truly lonely, that I may honestly pray. Let us be happy again somewhere, if it's only together, if it's only out of this terrible world. Destroy the world!' he cried in his heart.

Alcohol, therefore, takes a multiple role in *Under the Volcano*. It is certainly the instrument of destruction and of self-destruction, both metaphorically and literally, since it is intoxication that leads directly to the Consul's inability to handle his final interrogation and consequently to his execution. Equally, however, it is the instrument, as in the passage just quoted, of self-revelation and self-realisation. The

Consul uses alcohol in order to achieve fullest consciousness and, in so doing, accepts its destructive powers as the price which he has to pay. Alcohol is also, of course, the very fabric of reality in *Under the Volcano* and it would certainly be possible to chronicle the progress of the narrative in terms of a variety of more or less drunken states.

In terms of the relationship between alcohol and the family, alcohol continues to play the double role of making possible both damnation and revelation. The three central characters do, after all, form a curiously ambiguous family unit: the hero, his former wife and his half-brother. The drinking certainly reinforces that ambiguity, both in terms of the plot itself (what does Yvonne really think about Hugh and why does the Consul leave them alone together so much?) and in terms of the spiral of self-destructive addiction which, for the Consul, represents the only coherent response to a chaotic world. By meeting ambiguity with alcohol, by using alcohol to impose a view of things, however temporarily, upon the flux of complex relationships, the Consul is able to concentrate upon maintaining consciousness, which is, for him, a task so difficult in itself that love, for example, is simply impossible. The triumph of *Under the Volcano* is that it is able to create in Geoffrey Firmin a figure who is not only credible and, to an extent, attractive in his own right, but also a metaphor for the individual in society today. It is, finally, alienation which drives the Consul to drink, into himself. One of Lowry's biographers quotes the writer as saying: 'The real cause of alcoholism is the complete baffling sterility of existence as *sold* to you.' Thus, the conclusion of *Under the Volcano* is, in a profound sense, an affirmation of the values which the Consul knew but could not act upon. Foremost among these values is the strength of the family, a strength which the Consul, faced by the guns of the fascist police, expresses in even broader terms, recognising himself as both victim and, simultaneously, capable of redemption. The family becomes at that moment, the family of mankind, an endless succession of individuals, each totally isolated, each desperately seeking for that apotheosis of self that the Consul could not find in love. *Under the Volcano* is a modern tragedy which uses Lowry's own drinking as its baseline.

In this respect, it is remarkably similar to O'Neill's play. The difference, as was indicated at the beginning of this chapter, is that, whilst *Under the Volcano*, a novel, presents reality in terms of its relationship to a single character, *Long Day's Journey Into Night* (1941), a play, presents reality in terms of a number of alternative and simultaneous versions. The other characters in Lowry's novel are of significance only in relation to the Consul. In O'Neill's play, each character has independent validity and the family, as a living and drinking unit, is a greater force than the sum of its members.

Long Day's Journey Into Night is a largely autobiographical play about O'Neill's (1888-1953) own family. His mother became a drug addict shortly after his birth and he and his father were both alcoholics. Many of the events recounted in the play reflect in substance and in detail the history of the O'Neill family. The subject of the play is the complex web of interactions between the members of the family and the interdependence that binds them together and ultimately destroys them. The entire play is an exploration not only of the relationships between the family members in the present, but also the history which the family shares. This history is revealed to the audience gradually in the play through the accusations and blame that they hurl at each other, each seeing the other as responsible for his or her disintegration and alienation. In theme, this play can be seen as a variation of Sartre's *'L'enfer, c'est les autres'* ('hell is other people') (*Huis Clos*; English translation, *In Camera*, Sartre, 1946); in this case, 'hell is the family'. In spite of the good will, love and tenderness which underlie their feelings for each other and which intermittently emerge in their interaction, they are helplessly caught in a pattern of mutual destructiveness:

Mary   Do you know what I was telling her, dear? About the night my father took me to your dressing room and I first fell in love with you. Do you remember?

Tyrone   (*Deeply moved – his voice husky.*) Can you think I'd ever forget, Mary?

           (*Edmund looks away from them, sad and embarrassed.*)

Mary   (*Tenderly.*) No. I know you still love me, James, in spite of everything.

Tyrone   (*His face works and he blinks back tears – with quiet intensity.*) Yes! As God is my judge! Always and forever, Mary!

Mary   And I love you, dear, in spite of everything. (*There is a pause in which Edmund moves embarrassedly. The strange detachment comes over her manner again as if she were speaking impersonally of people seen from a distance.*) But I must confess, James, although I couldn't help loving you, I would never have married you if I'd known you drank so much. I remember the first night your barroom friends had to help you up to the door of our hotel room, and knocked

and then ran away before I came to the door. We were still
on our honeymoon, do you remember?

Tyrone   (*With guilty vehemence*.) I don't remember! It wasn't on
our honeymoon! And I never in my life had to be helped
to bed, or missed a performance!

Thus the action of the play can be seen as consisting almost solely
in a verbal sparring in which the family history is unfolded, so that the
movement within the play becomes purely interior action. Not only is
there no action outside of this dialogue, but O'Neill creates a feeling of
claustrophobia and isolation through his technique which, by observing the so-called classical unities of space, time and character, narrows
the focus of attention and simultaneously intensifies it. Structurally,
the play takes place within the confines of a single day, in one room
(the living room) of the Tyrone family's house, the only characters are
the members of the family and the family maid, and reference is often
made to the family's isolation from its community:

Try to go for — a drive this afternoon, you mean? Why, yes, if you
wish me to, although it makes me feel lonelier than if I stayed here.
There is no one I can invite to drive with me, and I never know
where to tell Smythe to go. If there was a friend's house where I
could drop in and laugh and gossip awhile. But, of course, there
isn't. There never has been.

The father's stinginess forces them to live in a shabby manner,
causing their mother to shun the outside world out of embarrassment
and shame. Another source of isolation is the family's secretiveness
about their mother's drug addiction; their need to hide it from the rest
of the world, again out of shame, sets them apart and so they live
locked in upon themselves. As in *Huis Clos*, hell is circumscribed: the
characters are interlocked in a series of verbal attacks, to which their
guilt makes them vulnerable and isolated, within the confines of a single
room. The unbearable tension of the situation is given as the cause of
the drinking that goes on in the play. The family as a unit emerges as a
destructive force, incapable of giving and sustaining nurturing, support
or nourishment, but rather as the instrument of degradation and destruction.

Alcohol is central to the action of the play in its role as facilitator
of the accusatory interactions, since being drunk enables the members of
the family to express how they are really feeling. It is also the external-

isation of their alienation and something concrete for which they can blame each other so that, for example, being drunk becomes an excuse to intensify the assault upon each other. It is seen as the result or effect of harmful past behaviour and therefore symbolises the crushing guilt which they all feel. It is a way of coping with the tensions of the situation and yet is simultaneously a cause of further destructive behaviour.

All three of the male characters drink. Although from time to time they attempt to hide their drinking, especially from their mother, as well as filling the whiskey bottle with water so it won't be apparent how much they've been drinking, for the most part, not only do they acknowledge their drinking (and drunkenness) to each other:

> Well, what's wrong with being drunk? It's what we're after, isn't it? Let's not kid each other, Papa. Not tonight, We know what we're trying to forget.

but they often drink together and encourage each other's drinking:

> Come along then. It's before a meal and I've always found that good whiskey, taken in moderation as an appetizer, is the best of tonics.

They drink in their home, they go to the bar together and they give each other money to do their drinking with:

> Put it in your pocket. You'll probably meet some of your friends uptown and you can't hold your end up and be sociable with nothing in your jeans.

Drinking provides both the context and the ostensible reason for the blaming and accusation of each other which is the substance of the action. The father and two sons drink to cope with the situation in the family and each blames the other for causing their drinking.

The destructiveness of the family unit is seen as the main cause of the alcoholism in *Long Day's Journey into Night*. The father, James, claims that he drinks to cope with the escape from his wife's drug addiction and the tension that it creates in the home. James accuses Jamie of being a poor influence on his younger brother Edmund:

> Even before that when he was in prep school, he began dissipating and playing the Broadway sport to imitate you, when he's never had your constitution to stand it.

Mary blames James for encouraging the boys to drink:

> Why is that glass there; Did you take a drink? Oh, how can you be
> such a fool? Don't you know it's the worst thing? (*She turns on
> Tyrone.*) You're to blame, James. How could you let him? Do you
> want to kill him? Don't you remember my father? He wouldn't stop
> after he was stricken. He said doctors were fools! He thought, like
> you, that whiskey is a good tonic!

Edmund accuses his older brother Jamie of having provided him with a
model of dissipation for him to emulate. Mary accuses James of having
given Jamie alcohol as a baby to calm him:

> You brought him up to be a boozer. Since he first opened his eyes,
> he's seen you drinking. Always a bottle on the bureau in the cheap
> hotel rooms! And if he had a nightmare when he was little, or a
> stomach ache your remedy was to give him a teaspoonful of whiskey
> to quiet him.

And Edmund reiterates this accusation against his father in relation to
himself:

> You did the same thing with me. I can remember that teaspoonful of
> booze every time I woke up with a nightmare.

Jamie accuses his mother of always favouring the younger brother and
blames his drinking on feeling unloved as well as on the need to escape
the tension causes by his mother's drug addiction.

Besides giving them all reasons to blame each other, being drunk
gives them the context to vent all their rage against each other. Mary
does not want Jamie to drink because, 'You know what a vile,
tongue he has when he's drunk.' They can say what they are really
feeling and get away with it under the guise of being drunk. Each member is dependent on the other, has an effect on the other and this
vicious circle of cause and effect (I drink because you're a drug addict,
I'm a drug addict because you drink . . .) creates the atmosphere of
entrapment and claustrophobia:

> Jamie   Want to warn you — against me. Mama and Papa are right.
> I've been rotten bad influence. And worst of it is, I did it
> on purpose.

Edmund (*Uneasily*.) Shut up! I don't want to hear —

Jamie Nix, Kid! You listen! Did it on purpose to make a bum of you. Or part of me did. A big part. That part that's been dead so long. That hates life. My putting you wise so you'd learn from my mistakes. Believed that myself at times, but it's a fake. Made my mistakes look good. Made getting drunk romantic. Made whores fascinating vampires instead of poor, stupid, diseased slobs they really are. Made fun of work as sucker's game. Never wanted you to succeed and make me look even worse by comparison. Wanted you to fail. Always jealous of you. Mama's baby, Papa's pet!

(*He stares at Edmund with increasing enmity.*) And it was your being born that started Mama on dope. I know that's not your fault, but all the same, God damn you, I can't help hating your guts!

Edmund (*Almost frightenedly*.) Jamie! Cut it out! You're crazy!

Jamie But don't get wrong ideas, Kid. I love you more than I hate you. My saying what I'm telling you now proves it. I run the risk you'll hate me — and you're all I've got left.

Thus, *Long Day's Journey Into Night*, just as much as *Under the Volcano*, is about the vicious circles of cause and effect which, on one level, form the narrative lines of the works and which, on another level, describe processes of alienation which force the individual in upon himself. Whether, as in *Long Day's Journey Into Night*, these processes are located with a family context, or whether, as in *Under the Volcano*, the processes occur within the consciousness of the protagonist, the central metaphor remains the same. Alcohol facilitates what is, finally, the conflict between self and otherness, between the individual and society. Drinking, therefore, which both creates the possibility of making contact with other people and promotes the urge to self-destruction, continues to act within the family as a double-edged weapon.

Like *Long Day's Journey into Night*, *The Little Foxes* (1939) by Lillian Hellman (1905-), is a play which revolves around a family, in this case the Hubbard family, and all the main characters in the play are a part of the family either by blood or by marriage. In this family, human values are subordinated to the drive for economic power and control so that, as in *Long Day's Journey into Night*, the family becomes a destructive force, causing the disintegration of its members. The three siblings, Regina, Oscar and Ben, ruthlessly sacrifice their spouses and children in their greedy rivalry for wealth and power. One of the characters, Birdie, is a victim of this process of dehumanisation and her alcoholism can be seen as directly attributable to it.

Briefly, the action of the play centres around a merger between the Hubbard family, which has married and bought its way into the southern aristocracy, and a northern manufacturing company. The two brothers and sister must put up $75,000 each in order to be equal partners. Regina's money is controlled by her husband, Horace, and she must convince him to invest their share in it. As the play opens, Regina has written to Horace, who is in a rest home in the north recovering from a heart attack, and she and her brothers are waiting for his response. As the play unfolds, Horace's motives for refusing his share of the money highlight the tensions in the relationships between the members of the family. We learn not only about the relationship between husband and wife, both past and present, but likewise of those between sister and brother, mother and daughter, nephew and uncle. Their interactions are revealed as ruthless manipulations in their own self-interest, each using the other to gain his/her own ends even if the result is harm or destruction of the other. Regina finally causes the death of her husband in her greedy struggle for wealth and economic supremacy over her brothers. She is also willing to sacrifice her daughter, Alexandra (Zan), by marrying her to her boorish, dissipated and dishonest nephew in order to keep the money within the family. Leo, the nephew, motivated by greed for himself and for his father, steals the bonds from his uncle's safe deposit box in order to ensure that the merger will go through. Thus, before the play is over, both a murder and a robbery have been committed within the family.

However, Lillian Hellman extends the scope of the play far beyond the realms of the personal, the individual and the psychological into that of social, political and economic realities. If the play is about the Hubbard family, it is also about the decay of an old social order and the rise of a new one. Interested only in expanding their wealth, the Hubbards have destroyed the genteel and peaceful culture of former times so that the humane values of the past have given way to economic and cultural exploitation.

Birdie, the alcoholic character in the play, is related to the Hubbard family by marriage, having been 'acquired' by Oscar Hubbard for her aristocratic connections and position. She cannot now tolerate the breakdown of the traditional values which places no value on human life and dignity.

She symbolises the destruction of the older order and her voice represents a last gasp of breath of the dying landed aristocracy and its culture. Her desperate futile dream is once more to be in possession of the family estate and restore it to its former condition. Her vision is of a better world where people are kind and compassionate to each other, where life is lived with grace and charm. She wants a return to the values of family warmth and love. Thus, if we can see her alcoholism as a bitter reaction to the loss of her culture's values, her drinking is even more a reaction to her loss of self, particularly within the context of the family, which, instead of offering support and love, is a bitter, grasping, destructive force in her life.

Since Oscar married Birdie for her position rather than out of love, she now realises she was acquired just like the rest of the property:

Ben   Perhaps, perhaps. (*He sees that Marshall is listening to the music. Irritated, he turns to Birdie and Alexandra at the piano, then back to Marshall.*) You're right, Mr Marshall. It is difficult to learn new ways. But maybe that's why it's profitable. Our grandfather and our father learned new ways and learned how to make them pay. They work. (*Smiles nastily.*) They are in trade. Hubbard, Sons, Merchandise. Others, Birdie's, family, for example, look down on them. (*Settles back in chair.*) To make a long story short Lionnet now belongs to us. (*Birdie stops playing.*) Twenty years ago we took over their land, their cotton, and their daughter. (*Birdie rises and stands stiffly by the piano. Marshall, who has been watching her, rises.*)

She is mistreated, ridiculed, scorned, humiliated and treated with complete lack of respect. She is considered an incompetent child who is in need of supervision and controlling:

Oscar   (*Taking a step to her.*) You have been chattering to him like a magpie. You haven't let him be for a second. I can't think he came South to be bored with you.

Birdie   (*Quickly, hurt.*) He wasn't bored. I don't believe he was bored. He's a very educated, cultured gentleman. (*Her voice rises.*) I just don't believe it. You always talk like that when I'm having a nice time.

Oscar   (*Turning to her, sharply.*) You have had too much wine. Get yourself in hand now.

Birdie   (*Drawing back, about to cry, shrilly.*) What am I doing? I am not doing anything. What am I doing?

Oscar   (*Taking a step to her, tensely.*) I said get yourself in hand.
Stop acting like a fool.

After constant humiliation by others, she begins to believe the others'
definition of herself — she is a silly, worthless 'ninny'. Her gestures,
words and actions in the play are self-deprecating. She giggles, flutters,
is over-anxious to please, apologetic about her behaviour, insecure. She
has no self-esteem or confidence left. Her way of coping with this loss
of self is to drink:

Addie   (*Moves to Birdie.*) Rest a bit, Miss Birdie. You get
talking like this you'll get a headache and —

Birdie   (*Sharply, turning to her.*) I've never had a headache in
my life. (*Begins to cry hysterically.*) You know it as
well as I do. (*Turns to Alexandra.*) I never had a headache, Zan. That's a lie they tell for me. I drink. All by
myself, in my own room, by myself, I drink. Then,
when they want to hide it, they say, 'Birdie's got a
headache again.'

Alexandra   (*Comes to her quickly.*) Aunt Birdie.

Birdie   (*Turning away.*) Even you won't like me now. You won't
like me any more.

Alexandra   I love you. I'll always love you.

Birdie   (*Furiously.*) Well, don't. Don't love me. Because in
twenty years you'll just be like me. They'll do all the
same things to you. (*Begins to laugh hysterically.*) You
know what? In twenty-two years I haven't had a whole
day of happiness.

Thus, Birdie's alcoholism can be traced on one level to her personal
loss of self, whilst, on another level, her destruction symbolises the destruction of an entire culture, an entire system of values.

Interestingly, Hellman embodies this phenomenon in a woman. It is
important to examine why a woman is chosen to symbolise cultural
powerlessness and loss of self. Traditionally, women have been acquired
as property, been in powerless positions in society and have represented
the humane values of kindness, compassion, warmth and family unity.
They have also traditionally taken their definition of self from these
cultural stereotypes, and have therefore been treated as incompetent
children. As a result, they have suffered loss of self-esteem from accept-

ing the definition of themselves as somehow less than their male counterparts, and have experienced considerable difficulty in escaping from their powerlessness in social and political spheres of life. In this play Hellman portrays the impossibility of escaping the trap of powerlessness and victimisation in a meaningful way, so that all that is left to Birdie is escape through alcohol. It is relevant in this context to note how the portrayal of female drinking in *The Little Foxes* differs substantially from the male drinking in *Long Day's Journey into Night*. O'Neill has his male characters drink together on the stage, openly supporting each other's drinking. Birdie drinks alone, secretly, offstage, and her drinking is considered a shameful secret to be hidden from the other members of the family and from the world at large. The rest of the family is told that Birdie 'has a headache' if her behaviour ever deviates from the standard of respectability demanded of her.

The novels of Jean Rhys (1893-1979) look at the female drinker less in relation to how she appears to her family and more in relation to how she appears to herself. In *After Leaving Mr Mackenzie* (1930) Julia's contacts with her real family are confined to a brief visit to London during which her mother dies and she quarrels with her sister. For the rest of the book, she is adrift in the hotels, bars and streets of Paris, drinking with desultory desperation and substituting for her family a succession of ineffectual and unsatisfactory lovers. They, like her family, fail to awaken in her the kind of sympathetic response to another person of which she knows herself capable but which nevertheless persists in eluding her. Her drinking, which cuts her off from human contact, is also her reaction to the inadequacies of the relationships in which she finds herself. The trap is not the rigidity of a grasping family; it is a trap which she carries with her always. Julia lacks freedom because she cannot finally escape from a self-image which is so impoverished that there can be no bridges between it and the powerful aspirations which she intermittently feels. Like Birdie in *The Little Foxes*, Julia is essentially a victim. The difference is that Birdie's victimisation is seen at its most vivid in the context of a family which excludes her but which she still, despite everything, believes in, at least as a structure which might contain the possibility of human contact. Such contacts as Julia achieves are so slight, so nearly accidental, so transitory and so tarnished, that there really never appears even a glimmer of hope that something like salvation will be achieved, either by her own efforts or through the fruition of a relationship with another human being.

In this regard actual reference to drinking or to drunken behaviour and the consequences of drunkenness are less specific than general.

Thus, alcohol seeps round everything in the novel so that its force is felt by accumulation rather than by individual statements. Take, for example the episode where Julia is in a hotel room in Paris with a man, Mr Horsfield, who has picked her up and is now rather confused about whether he really wants to become sexually or emotionally involved with her.

> She was swaying very slightly backwards and forwards, holding her knees, her eyes fixed.
> Mr Horsfield was filled with a glow of warm humanity. He thought: 'Hang it all, one can't leave this unfortunate creature alone to go and drink herself dotty.'
> He said: 'Now look here, I'm going to talk sense to you. Why don't you come back to London?'
> She looked at him steadily with her large, unwinking eyes. She said: 'I don't know. I might go back to London. There's nothing to stop me.'
> Then he thought: 'Good God, why in the world have I suggested that?' and added cautiously, 'I mean, you've surely got people there, haven't you?'
> 'Yes', she said. 'Of course. My mother and my sister. But my mother's pretty sick. She's been ill for a long time.'
> He felt that he could imagine what her mother and her sister were like. No money. No bloody money. Bloody money! You might as well say 'Bloody money.' They would be members of the vast crowd that bears on its back the label, 'No money' from the cradle to the grave . . . And this one had rebelled. Not intelligently, but violently and instinctively. He saw the whole thing.
> 'I'm tired', she said. And she was very tired. Her excitement and the relief of having got some money were both swallowed up. She wanted to sleep. She felt very cold — the cold of drunkenness — as if something huge, made of ice, were breathing on her.

In another Jean Rhys novel, *Good Morning Midnight* (1939), we see a similar situation when Sasha, a woman who like Julia is past the age when she felt herself to be attractive and who has lost contact with her real family connections, experiences through her drinking a kind of self realisation. It is a desperate and bitter image of self that emerges, but one which has persisted as a result of years of attempting to create the very relationships which it denies the possibility of achieving:

I stayed there, staring at myself in the glass. What do I want to cry about? . . . On the contrary, it's when I am quite sane like this, when I have had a couple of extra drinks and am quite sane, that I realise how lucky I am. Saved, rescued, fished-up, half-drowned, out of the deep, dark river, dry clothes, hair shampooed and set. Nobody would know I had ever been in it. Except, of course, that there always remains something Yes, there always remains something . . . Never mind, here I am, sane and dry, with my place to hide in. What more do I want? I'm a bit of an automaton, but sane, surely — dry, cold and sane. Now I have forgotten about dark streets, dark rivers, the pain, the struggle and the drowning . . Mind you, I'm not talking about the struggle when you are strong and a good swimmer and there are willing and eager friends on the bank waiting to pull you out at the first sign of distress. I mean the real thing. You jump in with no willing and eager friends around, and when you sink, you sink to the accompaniment of loud laughter.

If, therefore, we are looking at the causes of alcoholism, then the novels of Jean Rhys bear a more than superficial resemblance to Hellman's *The Little Foxes*. In both it is possible to attribute the compulsive drinking to some kind of personality abnormality. Birdie can be seen as weak, as failing to come to terms with reality, as clinging to a nostalgic and inaccurate view of an unattainable past. Julia and Sasha in *After Leaving Mr Mackenzie* and *Good Morning Midnight* respectively, who are, in a sense, two portraits of the same character, can be seen as unfulfilled, lacking in self-esteem, hopelessly seeking to achieve unattainable goals. Equally, however, these same personality factors described here as causative factors, could be seen as the effects of the alienating lifestyles which they have adopted.

Equally too, and of even greater importance, the sense of victimisation in the works of both writers can be attributed to forces working within society as well as within the individual. Julia and Sasha, just as much as Birdie, represent a set of human values which are being threatened and destroyed by a heartless social order. Qualities which have to do with human worth and sensitivity, with patience and with care, are shown as pitifully vulnerable to a society which values individuals for what can be got out of them. It is no coincidence that Hellman and Rhys are both women, just as it is no coincidence that Birdie, Julia and Sasha are all women. The difference between the novel form, where the alcoholic is seen in relative isolation, and the play, in which the alcoholic is seen in relation to a family, is certainly true for these works;

but more to the point, perhaps if we are considering the way in which women, and in particular women alcoholics, are portrayed, is the common theme of a lost individual subject to social, sexual and economic exploitation.

One way in which this is demonstrated in terms of family interaction is through what Scott Fitzgerald (1896-1941) calls the 'moral superiority' of the other family members. Thus, the position of the alcoholic within the hierarchical structure of the family is frequently seen in terms of a progress from a position of relative power and esteem to one in which the power wanes, the esteem of others and even of self is lost, while the other family members, by contrast, inverse their own power and esteem and achieve an important kind of superiority. This progress can result from a single drunken episode.

One of the most dramatic representations of the effects of what is actually a single episode of acute intoxication occurs in the opening chapter of Thomas Hardy's (1840-1928) *The Mayor of Casterbridge* (1886). A young man, accompanied by his wife and baby daughter, arrive on foot at a village fair. The strange inevitability of what follows is heightened by the fact that the protagonists are not at this stage given names, merely being identified as 'the man' and 'the woman'. Seeking refreshment, they enter the furmity tent (furmity is wheat boiled in milk) where the man arranges to have his helpings heavily laced with rum:

At the end of the first basin the man had risen to serenity; at the second he was jovial; at the third, argumentative; at the fourth, the qualities signified by the shape of his face, the occasional clench of his mouth, and the fiery spark of his dark eye, began to tell in his conduct; he was overbearing — even brilliantly quarrelsome . . .

'For my part I don't see why men who have got wives, and don't want 'em, shouldn't get rid of 'em as these gipsy fellows do their old horses', said the man in the tent. 'Why shouldn't they put 'em up and sell 'em by auction to men who are in want of such articles? Hey? Why, begad, I'd sell mine this minute if anybody would buy her!' . . .

She turned to her husband and murmured, 'Michael, you have talked this nonsense in public places before. A joke is a joke, but you may make it once too often, mind.'

But a quarter of an hour later the man, who had gone on lacing his furmity more and more heavily, though he was either so strong-minded or such an intrepid toper that he still appeared fairly sober,

recurred to the old strain, as in a musical fantasy the instrument
fetches up the original theme. 'Here – I am waiting to know about
this offer of mine. The woman is no good to me. Who'll have
her?' . . .

'Mike, Mike,' said she, 'this is getting serious. O! too serious!'
'Will anybody buy her?' said the man.
'I wish somebody would', said she firmly. 'Her present owner is
not at all to her liking!'

The episode is quoted at length because it demonstrates, through the
narrative and also through the device of avoiding naming the characters,
how the alcohol itself comes to take on the power of suddenly translating motive into action. There is no time to balance reasons for and
reasons against what the man is doing. He simply finds himself doing
it Alcohol, quite literally, breaks up the family.

Here, of course, the drinking, however catastrophic in its effect, is
not alcoholism in any shape or form. The man got drunk and although
there is an inference that it may not have been the first time, there is
certainly no suggestion that this episode related to any previous history
of alcohol abuse. Not that the absence of such a history does anything
to minimise the damage caused by his drinking on this occasion. The
violence of his action in destroying the family unit is beyond question.
It is interesting to compare the role of the woman here in Hardy's novel
with Hellman's portrayal of Birdie's alcoholism, discussed above. The
woman in Hardy is even more powerless even more of a victim, at least
at first sight, than is Birdie. The difference is that, although she is
treated as property to be bought and sold, just as in a way Birdie was,
Hardy's woman, even by choosing to go along with her husband's plan
('She bowed her head with absolute indifference'), takes up a position
of moral superiority.

Thus, when later in the novel, many years having passed during which
the man and the woman have had no contact with each other, they
meet again, it is to the role of alcohol in his life that Henchard (the
man) immediately refers:

Just before eight he approached the deserted earthwork, and entered
by the south path which descended over the debris of the former
dens. In a few moments he could discern a female figure creeping in
by the great north gap, or public gateway. They met in the middle
of the arena. Neither spoke just at first – there was no necessity for
speech – and the poor woman leant against Henchard, who supported her in his arms.

'I don't drink', he said in a low, halting, apologetic voice. 'You hear, Susan? — I don't drink now — I haven't since that night.' Those were his first words.

Despite the fact that he is, in social and economic terms, now extremely successful, that he is now, in fact, the Mayor of Casterbridge, whilst she has never achieved much in life and has only returned in the hope that he may be able to help their daughter, there can be no doubt that her very passivity adds to Susan's moral strength. It is not just that Henchard feels guilty, as he ought, but also that Susan, by agreeing to accept the role of victim, has gained control of the situation.

Control, after all, is a central issue when considering the effects of alcohol. Whether it is the control which the drunk man has over his action or the control the alcoholic has over his drinking, the idea that somehow control has passed from the individual permits authors to explore the nature of random events or of fate, depending upon how they care to define it. For Hardy it was not so much that fate, once the individual had lost control, was bound to exercise a malignant influence. It was rather that, given the range of possible outcomes, it was always most likely that consequences would be different from intentions. Looking at this issue in terms of the family and effects upon the family, Hardy certainly sees a complex web of interdependent, conscious, sensitive, continuous decisions as the basis of family life. The functioning family is supposed to represent fulfilment. Where that fulfilment breaks down, because of sexual threat or, as here, because of an apparently random drunken action, a chain of events is set in motion that takes the protagonists far away from the initial cause. They have ceased, therefore, in a fundamental sense, to have control over their lives. It may appear to them that they have freedom of choice and indeed, to an extent, so they do, but it is always in the context of the unanticipated consequences of events, often long ago, but none the less potent for that.

The core issue in Edward Albee's (1928-) play *Who's Afraid of Virginia Woolf?* (1962) is in a certain sense, the impact of *lack* of family, as Martha and George, the main characters, are unable to have children. Yet the parent-child relationship is an important issue in the play, as it was in *Long Day's Journey Into Night* and *The Little Foxes*, since George and Martha invent a fictitious child and enact an elaborate fantasy involving him. Thus, *Who's Afraid of Virginia Woolf?* is about an imaginary family rather than a real one. In a sense, of course, all the texts discussed in this chapter are about imaginary families since all are works of fiction rather than case histories. In this play, however, there is a fiction within the fiction. It is a play about the gap between intention and action, a gap which is emphasised by the way in which alcohol is used to reinforce the destructive interaction between the characters. Both George and Martha feel a sense of inadequacy stemming from the fact that they were never able to produce a child. This serves to reinforce a deeper and more general sense of inadequacy about themselves as people and especially in their roles as man and woman. Martha comments at one point in the play that someday George will leave her and that would be just what she would deserve. George, for his part, feels strongly his failure to live up to Martha's expectation that he should fill her father's shoes as president of the small college at which he teaches. However, even more important that the poor self-image that each one has and the lack of self-esteem that goes along with it, is the way that this sense of inadequacy is used in the play as an instrument for each one to attack the other with:

Martha   Ha, ha, ha, ha! Make me another drink . . . lover.

George   (*Taking her glass.*) My God, you can swill it down can't you?

Martha   (*Imitating a tiny child.*) I'm firsty.

George   Jesus!

Martha   (*Swinging around.*) Look, sweetheart, I can drink you under any goddamn table you want . . . so don't worry about me!

George   Martha, I gave you the prize years ago . . . There isn't an abomination award going that you . . .

Martha   I swear . . . if you existed I'd divorce you . . . Some day . . . hah! Some night . . . some stupid, liquor-ridden night . . . I will go too far . . . and I'll either break the man's back . . . push him off for good . . . which is what I deserve. I can't even see you . . . I haven't been able to see you for years . . .

George   If you pass out, or throw up or something . . .

Martha   . . . I mean, you're a blank, a cipher . . .

George   . . . and try to keep your clothes on, too. There aren't many more sickening sights than you with a couple of drinks in you and your skirt up over your head, you know . . .

Martha   . . . a zero . . .

Their constant verbal warfare creates the atmosphere of a battlefield in their home and anyone entering it is in danger of being drawn into the battle. Nick and Honey, the new young faculty couple, are unsuspectingly involved not only as observers, but as accomplices and victims as well. Nick, especially, is unwittingly used as a weapon against George by Martha in her sexual battle. She taunts George with reference to Nick's youth, strength, and potential for success and flirts with Nick, who in his naivete, succumbs to the seduction. However, Nick and Honey do not leave the battlefield unscathed. While Honey is out of the room, Nick reveals to George the intimate details of their courtship and marriage. Later George uses these confidences against his guests in order to dismay and to humiliate them.

For most of the action of the play, Albee allows residual tenderness to be totally obscured by the constant stream of verbal violence, much of it directed by Martha at George whose sense of inadequacy as a man is tied to his sense of professional failure, and this in turn is related to his and Martha's relationship to her father. Martha's father, though never actually appearing in the play, looms large as a powerful authority figure and role model:

> Martha   All right! Shut up! Both of you! (*Pause*.) All right, now. Mommy died early, see and I sort of grew up with Daddy. (*Pause – thinks*.) . . . I went away to school, and stuff, but I more or less grew up with him. Jesus, I admired that guy! I worshipped him . . . I absolutely worshipped him. I still do . . . And he was pretty fond of me, too . . . you know? We had a real . . . rapport going . . . a real rapport.

One of Martha's main motivations for marrying George was that as a promising young faculty member he seemed to be a likely candidate for taking over her father's position when he retired. Thus, *Who's Afraid of Virginia Woolf?* is about three generations – past, present and never-to-be. George's failure to fill his father-in-law's shoes reinforces the childlessness of the couple.

The parent-child relationship is developed in a circular fashion in the play. Early in *Who's Afraid of Virginia Woolf?*, reference is made to a novel written by George about a young man who inadvertently killed his mother with a shotgun and, later, learning to drive, crashed his car into a tree killing his father. Later, it becomes clear that the novel is an autobiographical one. And still later in the play, when George feels the need to terminate the fantasy that he and Martha have been perpetuating about their son, he kills him off by having him drive his car into a tree too. In a sense, then, he is responsible for the death of both his father and his 'son'. Clearly, the father-son relationship is a problematic one for George, and a crucial issue in the play. It is around this issue that George's inadequacy is the most clearly measured: he is incapable of living up to the father/authority figure of Martha's father, and incapable of producing a son of his own. To take revenge on George for disappointing her and to fill the emptiness of her life Martha flirts with, and even seduces, in George's presence, all the new, young, male faculty members who are sent to her, ironically by her father. These men take on not only the function of lover, and compensation for George both sexually and professionally, but of son as well. The Freudian interpretations of these parent/child relationships are inevitable and irresistible but fall outside the scope of the current discussion.

All the characters in the play drink, and they drink heavily. As in *Long Day's Journey Into Night* the drinking is both a result of their despair with their lives and a cause for further despair. The heaviest drinker in the play is Martha who several times refers to her own drinking and is described by George with heavy irony as a stereotypical alcoholic:

We've got half-filled glasses everywhere in the house, wherever Martha forgets she's left them . . in the linen closet, on the edge of the bathtub . . . I even found one in the freezer, once.

However, George drinks quite heavily himself. It is he who is in charge of the drinking in the play. From the moment the guests arrive he is busy mixing and pouring drinks for himself and the others and as soon as a glass is empty he rushes to replenish it. However, it is Martha who explains *why* they both drink:

I cry all the time too, Daddy. I cry allllll the time; but deep inside, so no one can see me. I cry all the time, and then, what we do, we cry, and we take our tears and we put 'em in the ice box, in the goddamn ice trays (*Begins to laugh*.) until they're all frozen (*Laughs even more*.) and then . . . we put them . . . in our . . . drinks.

The guests, Nick and Honey, drink as much their hosts. Although Honey claims that she drinks very little and wisely ('I never mix. And then, I don't drink much either.'), she spends almost the entire play in the bathroom, drunk and vomitting, only to come out and drink some more. As opposed to Martha's drinking which is overt, recognised and commented upon, Honey's drinking is a reflection of her life — it is a pretence. As her claim not to drink much is a sham, so is the way in which she got Nick to marry her, which was by having a false pregnancy. Their entire life is a hypocrisy; on the surface everything is perfect so that they present the appearance of an ideal young faculty couple — brilliant, happy and attractive. But under the surface we discover that Nick really married Honey for her money and their relationship is far from a happy and close one emotionally, intellectually or sexually.

All the characters, then, drink to cope with and forget their feelings of inadequacy, personal and professional failure and frustration, empty existences, and alienating work and love relationships. Drink insulates and numbs them. However, not only is drinking a result of their despair, but it also plays a role in perpetuating it. The drinking facilitates the destructive bickering — it acts as a disinhibitor allowing them to unleash all the hostility and resentment that they feel towards each other which they might have controlled, censored or not have had the courage to express had they not been drinking.

Another aspect of the effects of excessive drinking upon families is the way in which families attempt to cope with the problems caused by the alcoholic. *The Lost Weekend* (1945) is a less impressive literary work than many of the others which have been discussed in this chapter. Nevertheless, it is particularly interesting in this context and the fact that it gave rise to one of the most impressive feature films produced on the theme of alcoholism ensures that it is likely to remain, for many people, their most significant media representation of alcohol problems. It is, incidentally, curious to note that when Lowry sent the original manuscript of *Under the Volcano* to his publishers, it was shortly after the appearance of Charles Jackson's *The Lost Weekend*. Despite the fact that Lowry had been working for many years upon his novel, there were suggestions not so much of plagiarism as of riding on the bandwagon. Thirty-five years after the event, there is, of course, no doubt that *Under the Volcano* is one of the major literary works of the twentieth century, whilst *The Lost Weekend* would probably by now have disappeared from view totally had it not formed the basis for the filmed dramatisation starring Ray Milland which, in 1945, won the American Academy best picture award. *The Lost Weekend* is the story of a personal struggle and, as has been noted in relation to other novels discussed in this chapter, family interactions play a relatively minor role in the narrative. The elements of family are very peripheral to the personal struggle and are only mentioned to support or in relation to the main concern which is the struggle of the individual.

As the main character is not married, family refers to his brother and his brother's wife, and to his girlfriend. They can be seen as representing two different ways of coping with the alcoholic, and thus epitomise the main options open to the family or close relations of an alcoholic, as seen by the alcoholic. One way, symbolised by the brother, is to ignore the problem, all the time feeling impatient and annoyed with the inconvenience that this represents for his own life. For example, when they have planned a trip to the country for the weekend and the alcoholic does not show up, his brother goes on with his life as if nothing unusual is happening, as if nothing were wrong:

> He knew too well what he'd be coming back to, he knew he couldn't stop what had started, it was best to stay away and let the thing play itself out, pretending in the meanwhile that nothing was going on in the city or at least shutting it from his mind entirely. By deliberately not thinking of it Wick had learned not even to worry . . . to do that would be to suffer too much.

The alcoholic, inevitably feels that his brother does not understand but at the same time he also feels very guilty about the anguish he is causing him.

The other way of coping with the alcoholic's behaviour is personified by the attitude of his girlfriend, Helen. She loves him unconditionally, and as a corollary of that, she never reproaches him, never tries to reform him, never questions him, never tries to manipulate him into changing 'for her' or 'if he loved her.' She knows that anything he does in that direction must be for himself. She accepts him totally as he is, loves him for himself. Her only role is to make him as comfortable and safe as she can and is constantly picking up the pieces when he falls apart. His way of dealing with him gets more respect, admiration and approval from the alcoholic. She is the only person he trusts (except that he is ashamed even for her to see him as he is). However, her method of coping is no more effective in the long run than is his brother's. After she puts him back together again, he just goes out and starts to drink again. It is also unclear what Helen does for herself to cope with the alcoholism of someone she loves. It is only seen from the perspective of the alcoholic and what these different coping strategies do (or do not do) for him.

Helen hadn't uttered a word of reproach from the moment she

turned the doorknob and came through the door. She had never said you've been drinking. She hadn't asked how long have you been at it? Have you got any money left? Are you finished now, or are you going to start again tomorrow? She hadn't said where'd you get the black eye, or what in heaven's name happened to you? She hadn't mentioned the matinee he had missed or said sure, you weren't feeling up to it, you had other plans for that afternoon. She didn't remind him of the several dozen phone-calls she had been making for days. She hadn't said at least you could have answered the 'phone and saved me that much worry. She hadn't said look at you, look what a sight you are. She hadn't called you a fool or a drunk or a liar or anything. She didn't say why can't you think of your brother Wick if you don't care anything about yourself? And of course she would never have said what about me? She had merely said 'Let me help you, I'll take you down to my house, I'll put you to bed in a clean bed and your can sleep as long as you need to.'

In the end, the message of *The Lost Weekend* is that there is no effective way of coping for the family. Whatever is done is ineffective, unappreciated, if not actually resented, and causes nothing but increased guilt on the part of the alcoholic. It is implied that the family of the alcoholic would do best to take care of themselves and leave him alone. On a more complex level, of course, something of the same message emerged from *Under the Volcano* where the Consul chose to isolate himself and to reject, or fail to respond to, the attempts made by Yvonne, his former wife, to return to him and to help him. The difference is that, whilst in *The Lost Weekend* we see this conflict in terms of a case history, in *Under the Volcano* we see it in terms of the fundamental tension between an individual and society.

Conclusion

In this chapter, an attempt has been made to show that alcohol, when it appears in literature, is often shown in a negative context. Characters in the novels and plays which we have discussed drink because they are alienated, desperate, lonely, frustrated and sad. Drinking leads to bickering, vulgarity, disruption and destruction of the family, verbal violence, promiscuity and irresponsible behaviour. It is important, as we pointed out above, to distinguish between the way in which the alcoholic is located within the family in plays and in novels, since the differences apparent in the examples we have discussed make it clear that the question of emphasis is crucial to spheres of influence which drinking behaviour is seen to have. Nevertheless, despite these impressive differences, emphasising on the one hand the isolation of the drinker and on the other the disruptive consequences of excessive drinking, there is, of course, this central common phenomenon — that in both its causes and its effects alcohol and drinking are portrayed negatively.

While this is generally true, as we have seen, in English and American literature written in the last hundred years, if we take a more universal and historical perspective we find that this attitude is a fairly recent one. In the history of literature, more often than not, drinking enjoyed a far more glorious fate. It was of a celebratory nature: people drank to celebrate, and the very act of drinking itself was celebrated. Drinking was associated with joyful events and equated with pleasure, lack of inhibition, and the ability to reach the deeper regions of man's being — his irrational, spiritual, creative, intuitive side. And alcohol was considered a comforter for the anxious and weary, a lifter of spirits for the sad and downtrodden, a liberator of the repressed. It provided warmth, health and robustness, joy, relaxation, comfort, elevation of mood, sociability, fellowship, good cheer, camaraderie, and inspiration for creativity.

Frequently, of course, in general works on the effects of alcoholism, passing reference is made to the positive consequences of drinking. Such references are generally vague, ill-defined and tokenistic. Whilst it is outside the scope of this chapter to analyse in any detail the frequent references which exist in world literature to the celebratory aspects of alcohol, it would certainly be inappropriate not to point out how immensely widespread such references are. These celebratory components are not always or even generally, associated with family interactions as such. Where they are, the drinking itself is not usually stressed by the writer as being of particular significance, since it exists within the context of a number of other celebratory manifestations. It can be seen, therefore, as a narrative or stylistic device designed to reinforce the positive associations of a particular set piece in the narrative.

In the concluding section of this chapter, in order to make this contrast all the more vivid, examples have deliberately been chosen from outside the limitations imposed (namely, English and American novels and plays, written during the last hundred years) for the main part of the discussion. As early as the fifth century BC Euripides' tragedy *The Bacchae*, which shows the danger of refusing to acknowledge and recognise the uninhibited side of man's nature and the dangers of repression, celebrates Dionysius, the spirit of music, nature, emotion, lack of constraint, and the giver of wine to man:

> He was primarily a spirit of life, and of all that produces or liberates life; liberates it from pain or fatigue, from tedium or ugliness, from the bonds of responsibility, law, pity, or affection. One of his most obvious gifts was that of wine.

It is this gift which brings freedom from an easing of the pain and drudgery of life:

> Now corresponding to her came this son of Semele
> Who has discovered grape-juice for a drink, his gift
> Bestowed on mortals; he releases wretched men
> From pain, whenever they are filled with running wine,
> Gives sleep, oblivion of their daily miseries;
> There is no other remedy for weariness.

Twenty centuries later, in the mid-sixteenth century, during the French Renaissance — a time of humanism which glorified man, of optimism in the future, and of liberation from the constraints of the Middle Ages — Francois Rabelais (1532-64) wrote an immense work, *Gargantua et Pantagruel* (1962 edn), which stems directly out of the Dionysian tradition. Rabelais, a former doctor, had a firm belief in the goodness of man's natural being, and was against all that opposed and deformed nature and oppressed, restricted and inhibited man from full development of his potential. For Rabelais, if man is allowed to do as he likes, he will be virtuous. His work is a celebration of the richness of human experience, of freedom from constraint, and of joy in living. As in *The Bacchae*, wine is the symbol of and means to disinhibition, and drinking is the path to wisdom, virtuousness and openness to life. Rabelais' characters, a community of giants, celebrate life by excess in eating and drinking:

> As I'm a sinner, I never drink without a thirst, if not a present thirst a future one. I forestall it you see. I drink for the thirst to come. I drink eternally. For me eternity lies in drinking, and drinking in eternity. — Let's have a song, let's have a drink, let's sing a catch! Where is my tuning-fork? — What! I only drink by proxy. — Do you wet your guts to dry them, or dry your guts to wet them? — I don't understand the theory, but I help myself out by the practice. —

Enough! — I moisten my lips, I wet my thirst, and I gulp it up, all for fear of dying. — Drink all the time and you'll never die. — If I don't drink, I'm high and dry, as good as dead. My soul will fly off to some frog-pond. The soul can't live in the dry. — Waiters, you're good at transubstantiation, turn me from a nondrinker to a drinker! — A perpetual sprinkling for these parched and sinewy bowels of mine — Drinking's no good if you don't feel it.

And in the nineteenth century, the French poet Charles Baudelaire (1821-67) described the state of drunkenness as a means to reach a world superior to that of ugly and boring everyday reality. It permits an escape to the regions of the ideal:

One must always be drunk. That's the main thing: it's the only question. In order not to feel the horrible burden of Time which breaks your back and bows you to the earth, you must get drunk unceasingly. But with what? With wine, with poetry or with virtue, as you please. But get drunk.

Thus, when considering the place of alcohol in society and how it is reflected in literature, it is of central importance that we do not make the mistake of looking only at its negative aspects. Though these are important, and though they have informed much writing about drinking and the family, they are not in any sense the whole story.

3 SOCIAL INFLUENCES ON THE USE OF ALCOHOL IN THE FAMILY

Stan Shaw

The social influences affecting the use of alcohol in the family can be conceptualised as pulling in two directions at once. On the one hand 'the use of alcohol fulfils some function, which man, rightly or wrongly, values' (Jellinek, 1945). It has been approved for centuries in many societies and is associated in many people's minds with enjoyment, conviviality, and as a symbolic ingredient in social rituals, including special family occasions. On the other hand, alcohol is a potentially dangerous drug which can cause addiction and considerable disruption to drinkers and their families. Excessive drinking can lead to marital disharmony, crime, difficulties at work and a host of social, psychological and physical problems. The cost to society overall is dramatic. In 1977 it was estimated that the cost to Britain of lost industrial production, illness, accidents, fires, crime and property damage due to alcohol abuse totalled £1,000 million. Yet the economic effects of alcohol also balance out. For in that same year, total receipts from Excise and Custom duties and purchase tax (VAT) on alcoholic drinks amounted to over £2,000 million!

The use or non-use of alcohol within the family reflects these major contradictory forces. Indeed, it has often been assumed that the way in which families educate their chldren about alcohol determines how much disruption alcohol can cause or how its bad effects are prevented. For it has been hypothesised that groups and societies who 'get the balance right' can prevent the worst excesses of alcohol abuse if 'drinking custom, values and sanctions are . . . well established, known to and agreed upon by all, consistent with the rest of culture, and are characterised by prescriptions for moderate drinking and proscriptions against excessive drinking' (Blacker, 1966, p. 51). These balanced safe drinking customs are presumed to be established within the family as part of the socialisation process. For example, Americans of Jewish extraction have seemed much less susceptible to problems caused by drinking than have Americans of Irish ethnicity (Ullman, 1958). It has been theorised that Jewish children tend to be introduced to alcohol at a relatively early age by their parents, usually within the context of a religious occasion, and this has been presumed to lead to a more responsible use of alcohol amongst Jewish adults (Snyder, 1962). But this sort of analysis stops one step too soon. For it supposes that the use of alcohol in society is determined by how it is used within the family, without asking why these family attitudes and drinking patterns have arisen in the first place or why certain behaviours and attitudes related to alcohol have developed and been reinforced whilst others have been proscribed. The answers to these sorts of questions are only partly anthropological (such as the influence of religion on the use of alcohol in the Jewish family). There are other important factors which determine what degree of importance alcohol takes within the behaviour of any particular group. Indeed usually there are a whole series of ecological, historical and economic circumstances determining how alcohol has come to be produced, distributed and consumed in different ways from society to society. Ultimately it is these factors which affect how and when alcohol is used within the family. Let us first consider the range of factors which can determine the overall patterns of alcohol use within the family, and having then derived an overall theoretical framework, it will be possible to go on to consider how and why these factors are changing in our society at present, and what implications these have for the use of alcohol in the family.

Broadly speaking, societies in which the use of alcohol has been ingrained within a traditional family context tend to be those in which the production and consumption of alcohol is largely viticultural; for instance Mediterranean countries such as France and Italy, and Latin American countries such as Argentina and Chile. In societies in which the production, distribution and consumption of alcohol is largely concerned with beer and spirits, such as in northern European countries, there tends to be less stress on the use of alcohol in the family. There are various reasons for this.

First, the production of alcohol has tended to be of relatively greater importance to the economic framework of viticultural societies than it has in beer- and spirit-consuming countries. In wine-growing countries such as Italy and France millions of people earn their living from the production and sale of alcoholic drinks. It was once calculated that one-third of the French electorate were partly or entirely dependent on the production, processing and distribution of alcoholic drinks, whilst in Italy, some 10 per cent of all arable land is set aside for viticulture (Jellinek, 1960).

Secondly, the heavy production of alcohol in these societies tends to lead to high consumption within the producing society itself. Although export of wine is of vital importance to France, a massive amount of produce is still consumed within France itself.

The interests of groups dependent upon the production of alcoholic beverages contribute towards the general acceptance of large individual consumption. There exists an identification of the general population with these interests which they recognise as a national one. (In America there is no identification of the nation with a particular alcohol interest.) These interests demand a large number of outlets for alcoholic beverages. In France there is about one outlet for every 97 inhabitants (Jellinek, 1960, p. 22).

Thirdly, viticulture is only possible on a large scale anyway in a warm and sunny climate — a factor which also makes it likely that the inhabitants will be inclined to consume fluids, and to consume alcoholic drinks in particular if they are easy to obtain and cheap.

In some less developed regions, local wine is safer to drink than potentially polluted drinking water (just as beer was consumed with family meals in the past in Britain for the same reason).

For the above reasons, then, alcohol in wine-growing societies assumes a much greater importance in the national culture and in family life. Strong traditions have grown up of drinking within the family unit, especially during meals. Because viticultural societies have tended to endorse alcohol consumption on a widespread scale, it is only to be expected that they have favoured the use of alcohol in a family context and within the home, and the introduction of alcohol to children at an early age. Although, as we shall see, many children in British society take their first alcoholic drink in the presence of parents (Hawker, 1978; Aitken, 1978), it is usually at a later age, and often only at special family occasions such as weddings and parties. Alcohol consumption by all the family at once is rarely legitimised in the normal course of events. In northern European countries where beer and spirits are the more popular alcoholic drinks, and where wine has been until recently regarded as a diversion associated with special meals, normal social drinking tends to occur at well-spaced intervals, and usually not in the home but in a place set apart for alcohol consumption such as a bar or club. Alcohol therefore tends to be taken for its tranquillising and intoxicating properties, and as a symbolic element reinforcing peer-group rather than familial conviviality. Alcohol is consumed rather for the psychotropic drug effect of inducing a degree of altered consciousness in which the drinker will feel more relaxed and sociable. Not only does this tend to be segregated from a family context, but these are not seen as suitable aims for children. Because parents in Anglo-Saxon countries hold a different idea of the purpose of drinking alcohol, they are less likely to introduce their children to alcohol at an early age, to encourage the regular use of alcohol amongst children, or to provide a role model of drinking alcohol in a domestic or culinary context.

In viticultural societies, wine is consumed more for its own sake, for its taste and intrinsic value, as an aid to digestion and the culinary occasion. Drinking occurs in a slower fashion, over no set period and not in a place specially designed for it. Indeed in these cultures, alcohol is often touted as a general tonic and cure for all sorts of ailments. In countries like France people have been reluctant to accept that regular ingestion of large amounts of alcohol will be harmful. France has the world's highest rate of liver cirrhosis mortality, yet in one survey there, 80 per cent of respondents said they believed alcohol was good for their health and a quarter thought it was indispensable (Bastide, 1954). Mandelbaum (1967, p. 19) reported that whilst American airline pilots are forbidden alcohol before or during flights, French pilots have wine with their in-flight meals, since 'that kind of alcohol is defined as food by the French'.

The intrinsic use of wine for pleasure-giving in itself, rather than as a psychological release, is evidenced by the vast literature and activities surrounding the 'appreciation' of wine which has never held so strongly about beer and spirit consumption. There are of course schools of 'appreciation' of traditional beer and spirit drinks, such as those who consider 'real ale' aesthetically superior to keg beer, or malt whisky made with spring water superior to mass-produced Scotch. However, the mythology of different types of beer or spirits is not as complex as that surrounding wine. There are no rules about the 'correct' Scotch to go with different types of food (indeed it is assumed that spirits will likely be consumed without accompanying food); neither are there good years for real ale. In fact the appreciation of beer and spirits is as much preoccupied with superior alcoholic strength as it is with superior taste. The Campaign for Real Ale literature is quick to scorn the weakness of keg beer and lager, and 'real ale' surrogates prepared by the large brewers are invariably stronger than their usual product. A wine is never considered superior to another merely because it is stronger in alcoholic content. The further one moves from predominantly viticultural alcohol economies like say, France, the less the taste of alcohol *per se* is considered, and the more stress is placed, in say, Scotland, on the social symbolism of alcohol and on its drug effect as tranquilliser and intoxicant. Accordingly, the less of a family context is included in alcohol use.

It would of course be simplistic to posit a simple bisection between the viticultural and non-viticultural society. There are obviously differences of degree. Undoubtedly some of the more extreme differences in alcohol usage described by Jellinek (1960) have been eroded by advances in mass communication and mass travel, which have gradually reduced national differences in both attitudinal and consumption patterns. Thus the wine trade has been the most rapidly expanding sector in recent years in Britain, whilst countries like Japan have begun to manufacture 'Scotch'. Moreover, differences between types of alcohol use in the family can occur between societies who appear to lay similar stress on one type of drink. For example, France and Italy are relatively similar culturally, share a common penchant for wine-drinking, and have a considerably higher average alcohol consumption than other European countries (Bruun *et al.*, 1975). Yet the importance of family alcohol use is somewhat more pronounced in Italy than in France. This may be because the French economy relies not just on wine production, but is also heavily involved with the production and distribution of distilled spirits, particularly brandy and liqueurs. There is greater social pressure to drink amongst the French, particularly amongst French males who view heavy drinking as a symbol of virility and manhood, and there is more consumption of alcohol apart from at meals and outside the family. In Italy, wine tends to be considered a food and consumed almost exclusively with meals. Italians, therefore, like Jews, tend to be introduced to alcohol in moderate amounts in a family setting. Alcohol consumption in Italy is strongly home-centred and not surprisingly then, Italians view drunkenness, particularly in public, as bringing disgrace upon the family, whereas the French tend to be more accepting amongst adults of drunkenness in public (Shaw *et al.*, 1978; Sadoun *et al.*, 1965).

These factors also modify aspects of alcohol addiction, as pointed out by Jellinek (1960, p. 24):

> As a vast majority of Frenchmen approve of a daily intake of approximately 2 litres of wine, it is quite understandable that French alcohol addicts feel no guilt about their drinking . . . In Chile, where male society has a high degree of acceptance of large alcohol intake, comparable to that in France, but the great majority of women are opposed to it, alcoholics show no guilt about drinking towards their fathers, brothers, sons . . . but do show marked guilt feelings towards their mothers, wives, daughters . . . on the other hand, in America

and other predominantly Anglo-Saxon countries, the guilt abou
drinking felt towards both sexes is highly characteristic of alcohol
addicts.

Just as France and Italy differ somewhat in the use of alcohol within
the family, so non-viticultural societies also have their idiosyncracies.
In Britain, it is not simply the means of *production* of alcohol which has
served to segregate alcohol consumption from the family context. Much
more important historically has been the pattern of alcohol *distribution*
in Britain. For the traditional outlet in Britain has been the public
house, which originated in Saxon times and has been the usual drinking
venue for the majority of the population ever since. However, in the
Middle Ages, wine-drinking was common in Britain and consumption was
relatively high, but the dissolution of the monasteries effectively ended
British viticulture (Wilson, 1973). 'As a result, the pattern of consumption has since been largely determined by treaties, wars and tariff
levels' (Spring and Buss, 1977, p. 569). Indeed, in Britain, adults have
always been obliged by custom, law and convenience to do most of
their drinking in places granted a special licence to serve alcohol.
The importance of the public house in British society was confirmed
from the seventeenth century onward when the pub began to operate
as a labour exchange, centre of transport and even, occasionally, court
and prison. The pub was the centre of entertainment, providing gaming,
plays, cock and prize fighting, and bear baiting. The public house became a community centre, and there were vast increases in their numbers in the nineteenth century. Although the modern public house
now vies with other types of entertainment, the mythology of the
public house as the natural centre of the community lives on in the
popular imagination, and is particularly reinforced by the mass media
image of 'normal British life' as portrayed in popular British television
and radio serials. This has been true since the days of The Bull in 'The
Archers', and the present crop of soap operas revolve round the Crossroads Motel, the Wool Pack in 'Emmerdale Farm' and The Rover's
Return in 'Coronation Street', all presented as the natural social centres
of their environment. Everyone in 'Coronation Street' is a daily drinker
at The Rover's Return. The media presentation of public houses thus
exaggerates their importance, and presents an idealised picture which
avoids contradicting social attitudes which actually apply in real life.
For example, it is presented as non-problematical for an unaccompanied
woman to enter The Rover's Return and buy a drink, whereas this
might not be approved of in normal circumstances (King, 1979).

ɔ true that the presentation of the pub as the usual
ɔ reflected in the results of social surveys. In 1978, 78
ɹe adult British population went into a public house at
, 54 per cent went once a month, and 37 per cent attended at
.ce a week (FARE, 1979). The ingrained nature of the public
.e system in British life tends to segregate family members from
t.ch other when it comes to consuming alcohol. First, pubs attract
men rather than women (Wilson, 1980). This partly reflects the distribution pattern of alcohol in that a majority of men prefer to drink
beer, while women prefer other drinks, and pubs are the usual source of
draught beer. But an OPCS survey in Scotland where spirit consumption is more popular, also showed that 'regular pub going is predominantly a male activity . . . almost two-thirds (63 per cent) of men come
into the "regular" category, compared with less than one-fifth (18 per
cent) of women' (Departmental Committee, 1973). However, the
survey found that this differed between classes. 'In Scotland, only 25
per cent of those in the professional or intermediate group drink regularly in a public house, compared with between 40 and 45 per cent in
the other groups'. But 'well over a half (56 per cent) of those in professional and intermediate occupations have a drink at least once a
month at home, compared with less than a third of those in other occupational groups' (Departmental Committee, 1973). This tendency of
the middle class to drink more at home and in a family situation than
does the working class, tends to be typical of non-viticultural societies.
A 1980 survey of England and Wales confirmed that middle-class
people drank relatively more wine and spirits and did more of their
drinking at home than working-class people (Wilson P, 1980).

Where the British public house system does cut across demographic
and regional differences in one very important respect is that it effectively precludes the family setting — because children are banned from
public houses. Early in the nineteenth century, all kinds of alcoholic
drinks were legally sold to all age groups (see Chapter 1). Evidence presented to parliament in 1834 found that customers attending 14 public
houses over the course of a week included 142,000 men, 108,000
women and 18,500 children. In 1839 the Metropolitan Police Act pro-
hibited sales of spirits in London to children under 16 years, and this
prohibition was extended over the whole country in 1872. By the 1908
Children's Act, children under 14 were not allowed to enter bars.
People under 18 are not allowed to buy or consume liquor in a bar,
except for persons at least 16 years old who can have beer or cider with
a meal, provided the meal is not served in the bar. Britain's licensing

laws have thus effectively precluded the pub being a setting for alcohol consumption within the family.

Yet if we move on to consider social influences creating *changes* in alcohol use in the family, it becomes obvious that major changes are occurring in the clientele and the importance of public houses. More young people and women now frequent them, which reflects first the growing economic importance of these demographic groups, and secondly, a process of acculturalisation in which patterns of alcohol consumption in Britain have been moving away from a male, adult beer- and spirit-dominated culture based on the public house – a pattern which applied from the late-nineteenth to mid-twentieth century – towards drinking habits which have increasingly taken on certain aspects of viticultural drinking societies, with greater accent on availability of alcohol apart from public houses, more home consumption, more consumption by women and more wine consumption. Ironically, most of these moves have been touted as safer and healthier alternative modes of drinking patterns, but as we shall see, these changes have not been so much alterations as rather additions to an already existing pattern. As such it must be doubtful how far growing social influences encouraging more alcohol use in the family are actually trends leading to safer drinking habits.

In one sense, Britain's drinking habits have been changing since the beginning of the twentieth century. In 1900 there were over 90,000 public houses, but by 1977, despite the massive rise in population, the number of pubs had fallen to under 75,000. This trend was initiated by the introduction of licensing laws in World War I, but accelerated recently due to the growing number of alternative places and types of entertainment, and also the rise of home entertainment, and particularly television. Indeed, since the innovation of mass television, coupled with the rise of young people as a group with relatively high disposable income, the British public house has become less geared to the older person and more and more to attracting younger persons, often of both sexes. A Scottish OPCS survey found that in the 18 to 24 age group, about three-quarters visited a public house at least once a month, much more frequently than amongst older age groups (Departmental Committee, 1973). Wilson (1980) found that 70 per cent admitted having a drink in a public house before they were 18. 'Contrary to the widespread belief that supermarkets are the sources of supply for young people, the majority choose to buy their drinks in pubs or from off-licences. Young people who drink from choice in a pub, club or discotheque probably see the place where they drink as important as the drink itself' (Hawker, 1978, p. 14). Discotheques, certain pubs and licensed clubs are primarily designed to attract younger persons from both sexes. Hawker has pointed out that,

> reasonable drinking or limited drinking is certainly, as a form of entertainment, less expensive than going to cinemas, theatres, or concerts. Most of the young people in this sample had quite generous incomes from pocket money and part-time jobs and presumably made this decision about how to spend their money. Any commodity, which in addition to its other attractions, is available and comparatively cheap has a wide appeal and this must partly account for the increase in per capita consumption amongst both adults and young people (pp. 14-15).

She found that the price of alcohol was relatively low compared to the personal disposable income of the young people. In her study, only 3 per cent of both sexes thought that alcohol was too expensive for them.

Paradoxically, the trend away from older people's patronage of public houses to that of younger customers is partly a role model learned from parents. Amongst the current generation of young adults, that is parents with young children, 91 per cent of mothers and 92 per cent of fathers drink (Hawker, 1978). This means that the majority of children will grow up in homes where alcohol is accepted socially and parents will undoubtedly provide the models for their children's future drinking behaviour. A major study by O'Connor (1975) shows that English parents and young people hold positive and permissive attitudes towards the use of alcohol and the majority of parents approve of their children drinking, especially in a family and peer group context. Indeed this overcomes a certain amount of negativity towards alcohol and drinking which Jahoda and Crammond (1972) found in the attitudes of children aged 6-10. Hawker found that amongst her sample, almost half, both girls and boys alike, had been given their first drink by their parents at home. But 'it was noticeable when place of drink was looked at in relation to age, the drinking at home decreased amongst the older age group'. Aitken (1978) found that only 2 per cent of 10 year olds and 3 per cent of 12 year olds had taken a drink outside of the parental home or home of adult relatives or friends of parents in the absence of parents. However, 20 per cent of 14 year olds said that they had done so.

Thus drinking in the absence of parents appears to increase over the first two years of secondary schooling. So although parental influence is important in providing some role model for drinking, and often for introducing children to alcohol in our culture, crucial changes occur between the ages of 12 and 14 when peer group influence begins to exert itself. Nevertheless most studies confirm that adolescents retain a negative view of drunkenness and, to some degree, of heavy drinking and spirit-drinking. It would appear that parental influences remain influential in such areas as moral beliefs, whereas peer influences become of increasing importance in such areas as fashion and entertainment. Stacey and Davies (1970) found that the swing towards peer-group drinking behaviour was increasingly confirmed between the ages of 14 and 17. With increasing age, more and more alcohol was consumed in the company of peers. Peer pressures influenced pastimes and expressions of taste which up to about age 14 are to a considerable extent still under the control of parents. After about age 14 the influence of parents decreases and the rise of disposable income, via full- and part-time jobs, besides pocket money, are reflected in the changing drinking patterns amongst young people. Given the availability and attraction of pub, club, and discotheque to this group, it is little wonder that a pattern of very regular drinking is entrenched among many people of both sexes by the time they are 18 to 21.

Having discovered their market potential, brewers have reinforced it through the development of disco pubs, installing juke boxes in bars and so on. It is almost certainly the case that the commonly-offered scapegoats for the increase in youthful drinking in Britain — the rise in the number of supermarkets and off-licences and the influence of drinks advertising — are probably of relatively little consequence and outside the major forces at work. The willingness of brewers to invest in attracting young people to public houses and into changing the role of the public house into a quasi-entertainment centre has also been encouraged because there is a relatively low rate of profit derived from retail sales alone in public houses. There is consequent necessity for investment in other spheres, and for branching into live entertainment, discotheques, catering, and various types of games. By and large these trends have not been designed to promote greater family use of the public house, but to attract younger customers. As the number of public houses has decreased and a high percentage of them have become the domain of younger customers, alternative outlets for alcohol distribution have become increasingly important.

One recourse for the 'serious' beer drinker who prefers to not have to drink to the sounds of juke boxes and video game machines is of course to brew his own beer at home, and indeed this has become an increasingly important market. Whereas home brewing was dismissed by H.M. Customs and Excise in 1970 as 'of no social or revenue significance' (Zacune and Hensman, 1971, p. 7), enough home brew kits were purchased in 1978 to produce 52 million pints (FARE, 1979). This development has been allowed in Britain because home brewing is perfectly legal. Domestic wine production is also legal but its extent is unknown. However, home distillation of spirits is illegal in Britain and is thought to occur only very rarely. Between 1966 and 1969 inclusively, for example, there were a mere 52 convictions for illicit distillation (Zacune and Hensman, 1971).

Still more important than the rise in home brewing has been the change to the taking home of alcoholic drink for domestic consumption. On average, a quarter of male drinking occasions and 39 per cent of female occasions now occur at home (Wilson P., 1980). Again one must look to changes in the law and the alcohol distribution system for an explanation. The trend was basically triggered by the 1961 Licensing Act which allowed off-licences to open during normal shopping hours, followed up by the 1964 Resale Prices Act, which abolished retail price maintenance on alcoholic drink, a decision accepted by the distillers in 1966 and by the brewers in 1970. The result was that by 1977, half of Britain's supermarkets had licences to sell alcohol, and the number of off-licences (including supermarket outlets) which had remained virtually static between 24,000 and 26,000 for over 39 years, suddenly started growing from 1961 onwards each year until it had reached nearly 40,000 by 1978. The trend is still accelerating. There were exactly twice as many new off-licences granted in England and Wales in 1978 compared with 1968 — 2,437 compared to 1,218. The effect of this important shift in the retail distribution of alcohol has been to make alcohol purchase often a part of routine shopping. Accordingly then, women have become much more important in purchasing alcohol and women's decisions and tastes have become more and more prominent. *Women's Market* magazine stated in 1976 that 'with grocery outlet accounting for almost half the current £860 million drinks trade, it is clear that women have become the big spenders in the alcoholic drinks market' (Otto, 1977, p. 25). However, it would be wrong to accept the implication of this statement that the growing importance of women in alcohol use in Britain is only due to the rise of supermarket outlets for alcohol. A number of commentators have erroneously believed the changes in retail distributon have been the sole trend affecting alcohol purchase and consumption in the

British family. It would be more realistic to see this change as part of other wider changes which affect the economic position of women, drinking patterns in general, and in the final analysis changes in the whole structure of the British economy and family system (Shaw, 1980).

In fact, alcohol consumption in general in Britain has been rising dramatically ever since the changes in the law in 1961. Consumption rose consistently throughout the 1960s, and when the drinks industry accepted supermarket distribution and price cutting by the end of the 1960s alcohol consumption accelerated massively between 1969 and 1974. It then reached some sort of plateau, falling slightly up to 1976 and accelerating slightly up to 1979. The net result of the whole development has been a rising family expenditure on alcohol. In 1968, the average weekly household expenditure on alcoholic drink was £1.03 but this had risen to £3.92 by 1978. Alcoholic drinks had also risen as a percentage of total household expenditure over these ten years — from 4.1 per cent of the family budget in 1968 to 4.9 per cent by 1978 (Annual Abstract of Statistics, 1979). But, as one would expect from the increase in off-licence retailing and the slight decline of public house marketing, the relative importance of the type of drinks purchased has changed dramatically. Between 1969 and 1979, beer consumption increased 23 per cent, but the average consumption of wine and spirits each more than doubled. Indeed in the crucial years 1969 to 1974, wine consumption increased 83 per cent in a mere five years, a trend accelerated by a further fall in the duty on wine in 1973, but halted by rises in duty in 1976 and 1977.

In terms of drinking patterns, this tends to reflect the process of 'aggregation'. It confirms the findings in various societies that a large increase in consumption is not usually the result of a complete alteration in a society's drinking pattern, but rather represents the aggregation of new elements added on to already existing stable drinking patterns (Makela, 1975; Sulkunen, 1976). Thus most alcohol in Britain is still consumed in the form of beer, but beer consumption has been only maintaining a slow growth, whilst at the same time, other drinking habits have been developing rapidly. A survey of drinking habits in a London suburb in 1965 (Edwards *et al.*, 1972) found that alcohol use in social classes below I and II, as defined by OPCS (1970), was segregated from the family and confined almost exclusively to the public house, whilst classes I and II tended to have a more continuous pattern of drinking with more versatility in the type of drink consumed. By the time the survey was replicated in 1974 (Shaw *et al.*,

1978), it was clear that the drinking habits formerly typical only of classes I and II had also spread throughout the population, including more wine and spirit consumption, and more drinking at home. It was as if the drinking habits and general shifts in consumption patterns reflected a growing taste among the population in general for the 'good things' in life. Their expenditure on alcohol was increasing, and the real price of wines and spirits was falling much more than was the real price of beer. Combined with an increasing availability of these materials in terms of their outlet, and the growing knowledge of different types of drink which developed from the 1960s, it is not surprising that the working- and middle-class family began to broaden its drinking habits.

In the 1960s also, the development of cheap package holidays made holidays abroad available to many below classes I and II and doubtless this introduced many people to newer drinks, such as white rum, table wine, liqueurs, etc. The appreciation of good living and conspicuous consumption also changed attitudes to the purpose of alcohol consumption, away from its usage purely as an intoxicant, or social and psychological lubricant used only on special occasions, to a more continuous appreciation of alcohol for its own sake – an appreciation of its intrinsic value, taste and quality, particularly as regards wine. In effect, alcohol use in Britain began to take on some of the characteristics of a semi-viticultural society. Thus in 1968, 35.4 million gallons of wine were imported into England; by 1978 this had rocketed to 79.6 million gallons. Between 1970 and 1976, table wine sales rose 45 per cent, and a survey in 1976 showed that there were 18 million table wine drinkers in Britain – a vast new addition to British family drinking habits in that it was fast becoming normal to consume alcohol at home in a culinary context. It was also important in the redistributon of alcohol consumers between the sexes, since 9.5 million were found to be women drinkers, compared to 8.5 million men. Within the same period also, sales of vermouth (such as Martini and Cinzano) rose 118 per cent, but the number of women vermouth consumers rose 140 per cent. (Shaw, 1980).

This process of family drinking habits adopting the characteristics of other cultures can also work the other way round. Simboli's (1976) study of third generation American Italians found that they retained the family wine-drinking habits of their forefathers, but added a substantial amount of spirits and beer consumption to their drinking, particularly amongst males, and usually in non-family situations. However, in the case of both Britain and the Italian Americans, the general relationship between wine consumption and the family context for drinking remains. Although one could relate the British aggregation of wine drinking to an increasing knowledge of continental customs through holidays, EEC membership and so forth, it is necessary to remember that this process has been accelerated most of all because the commodities involved have fallen so much in real price. For it has been calculated that between 1967 and 1977 the real price of beer, as a percentage of disposable income fell 4 per cent, but the real price of wine fell 14 per cent and the real price of spirits 21 per cent (ACCEPT, 1977). Had it been beer that dropped dramatically in real price, then the increased versatility in drinking habits in Britain might not have occurred so strongly. For example, when Finnish law was changed in 1969 in order to make more medium-strength beer available and cheaper, the result was that Finnish heavy spirit-drinking continued, but the Finnish family also began to consume, in addition, medium-strength beer with their meals (Makela, 1970). Thus the change in use of alcohol in Britain must be explained in terms of increased supply certainly as much as, if not more, than changes in demand.

It is also important to note that the type of drinks which fell most in price and the changes in retail distribution made it likely that women would become more influential in the purchase and consumption of alcohol. Not surprisingly, then, a market research survey noted that 'the ladies have become the major factor in the increasing prosperity of the wine trade' (*Alliance News*, 1976, p. 19) and by 1979, an IPC drinks sales executive included that 'the growth amongst women drinkers is the most significant factor affecting the drink market as a whole (Ratcliffe, 1979, p. 6). Yet the reasons for this development, with its important implications for greater use of alcohol in the family and the home context, must be sought not just within the retailing of alcohol, but rather in the whole position of women within the economic structure, and indeed consequent changes in British family structure itself. For not only has the real price of alcohol been falling, particularly that of wines and spirits, but at the same time women's disposable income has been rising. The average wage of women trebled between 1972 and 1977. In 1972, it was only half that of an average man's wage, but by 1977 it was two-thirds. The actual number of men in employment has been dropping, whilst the number of women has been increasing, reaching 9 million for the first time by 1972, and then over 10 million by the middle of 1977 (Shaw, 1980). The Department of Employment (Information Division of the Treasury, 1974, p. 2) concluded that:

The cause of these developments are complex and not all can be quantified. In the past, it was usual for a woman to leave work when she married. Now it is more usual for her to stay at work until the first child is due. With smaller families and less time between children, the period of time while a woman has children under school age has considerably reduced and her total absence from the work force to bringing up her family is much shorter than in previous generations. It is also now more socially acceptable for a woman with dependent children to be in employment.

The changing role of many women in the family structure, from housewife to breadwinner, has naturally involved greater control over her family's spending. With more and more women having a rising disposable income and contributing significantly to the family's income, and with less couples using the system of the male allotting a fixed amount to the wife for housekeeping, the commodities bought, including alcohol, have begun increasingly to reflect the taste of women consumers. At the same time alcohol has more and more become a commodity included within housekeeping expenditure because of its increasing availabilty during routine shopping. It is pertinent also to note from the Treasury Report (Information Divison, 1974) that the major increase in women's employment has been amongst married women. In 1921, only 10 per cent of young married women were employed, but by 1971, nearly half the married women under 30 were, and 'the 1971 figures show a continual increase in the economic activity of married women between the ages of 30 and 50' (p. 3). One should also note here that American surveys have shown that the higher a family income, the less likely women are to abstain, and that employed women are more likely to drink and purchase alcohol than a housewife. The author has noted that trends have particularly affected young women, whose income is now actually at its highest between the ages of 25 and 29 (Shaw, 1980). The ability of young people and young married couples to develop their own drinking habits and their versatility in trying out various types of   alcoholic drink have been accelerated again by the segregation of many young people and young couples from their immediate previous generation, because of the post-war trend in our social structure away from the extended family towards a nuclear family structure, and the greater geographical and economic independence of young single people – a move reflected and reinforced by housing and education policies and greater geographical occupational mobility which allow more adolescents and young married couples to leave the parental home and its environs.

Advertising campaigns for alcoholic drink have duly changed to feed off all these new trends. For example, the touting of the 'bright lights taste' of Martini and the 'shattering' effect of Smirnoff encapsulate the increasing emphasis on young women drinkers, the intrinsic taste value of alcohol, continental habits and the upper-class 'good life' sophistication and economic and sexual independence of which alcohol is promoted as a natural component.

Yet confirmation of the growing importance of women as purchasers and consumers of alcohol, the developing versatility in choice of drink and the growing relationship between these factors and consumption in the context of home and family can be seen even in more staid media products like *Homes and Gardens* magazine, which can carry advertisements for twenty or more different types of alcoholic drink.

What then can be said of the future? In which direction are social influences likely to send the use of alcohol in the British family? It is probable that influences like the above mentioned case of advertising will gradually be curtailed, but this will probably be a cosmetic move aimed at the most obvious target. Advertising has been continually cited as one of the 'causes' of increased drinking, yet in the case of the women's market the drinks trade has been considered by the advertising trade to have been slow to pick up on changes in consumption pattens and to alter their campaigns accordingly (Ratcliffe, 1979). Advertising *per se* reflects social trends rather than originates them; the more important determinants of alcohol use in the family lie in the supply of alcohol — its type, production, distribution, and price — and the demand for alcohol as fixed by broad cultural influences and the degree of disposable income. It can be discerned that certain economic conditions may likely reduce alcohol consumption — high unemployment and rising price of alcohol for example. Yet at the same time there are other influences which may come into operation which may make increased alcohol consumption likely — and ironically these influences are moves to make greater family consumption with viticultural characteristics more likely. For example, both the Departmental Committee on Liquor Licensing in England and Wales (1972) and in Scotland (1973) recommended the relaxation of licensing law and that children should be allowed into certain licensed premises. The England and Wales Report recommended that the legal drinking age should be dropped to 17. The EEC has recommended moves to harmonise official policies on drink throughout the community. Such moves are assumed likely to create more flexible but at the same time more responsible and sensible drinking habits. But as we have seen, these social forces, *ceteris paribus*, merely tend to add on new drinking habits and situations to already existing consumption. The acquisition of continental drinking habits will certainly not be 'safer' or more sophisticated. If one looks at current per capita consumption in EEC countries, France drinks heaviest, followed by Italy, but Britain is second from the bottom (Brewers' Society, 1979). But as the traditional British segregation of regular drinking from home and family becomes increasingly blurred, it is possible that Britain may move more into line with its European partners in the area of alcohol consumption, and the already high prevalence of alcohol-related problems can then be expected to follow suit.

4 THE TRANSMISSION OF ALCOHOL PROBLEMS IN THE FAMILY

John B. Davies

That children sometimes resemble their parents is a commonplace observation. But, whilst similarities in appearance are generally of little consequence, similarities in behaviour are more problematic, especially in cases where the behaviour in question is considered 'deviant' or undesirable in the society in question.

Where a child bears a striking physical similarity to one of the parents, perhaps involving duplicating a particular facial feature, we say things like, 'She has her father's nose', or 'She has her mother's smile.' What is implied in these statements is that the characteristic or group of characteristics in question is a consequence of genetic transmission from one generation to the next. The transmission of particular physical characteristics has been much studied, and where pure strains and single genes are involved the processes are, in terms of broad principles, well understood.

Unfortunately, not all examples of genetic transmission are so simple. Certain characteristics may be underlain by a genetic combination involving a number of elements, rather than by a single gene. Thus, the 'mother's smile' might involve components for lips, teeth, tongue and facial musculature, and each of these might in itself be multi-determined by several interacting genes.

When we talk about ways of *behaving*, the picture is even more complicated. Whilst no one would sensibly suggest that a girl obtains her 'father's nose' by learning it, the girl's behaviour is very much subject to the learning process. Consequently, a similarity between her behaviour and her father's might, it appears, have come about in one of two ways: she might have inherited it from him, or she might have learned to behave like him. In actual fact, both learning from the environment and a genetic basis are demanded for any piece of behaviour. A behaviour cannot take place in the absence of the genetic basis which makes the behaviour possible. (Thus flying is outside the human repertoire, and we cannot learn that behaviour.) Conversely genes only express themselves in a given environment, which usually determines, in part at least, the way in which they express themselves. The argument thus hinges on which is the *most important* contributor

73

to a given piece of behaviour: genetic constitution or environmental learning.

Evidence is often ambiguous. For example, music scholars have many times speculated about the Bach family, in which an inordinate number of family members had a high degree of creative and performing ability. The family tree has been much studied, with a view to demonstrating how the 'musical gene' could have been transported into and between different branches of the family. Unfortunately, the evidence remains largely ambiguous, since it is possible not only that the talent was transmitted genetically, but also that it was transmitted through social and cultural channels existing in the family. The family was largely preoccupied with music and valued it highly, so that any new members coming into the family would be brought up in a musical atmosphere, where opportunities for musical pursuits of all kinds existed, and where a young child would receive encouragement to take part in such activities, and praise when he/she did so.

Whilst not everyone likes music, few would argue that it is a bad thing, or that the world would be a better place without it. This is not the case with other kinds of behaviour. For example, kinds of behaviour that we label schizophrenic, or psychopathic, or alcoholic are often harmful to the individual concerned, and to others. The difficulty is that a view of, for example, alcoholism as being *primarily* caused by a genetic predisposition suggests quite a different approach to the problem than that suggested by a view of alcoholism as being primarily due to environmental learning. The former suggests that there is something very wrong with the individuals displaying the behaviour, whereas the latter suggests that there is something very wrong with the world in which they live.

There is an accumulating body of evidence attesting to the fact that a hereditary component exists in alcoholism. Many workers, particularly those engaged in the social sciences, or who prefer social explanations for whatever reason, are rather dismissive of this evidence, some of which shows not merely a hereditary component but also indicates limits to the environmental learning explanation. The dilemma stems from the fact that one cannot do very much about altering genetic predispositions, whereas there is, in principle at least, slightly more hope of changing the environments in which people grow up and live. A much quoted extract from Edwards (1971) states:

> Since we are not able to manipulate personality and produce a race with no neurosis, the only realistic method of exerting a benign

influence on the prevalence of alcohol addiction is by control of the environmental conditions of drinking . . .

Without entering into discussion of the interdependence of personality and environment, the above statement is not used logically when employed as *prima facie* support for the environmentalist position. The fact that only the environment offers any practical hope for manipulation does not demonstrate a satisfactory theoretical basis for the effectiveness of such manipulations; nor does inability to do anything about it demonstrate the lack of validity of a hypothesis (in this case the 'genetic' hypothesis).

On the other hand, there is also a great deal of evidence demonstrating the effects of social pressures and norms, both within and outside the family, upon the development of drinking behaviour. This view does not meet with approval from those who favour an undifferentiated 'disease' notion of alcoholism, and who would prefer 'treatment' to fall within an exclusively medical framework. Nor do producers of alcoholic beverages favour the notion that people can become alcoholics due to environmental pressures (such as alcohol advertising, cheapness, or easy availability); they prefer the notion that alcoholics have a genetic basis for their alcoholism, which if true would place alcoholism outside their sphere of responsibility.

Genetic and Hereditary Factors in Alcoholism

The genetic theory of alcoholism centres around the idea that certain individuals are born with a metabolism which is abnormal, and which requires the ingestion of alcohol for its 'normalisation' in much the same way that a diabetic 'normalises' him/herself with insulin. There is much evidence showing that alcoholics do indeed differ from non-alcoholics in terms of a number of bodily states or modes of functioning; and to a lesser degree psychological differences have also been identified. The problem with all this information is that *causes* are difficult to differentiate from *effects*. The findings *might* pinpoint those things which predispose a person to become alcoholic, but equally likely, they may indicate what excessive alcohol consumption can do to people.

Animal studies have been carried out to attempt to clarify these issues. A number of workers have shown that it is possible to produce strains of animals, usually mice or rats, which have different degrees of preference for alcohol, thus demonstrating a genetic basis for different alcohol consumption patterns (e.g. Eriksson, 1968). The difficulty here, and one that is readily acknowledged by the author quoted above, is that the demonstration that ingestion of alcohol in rodents *can* be made contingent upon genetic differences through selective breeding is not a demonstration that ingestion of alcohol is *necessarily* of genetic origin in rodents, even less so in human beings. Humans, and apparently even rats, can have a number of reasons for drinking.

A study frequently cited was carried out by Wolff (1972) in which comparisons were made of the physiological effects upon the body of alcohol ingestion, between Caucasians and certain Mongoloid races (Japanese, Taiwanese, Korean). Wolff studied the reactions of both adults and infants. In terms of a number of measures, Wolff found that the Mongoloid sample showed more marked reactions to alcohol than did the Caucasoids, and also that they showed reactions to quantities of alcohol which had little effect upon Caucasoids. The above is sometimes assumed to be a general demonstration that alcohol consumption patterns are necessarily a product of genetically-determined differences in susceptibility to alcohol; but once again the evidence is ambiguous when taken as support for this proposition. In the first instance, the demonstration of between-racial-group differences in reactions to alcohol does not necessarily have any bearing upon within-group alcohol consumption. Secondly, alcoholism is not just a physiological reaction but a form of behaviour; and as stated above there can be a great number of reasons of varying origin for indulging in this form of behaviour.

The most powerful evidence comes from studies of heritability using rather special samples, such as monozygotic and dizygotic twins born to alcoholic or non-alcoholic biological parents (n.b. monozygotic twins come from a single fertilised ovum, and thus have identical genetic constitutions; dizygotic twins come from separate ova and are not genetically identical); half-sibs; adoptees; and other groups who by their nature allow environmental components to alcoholism to be separated out from hereditary components. Good reviews of this and other genetic evidence have been compiled by Goodwin and Guze (1974) and by Shields (1977). Examples of the kinds of things which have emerged from these studies include: the finding that the offspring of alcoholic biological parents, adopted from an early age by substitute parents with no reported alcohol problem, still manifest a higher rate of alcoholism in later life than does a matched sample of control adoptees; the finding that concordance rates for alcoholism are significantly higher in monozygotic twins than in dizygotic twins; and a study of half-sibs (Schuckit *et al.*, 1972) in which the factor of having had an alcoholic biological parent seemed most influential in determining an alcoholic outcome. This study showed that amongst half-sibs with an alcoholic biological parent the fact of actually living with an alcoholic parent made no significant difference to the chances of becoming alcoholic. Given an alcoholic biological parent, a half-sib reared by an alcoholic parent figure was not significantly more or less likely to become alcoholic than a half-sib reared by a non-alcoholic parent figure. This study appears to show that having an alcoholic biological parent was an important factor in predicting alcoholism, but whether the half-sib was raised with an alcoholic parent figure or not made little difference. Whilst the study is not entirely beyond criticism, Winokur (1976) in a paper discussing this type of evidence generally states, 'Were alcoholism not to be a behavioural illness but rather to be an illness with known organic pathology, such findings as these would make one very suspicious [i.e. suspect the presence] of a genetic etiology.'

There is one other special case which, whilst not strictly genetic, is none the less probably more sensibly discussed here than under an environmental label. This is the foetal alcohol syndrome, which is the subject of much recent interest. It appears that children born to mothers with an excessive alcohol consumption pattern sometimes show a cluster of characteristics including cardiac murmers, joint malformations, low measured intelligence (IQ), epicanthic fold, hirsutism, a generally altered pattern of morphogenesis, growth deficiency and failure to thrive. A recent paper by Streissguth (1976) discusses these symptoms in some detail, and includes some powerful photographs of the faces of children born with the syndrome. These findings are of interest here insofar as the foetal alcohol syndrome is an instance in which parental drinking behaviour clearly has had terrible consequences for offspring, though it is not evidence for the transmission of alcoholism *per se*. The possibility that milder forms go unnoticed, and might manifest themselves in limited attention span or learning difficulties at school, remains a topic for speculation.

Setting the foetal alcohol syndrome aside as a special case, the general conclusion from the evidence must be that a genetic component is clearly implicated in alcoholism. In other words, *to some degree*, alcoholism can probably be transmitted from one generation to the next by a genetic mechanism. Its effect is to *increase the probability* that offspring will encounter problems with alcohol in later life.

Importantly, however, the evidence also suggests that this process is not an inevitable one; not all offspring of alcoholics become alcoholics themselves, even in studies of monozygotic twins where genetic constitution is identical. Alcoholism cannot therefore be determined solely or uniquely by genes. Consequently, it seems likely that what we are talking about is not a constitution which *determines* alcoholism, but a continuous distribution of 'predisposition', ranging from 'high' to 'low', which does not make an alcoholic outcome inevitable. Environmental pressures and life events may ensure that an individual with a 'high' predisposition becomes a tee-totaller, whilst someone with a basically 'low' predisposition none the less becomes alcoholic. Furthermore, the difference between these postulated 'highs' and 'lows' might generally be rather slight and consequently of little substantive importance, except perhaps in a few extreme cases. The belief that anyone can become an alcoholic if he or she drinks enough is substantially true despite the genetic evidence. In summary, whilst the above evidence strongly supports the idea of a genetic component in alcoholism, the extent of this involvement relative to other factors is still a matter for some debate.

As a footnote to this section, it should be noted that learned behaviours are not transmissable through genetic mechanisms. Thus, learning to become a violinist, a teacher, a gymnast or an alcoholic in no way affects the genes a person will pass on to his/her offspring (unless they become accidentally damaged in the learning process, when the outcome will probably not be beneficial).

Social and Environmental Factors in Alcoholism

As we shall see, there is recent strong evidence that the number of alcoholics in a country bears a relationship to the mean *per capita* consumption in that country. This is not surprising, and merely suggests that people drink more, and are consequently more likely to suffer from alcoholism, in some countries than in others. Studies of heredity are not designed to take into account such general influences of drinking culture on alcoholism 'base rates', so that sometimes we mistakenly assume that confirmation of a genetic hypothesis is 'proof' that other factors are not important. For example, twin studies like those described in the previous section may be carried out in different countries with high and low alcoholism prevalence rates respectively. Once samples have been obtained, the results might well be substantively identical, and a genetic or heredity type hypothesis again be supported. It should be remembered, however, that the aim is to test this type of hypothesis rather than a social/environmental one. The fact that, in the 'high consumption' country the experimenter found it far easier to obtain his quota of 100 alcoholic twin pairs (or whatever) than did the researcher in the 'low consumption' country, is unlikely to be reported. Indeed, since researchers seldom work on a cross-national pairing basis, the extent of the influence of general consumption patterns on alcoholism rate will normally be unknown in such studies. Unfortunately, in research into the genetic basis of alcoholism, the relative ease of obtaining samples is readily lost sight of since it is peripheral to that line of research. The effects upon individual drinking of different types of 'drinking culture' cannot be illuminated by studies carried out within a single culture.

The conclusions from the genetic studies, however, suggest that parental influences with respect to alcohol are by no means as automatically pervasive, straightforward or specific as might have been imagined. Influences of a widespread nature outside the immediate family circle are important in shaping drinking behaviour. In other words, the nature of the drinking culture is of fundamental importance. A recent study by Davies (1979) shows a very high association between indices of the prevalence of alcoholism and the general level of consumption in 16 different countries, a finding which is difficult to reconcile with an argument for strong genetic determination, particularly as there is limited evidence to suggest that these things co-vary over time *within* countries. Consequently, the starting point for parental influence is not the obvious one of merely providing a non-alcoholic model of alcohol consumption, but the much more subtle problem of endeavouring to raise offspring who will successfully guide themselves through, and selectively perceive, the drinking environment generally, both within and outside the home.

Recent investigations of the precise relationship between parent's drinking behaviour and children's knowledge of alcoholic drinks are virtually non-existent, but two studies provide some food for thought. The first piece of work is a PhD thesis by Penrose (1978) at the University of California. In this study, children aged 5-6 years old were asked to guess the drinks (both alcoholic and non-alcoholic) that were likely to be consumed by various child and adult figures in a number of party situations. In addition, each child's parents filled in a questionnaire about drinking patterns in the home. No relationship was found between the children's responses and their parent's answers to the drinking questionnaire. A roughly similar type of study by Jahoda *et al.* (1980) related children's knowledge of various alcoholic and non-alcoholic drinks, and the people likely to use them (including father- and mother-type figures), to parents' questionnaire answers about their own consumption. As in the previous study, no relationship emerged between the parents' questionnaire answers and the children's knowledge of drinks and who used them. The children were not more knowledgeable about the drinks their parents usually drank; neither did a high or low reported parental consumption lead to lesser or greater accuracy of responses by their children. Since 91 per cent of the children in this study (N = 113) discriminated correctly overall between the use patterns of alcoholic and non-alcoholic drinks, the conclusion appears to be that the general drinking culture is often sufficiently powerful to swamp any specific effects that might occur due to parents' own consumption patterns.

During the last seven or eight years, a number of normative studies of children's drinking behaviour have been carried out. In 1972 Jahoda and Crammond produced the report *Children and Alcohol*. One aim of this study was to determine whether young children of primary school age would understand and benefit from education about alcohol. Amongst other things, it emerged that, even at age 6, a substantial number of children possessed a working concept of alcohol, could identify alcoholic and non-alcoholic drinks, knew something of conventional usage patterns, and could identify drunken behaviour. In the light of the preceding paragraphs, it may be concluded that much of this information is gleaned from children's observation of the media and other environmental influences, and is not solely a function of their experience of drinking patterns in the parental home. On the other hand, this study found that about two-fifths of the children in the sample (the children were aged between six and ten years) reported having tasted alcohol at some time. This was usually in the home, under parental supervision (usually the father's). Parents were also an important reported source of attitudes and opinions about alcohol; either through explicit exhortations, or *implicit* messages deriving from their own drinking.

Because studies have revealed parental influences upon certain attitudes in children, it has sometimes been assumed that the model of alcohol consumption provided by parents might in itself be the most important influence in shaping children's knowledge of alcohol and its use. Recent evidence suggests, however, that the influence of parents' own consumption is by no means as direct and specific as has been assumed; it seems likely that the general culture provides a background against which specific home models become somewhat blurred. Common sense suggests that a model of parental alcohol consumption which is uncontrolled can hardly be a beneficial influence, but it appears that children's knowledge of alcohol and its use bears no straightforward relationship to parents' own consumption.

The children's study by Jahoda and Crammond cited above is the first of three volumes tracing the development of normative drinking among growing children and youth. The other volumes are *Teenagers and Alcohol* (Davies and Stacey, 1972), which is a study of teenagers aged fourteen to seventeen, and the recent study filling in the age gap between the previous two, *Ten-to-fourteen-year-olds and Alcohol* (Aitken, 1978). Taken together, these latter two studies show a general trend for parental influences to become less powerful with children's increasing age, and for their behaviour to become increasingly responsive to the demands and pressures of the peer group. Drinking follows this pattern for most young people, who make the transition from occasional sips on special occasions under parental supervision, through parties and other early experiments with drink at which parental influence is less strong and peer group influence stronger, to a situation at age 17 or 18 years where most drinking takes place outside the home in pubs or bars or other licensed premises. This appears to be a normative pattern in the development of drinking behaviour, and in itself is entirely to be expected as part of the anticipatory socialisation process operating in our society. The parental task is thus to provide an early drinking environment, when parental pressures are most strong, which will 'inoculate' the child against and enable him/her to perceive and withstand, those occasions outside the home on which a deviant model of alcohol consumption is presented, in later life. Other important studies of normative alcohol use have been produced by O'Connor (1978), again with young people, and by Dight (1976).

The Social Context of Drinking

An approach which stresses the influence of any kind of environmental factors, be they social or otherwise, places emphasis upon the ways in which behaviour is modified as a result of previous reinforcement history, or 'experience'. In psychological jargon, this is a definition of learning. When the process appears to depend centrally on other people rather than on inanimate objects, 'social learning' is said to be involved.

Social learning is of considerable importance in the shaping of drinking behaviour, since the consumption of alcoholic drinks by adults is observed by youngsters both in real life and in the media, and affects their views of drinking and their attitudes towards drink. If observation encourages the belief that consuming drinks leads to being a 'real man', or a 'mature person', or whatever else, then drinking may come to be perceived as a route to the achievement of these desired goals through a process of association.

The tendency for youngsters (and adults) to behave in ways which resemble the behaviour of others has often been described by psychologists, and whilst a number of slightly different theoretical positions have been adopted, it appears that in common parlance the copying tendency can vary along a kind of 'strength' continuum. At one extreme, there is simple 'imitation' in which a child (usually) simply replicates fairly closely a specific piece of observed behaviour; such imitation very often ceases if the model is observed to receive a negative outcome for the behaviour in question. Next comes 'modelling', a broader concept involving a larger repertoire of behaviour, in which the observer's actions do not precisely mimic, but go beyond, those of the model. Finally, there is 'identification', a less clearly defined idea which involves the whole individual, a *type* of responding rather than a set of specific acts, and a psychological attachment to a particular type of model which is chosen in preference to other available model types. Whilst it may be fairly easy to alter specific non-desired imitative acts, types of behaviour which have their roots in identification with a particular type of model may be much less easy to change with simple specific interventions. As will be seen later, alcohol consumption by youngsters develops from simple imitation (perhaps), into one aspect of a learned identification process which permeates a wide range (possibly all) of the individual's behaviours, attitudes and values. As with delinquency, it is conceivable that the performance of acts which attract negative comment, sanctions or punishment from other groups is *congruent* with the model with which the individual identifies.

Studies have demonstrated that the young person who drinks heavily in comparison with his fellows differs in a number of ways from those who drink less heavily. The style of drinking is thus not a separate and isolated element in the attitudinal/behavioural 'repertoire', but is one element in a general pattern of behaviours and attitudes. Providing 'inoculation', therefore, requires parental models and influences which attempt to shape the 'repertoire' generally, rather than a specific drinking model. This fact is often not comprehended. 'I don't know where he gets it from,' resigned parents sometimes say. 'We hardly drink at all, and yet our Jimmy (or Susan) comes home drunk nearly every night.' Because drinking heavily is only one behaviour in a cohesive set of attitudes/behaviours which amount almost to a 'view of the world', one can venture the following: it may be possible for parents who drink very little (or perhaps do not drink at all), as well as for those who drink more freely, to provide models for a variety of behaviours which can form a context appropriate to the development of excessive alcohol consumption in their children. It is not sufficient merely to drink little or nothing, as though this were the only concession necessary.

Alcoholism is not inevitable. Consequently, if a child seriously abuses alcohol in a way which gives rise to concern it will be because of the things that happen to him/her, and will be related to the life 'philosophy' which he/she learns, the basis for which is laid down during the early home years during which parental influence is strongest. If the parental 'philosophy' resembles in subtle ways the one of the adolescent peer group, as it does perhaps in some cases, or if the 'philosophy' is simply one of indifference or not caring, then the peer group model will offer attractions for which there is no counter influence. The same result may occur if the 'philosophy' offered is so rigid and strict that it becomes perceived as impossible to attain.

In studies of drinking amongst teenagers, it is frequently found that those who drink the most tend also to be those who smoke the most. A detailed study of smoking, 'The Young Smoker', was produced by Bynner in 1969. This study makes an interesting comparison with drinking studies, especially the Davies and Stacey, and Aitken studies referred to above, because it appears that many of the things which turn out to be characteristic of the heavy-drinking (in relation to others of his/her own age) teenager turn out also to be characteristic of the heavy-smoking teenager. In other words, there is much in common between smoking and drinking in terms of the symbolic attraction of these activities and the view of the world which goes with them. The notion that drinking is one aspect of a broader cluster of attitudes and behaviours is thus reinforced. This notion is by no means new; a recent paper by Zucker on parental influences on children's drinking patterns (1976) emphasises a general social-learning theory approach, but more interestingly, discusses the development of problem drinking in children almost entirely within a general 'deviancy' framework. This author asks the following question (p. 233): '. . . to what extent is a general theoretical framework of socialisation to deviance appropriate in explaining the specific learning of one behavioural repertoire having to do with alcohol consumption in adolescence?' From a summary of available evidence, he concludes that 'general deviance', and problem drinking are alternative ways of expressing 'similar need systems'. (The main point stands, without the need to accept literally the phrase about 'need systems'.)

The position taken here is that problem-drinking by teenagers is certainly only one facet of a more general repertoire, but that whether one views this repertoire as appropriately described as 'deviant' depends very much on who you are, and what you regard as (or what you would like to see imposed as) 'normal' behaviour. The label 'deviant' implies that there is something specific and identifiable wrong with the people displaying the behaviour *other than the behaviour itself* (i.e. the behaviour is seen as a manifestation of 'deviance' as a property of the person), and thus overlooks the possibility that certain so-called 'deviant' behaviours are in fact logical and adaptive forms of adjustment to given situations. In other words 'deviance' always raises the question 'Deviant from what?' It may be somewhat unrealistic to urge certain parents to adopt a more middle-class (i.e. 'non-deviant') view of the world, in the interests of their children's welfare, in circumstances where the influences which shape their children's behaviour are the same ones which have also shaped the parents' behaviour, and when the resultant attitudes and behaviours are reinforced by the (perceived) world in which both the parents and children live. The notion that serviceable attitudes and beliefs can be altered by simple verbal messages, without altering the environmental conditions which reinforce the attitudes, is naive.

What Could Parents Do to Help?

This final section serves as a more optimistic antidote to the gloom of the previous paragraph, the gist of which was that some parents are in no position to help themselves, let alone anyone else. Those parents who are more fortunate might help, not by immediately considering what is actually or potentially worrying about their sons'/daughters' behaviour, but by first taking a close look at themselves. The studies referred to previously have shown that many adolescents and older teenagers believe that the consumption of alcohol bestows upon the consumer certain prized characteristics which make the consumption of alcohol highly desirable. The Davies and Stacey study isolated two factors associated with the perception of teenagers who drink. The first of these concerned 'toughness'. Drinkers were perceived as being more mature, more able to look after themselves, tougher, harder, and more interested in the opposite sex, than were non-drinkers. (Being *bad* at schoolwork also emerged as a component of this factor.) A second factor concerned 'sociability'. The most important aspects of this factor were having lots of friends and being attractive to the opposite sex. By and large, teenagers perceived the non-drinker as having negative 'toughness' (i.e. as being, in plain words, a bit of a 'wet' or a 'cissy') and as having insufficient sociability. Relationships of the above type have emerged in other studies. In considering these findings we adult males might like to consider how important it is for us to present a masculine and husky image to the world. The fact that many males give some considerable priority to presenting an appearance of being 'all male' is suggested by the way advertisers have in the past fed this conceit with messages like 'Guiness for strength' (why not Guiness for gentleness?) or 'Bass for men' or 'The one you don't down in one'; and for males in higher occupational groups deodorants called Brut, cars called Stag and Mustang, and so on. We might also ask ourselves more generally how much we are attracted by aspects of the 'sociability' message. In advertisements, this is sometimes portrayed as a kind of sexually polarised fantasy world in which everyone seems to be superficially having a good time, although the reasons why this is so are not apparent, since no one is doing anything constructive, worthwhile, or even moderately enjoyable, apart from looking sexy and drinking drinks. The people in the advertisements appear both normless and aimless, as though they suffered from some type of 'psychopathic sociability', and the achievement of the surface appearance seems to be an end in itself.

In other words, before we adults start an attack upon the immature and childish beliefs and stereotypes of the younger generation, we ought to be quite sure that we don't actually subscribe to some very similar ones ourselves. The association between these beliefs and heavier drinking in young people suggests that alcohol consumption will be perceived by offspring as a necessary means for their realisation, if the parents create a home atmosphere in which the child learns that such myths relate to valued and prized goals. Much alcohol advertising actually seeks to surround the consumption of particular beverages with one of these factors of either hypermasculine toughness, or fantasied sexual sociability – and it sells drink to adults.

A study by Davies (1981) of workers in five industries on Clydeside made use of scales which had been employed previously in an adolescent study, to see whether adult views in fact related to the 'immature' views of adolescents in the way suggested. The results confirmed the relationship within the limited scope available in an industrial study, though broader investigations of these matters are required. Both the adult and the adolescent study showed a tendency for those adolescents and adults who drank the most to subscribe more strongly to an 'alcohol myth' factor than did those who drank less. Components of this factor included agreement with statements like 'People who drink are more attractive to the opposite sex', 'People who drink are more friendly than those who don't', 'There's something mature and manly about men who drink', 'It's only natural for a man to like his drink', and 'People who drink know how to look after themselves'. In this instance, there is evidence that the 'immature' views of youth, and the 'mature' views of adults are pretty much the same in some cases.

The adolescent study also showed that the heavier drinking teenagers tended to have lowered respect for authority figures (not *necessarily* a bad thing), had higher scores on a 'materialistic/cynical' factor (which involved agreement with items like 'The most important thing in the present day is to have lots of money', 'People with lots of money have the best of everything', 'It is funny when people get angry or annoyed' and 'It is sometimes funny when a person gets injured'), tended to be heavy smokers, and had lots of friends who drank. Amongst the boys and girls in this study the heavier drinkers also had higher scores on a 'trouble/precocity' factor, (which included items about conflict at home, trouble with the police, and reports of having been on probation) which seems, possibly, to have some relationship to delinquency.

From the above it should be apparent that the idea that drinking is only one part of a constellation of beliefs and behaviours is not mere speculation, but is strongly supported by evidence. With respect to these latter variables, what are lacking are comparable data for adults, but at risk of being wrong, one might be willing to speculate that views of this type can frequently be found amongst parents as well as amongst young people.

In short, the task of parents is not simply to provide a specific model of controlled drinking behaviour (though this is probably quite a good start), but the more difficult one of providing an environmental context and a view of society within which the heavy consumption of alcohol is not a functional form of behaviour, and within which alcohol is not used for implicit socially symbolic reasons.

Finally, although certain attitudes and beliefs have been shown to be associated with heavier drinking, both amongst teenagers and adults, it is not the suggestion that the attitudes automatically *cause* the drinking. Both drinking patterns and attitudes are frequently formed in response to particular social and environmental influences and pressures. Changing attitudes is thus most effective where the attitude change is brought about by alterations to those circumstances which actually reinforce the attitudes and the related behaviours. People do not acquire beliefs and attitudes out of thin air, or just because they feel like it. The attitudes and beliefs serve real functions, and help people to make sense of the world in which they live. If you can apparently make a person 'change his mind' about something merely by persuasion, it probably means that the belief in question has few immediate consequences for that person. Changing attitudes which have been formed as a result of repeated life experiences with important consequences is rather more difficult. Not all parents are in a position to provide the type of life 'philosophy' or 'view of the world' implied in the preceding paragraphs. This is so because for many adults alcohol provides not only a real release from tensions, pressures and troubles encountered in the world, but equally important the myths and images associated with alcohol consumption enable many people to achieve, albeit in a restricted sphere, some self-esteem and to come a little closer to their 'ideal self' — things which are perhaps less readily available to them in the other aspects of their lives. Consequently, to see the problem of 'transmission of alcoholism' as basically revolving around the way in which something is or is not transmitted from parents to children, is to see only part of the process. Today's children become tomorrow's parents. We can make suggestions about the transmission of alcoholism from parents to children, but what shall we do about the things which influence both the children and their mothers and fathers too?

5 SEX ROLES, FAMILY ORGANISATION AND ALCOHOL ABUSE

Joy Leland

Background

Sex roles have been implicated as an influence on alcohol use throughout the course of modern alcohol studies, especially in recent years. The logical impetus for the idea grows out of reported differences between the sexes in the incidence, antecedents, manifestations and results of drinking and various associated problems. To account for these differences, two broad types of explanations are possible. The first and probably simplest would be to identify sex-linked physiological traits which induce a genetically-transmitted differential response to alcohol. The alternative would be more complicated — other differences between the sexes growing out of their life experiences as individuals and/or as members of social groups, especially the family.

Sex differences have served as an organising principle in all known societies. Although the degree and the details of sex differentiation vary greatly among groups and over time, humans have consistently assigned different sets of responsibilities and privileges to men and women. In everyday English speech, we refer to these sets of responsibilities and privileges, plus the attitudes, behaviours and appearances which are associated with them, as sex roles.

The origins of sex-role differentiation are obscure. Some people argue that only genetically-determined differences in psychological make-up could account for the regularities in the content of sex roles that occur across cultures and over time, particularly the widespread sexual division between home and family activities for women and outside pursuits for men, which has been attributed to differential aptitudes between the sexes.

At the other extreme, while conceding a limited set of inherent sexual differences such as the greater physical strength of men and the child-bearing function of women, other people argue that sex roles must be more constructed than innate in order to account for the variable content and degree of sex differentiation among cultures and throughout history. According to this view, sex roles are primarily an

88

outgrowth of cultural forces, including economics and politics. These in turn produce responses which become institutionalised and transmitted across generations through family child-rearing practices preparing children for their roles as adults. Thus culturally derived and propagated differences between the sexes are incorporated by family socialisation into the individual personalities of group members and may persist long after the conditions which made them functional have disappeared.

A mixed model incorporating aspects of both nature and nurture seems most plausible. Even if some differences in the roles assigned to men and women have a genetic basis, the nurture element in the equation is likely to remain large, given the abundant evidence (1) of humans' astonishing adaptability to social forces and (2) of culture's role in translating physical characteristics into behaviour. Here our discussion will emphasise the influence of nurture, rather than nature, on sex roles and drinking behaviour.

Divisions along sex lines are less pronounced in the world's 'tribal' societies than in modern Western nations. The restrictions of women to the family and men to the public sphere developed late in human history in association with the industrial revolution and has tended to be restricted to the urban middle classes of Western countries. Sex differences currently are said to be blurring in these very groups. Rather than modernisation, this trend might be more correctly viewed as a conservative move, back to the way we used to be and the way much of the world has remained.

Sexual differences in drinking follow similar patterns; they are less prevalent in 'tribal' societies and more pronounced in modern Western societies. In 'tribal' societies, men are reported to drink more than women in only about 60 per cent, while the sexes drink equally in the remainder (Bacon, 1976). In all Western societies for which we have data, more men than women drink heavily and experience drinking problems, though the sex ratios vary among nations and subgroups within nations.

The tendency for strong sex differences in drinking to co-occur with strict sexual divisions in other facets of life reinforces the notion that sex roles might have something to do with patterns of alcohol use and abuse. In fact, these parallels would seem to present ideal conditions for exploring possible relationships between sex roles and drinking. Unfortunately, however, we have not been able to take much advantage of this 'natural experiment' of cross-cultural comparison because so far we have little detailed information about alcohol use in tribal societies. Even for Western societies, the drinking data available for different nations are seldom comparable. Consequently, most investigations of the association between sex roles and drinking have focused on single nations, and primarily the United States.

Sex Differences in Drinking

The most obvious way to explore the part sex roles play in alcohol use would seem to be to begin with documentation of actual differences in drinking behaviour and consequences between the sexes and of other sex differences which could account for these. Gomberg (1979) and others have provided recent, concise reviews of this literature. Here we will cover only one recent study (Beckman, 1978b), which addresses many of the pertinent issues. Using a large sample (477) and adequate controls, Beckman confirmed earlier clinical indications that alcoholic women in the US exhibit important differences from alcoholic men in the course and pattern of their drinking. In comparison to alcoholic men, alcoholic women reported: (1) a later onset of heavy drinking; (2) more frequent association between initiation of heavy drinking and a specific stressful event in their lives; (3) more rapid development of problem drinking; and (4) more solitary drinking at home, but also more drinking in the company of their spouses.

Although the study revealed no significant differences between male and female alcoholics in age, religion, education, marital status or the presence of children, it did identify some personality differences which might shed light on the contrasts in the sexes' drinking histories and behaviour. The alcoholic women showed lower power needs, higher dependency needs, and a more external locus of control than the men. These traits dispute the common notion that alcohol abuse blurs sex differences in personality. Also, they fit the folk sex-typed roles in our society — that women prefer to be cared for, while men like to control. In fact, the first two traits are central to separate predictions of lower problem-drinking rates in women than in men, derived from two general theories of alcohol abuse to be described here later — the power theory and the dependency theory. The fourth personality difference reported by this study was that alcoholic women exhibit less traditional sex-role attitudes than men.

Sex-role Conflict

This brings us to a curious preoccupation by an important body of research with the relationship between drinking and sex-role conflict in women. Since a main rationale for the notion that sex roles have something to do with drinking is derived from the tendency for men to abuse alcohol more than women, we would expect the work to concentrate on a search for role differences between men and women which could explain sex differences in drinking behaviour. Instead, more attention has been given to co-variation within the female sex between alcohol abuse and sex-typed attitudes and performance.

Over the course of our discussion of this research, it is of interest to note that the strategies employed pay little attention to the family context. This seems strange, since the family is not only the main source of sex-role instruction, but also the setting where much sex-typed behaviour takes place, particularly for women.

Over several decades, many studies have alluded, with varying degrees of documentation, to a spectrum of sex-role problems in women who abuse alcohol (see reviews in Beckman, 1978a; Wilsnack, 1976; Gomberg, 1979). However, actual tests of a possible association between female drinking and sex roles have appeared only recently. Perhaps the most prominent of these have been conducted by Sharon C. Wilsnack, a psychologist now at the University of North Dakota School of Medicine. Overall, Wilsnack interprets her results: (1) as providing empirical support for the previous clinical observations of disturbed feminine identification in adult (but not teenage) alcohol abusers; (2) as suggesting conflict between conscious femininity and unconscious masculinity as the particular form of sex role conflict which may contribute to adult women's alcohol abuse; and (3) as indicating that drinking makes women (normal, as well as problem drinkers, younger as well as older ones) feel more womanly and thus provides them with an instrument to reduce temporarily their sex-role conflict.

Confirming earlier results by other investigators, Wilsnack's alcoholics did not differ from the normal women in their responses to a number of questions concerning *conscious* sex-typed feminine attitudes, interests and values, or on a check-list concerning attention to physical appearance (greater attention thereto assumed to reflect greater conscious interest in traditional feminine values). Furthermore, the alcoholics responded in a more 'feminine' manner than controls to interview questions concerning motherhood; they wanted more children and more additional children than controls, perhaps reflecting the fact that on the average they had produced fewer offspring than the controls. However, on less conscious levels, indications of masculine tendencies did emerge among the alcoholic women. They gave more 'masculine' assertive responses than matched non-alcoholic controls to most of the questions designed to investigate sex-role style (willingness to accept leadership, desire to achieve, assertiveness, frankness, etc.). In addition, their responses were more 'masculine' than controls on the Frank Drawing Completion Test. That is, they used sharp angles to close off open areas of stimulus drawings, as men do, as opposed to using round shapes, curving lines, open spaces and elaborated inner areas of the drawings, as women in general do, including the non-alcoholic controls.

From these results Wilsnack inferred that the alcoholic women were torn between strong conscious preferences to be feminine, and unconscious masculine feelings, i.e. they exhibited sex-role conflict *between* levels of consciousness, and to a greater degree than the non-alcoholics.

Further evidence of sex-role disturbance was inferred from the alcoholics' reports of higher rates than controls of gynaecological and obstetrical disorders before the onset of alcohol abuse, which could reflect stress to her self-concept resulting from conflict between conscious desires to perform adequately traditional feminine roles, such as motherhood, and unconscious leanings toward masculine roles.

Thus far, Wilsnack's results merely indicate that women who drink too much exhibit greater sex-role conflict than controls. But why should sex-role conflict manifest itself in alcohol abuse in particular?

Wilsnack's next study (1974) proposed a plausible explanation: drinking reduces sex-role conflict by making women feel more womanly, thus lessening the dissonance between their unconscious masculine inclinations and their conscious desires for femininity. In an earlier pilot study (reported in Wilsnack, 1974), drinking had also seemed to increase womanly feelings in 20 non-alcoholic young women. That is, after two drinks, they reported such feelings as 'warm, loving, considerate, expressive, open, pretty, affectionate, sexy and feminine' — assumed to reflect 'traditional femininity'.

To test further the notion that women drink to feel more womanly, Wilsnack looked for evidence of unconscious deviations from traditional sex roles in the responses of 25 young female social drinkers in an experimental party setting. Imaginative stories written by the women before drinking contained more 'masculine' (power) themes than those they wrote after drinking, which included more 'feminine' themes, i.e. themes which in other research had characterised fantasies during breast feeding — assumed to represent an archetypical female activity. She interpreted this evidence as indicating that alcohol brings the unconscious self into line with the more feminine conscious self. However, one might note that Wilsnack's argument would be more convincing if she had shown that drinking increased feminine feelings in alcoholic women, as well as in these female social drinkers.

Wilsnack's formulation was strengthened by her findings that, before drinking began, the women who exhibited the most sex-role conflict, and hence the greatest need to reduce it, were the ones who eventually drank most heavily in the experimental setting.

Wilsnack would be the last to suggest that the above findings definitively implicate sex-role conflict in excessive drinking among US female alcoholics. Obviously, the small sample sizes, alone, would preclude such a generalisation, as would the complicated chain of assumptions and inferences underlying the interpretation of subjects' responses to the various measures, particularly the assumption that items which have in the past distinguished men from women reflect the actual content of current US sex-role differences.

In fact, the Wilsnacks' (1978) subsequent work suggests that the relationship between sex roles and drinking in females is more complicated than her previous studies had indicated. Among white, black and Spanish girls who drink, they found that those who reject traditional femininity are likely to drink more and have more drinking problems than those who value it, but this relationship did not hold for Oriental and American Indian girls. In fact, for Indians the small associations were in the wrong direction— drinking problems were more frequent in those who most valued traditional femininity. These (and other) qualifications, which emerged from the Wilsnacks' 1978 work, concerning the possible relationship between sex roles and drinking, probably are in part a reflection of the later sample's greater size (13, 122 vs. 28) and ethnic variability than the earlier ones. Note that the relationship between rejection of traditional femininity and problem drinking in these *young* girls is in striking conflict with findings of the opposite association in Wilsnack's (1973) *adult* women. To reconcile these contradictory findings, the Wilsnacks (1978, p. 871) suggest that sex-role conflict may contribute to drinking problems in different ways for young women than for older ones:

Adolescent girls who reject traditional femininity and drink heavily for symbolic reasons and relief of stress may progress from early drinking experience to dependence on alcohol. Girls who adhere to traditional femininity may be better protected from early drinking problems, but later in life the commitment to femininity may expose some of them to role crises and conflicts which they may cope with by drinking.

Qualifications on the idea that sex-role conflict encourages women to drink emerge from the work of Parker (1972, 1975) and Beckman (1978a). The most serious challenge to the idea of an association between sex-role conflict and female alcohol abuse emerges from Beckman's analysis of the patterning of conscious versus unconscious femininity within each woman. Although conflict between conscious femininity and unconscious masculinity was the most prevalent form of sex-role conflict in these alcoholic women, it occurred in only about one-quarter of them (compared to one-eighth of the controls). If such conflict is not present in a majority of alcoholic women, obviously it cannot contribute to an explanation of female alcohol abuse in general.

Furthermore, like Parker (1972), Beckman found some examples of the logically possible opposite form of sex-role conflict — conscious masculinity versus unconscious femininity was exhibited by 6 per cent of the alcoholics (compared to 10 per cent of the controls). When the two forms of conflict were combined, disregarding the direction, differences between the alcoholics and the controls in the proportion of subjects exhibiting some form of sex-role conflict were no longer significant (31 per cent of the alcoholics, 28 per cent of the normals and 22 per cent of the non-alcoholic psychiatric patients).

Gomberg (1979) distinguishes between early and late onset problem-drinking women on the basis of their handling of sex roles. The early onset drinkers are 'overtly rebellious' and have impulse control problems, while the late-onset drinkers: 'identify strongly with traditional roles, wife and mother . . . find that marriage and motherhood do not yield fantasies of happiness . . . feel depressed and guilty . . . '

Additional complications in the relationship between sex-role conflict and alcohol use in women are illustrated in a 1979 study by Scida and Vannicelli. Subjects (students, alcoholics in treatment and college employees) were classified into three types of drinkers (Park Problem Drinking Scale): 26 alcoholics, 35 problem drinkers and 40 normal drinkers. They described their conscious sexual self-images by means of the Bem Sex-role Inventory (which Beckman had used to measure an intermediate level of consciousness): (1) as they perceived themselves to be when they had not been drinking; (2) as they perceived they would be if they had been drinking; and (3) as they would like to be.

Confirming previous findings by many researchers, at the *conscious* level for the non-drinking state, the heavier-drinking women did not perceive themselves as being, or desiring to be, any more feminine (or masculine) than normal drinkers (inferred from the sex which predominated in their Bem scores), nor were they any more rigid or extreme than normals in their sex images (inferred from the magnitude of their scores). However, the greater the difference between a subject's 'not drinking' sexual self-image and her 'ideal', the greater her tendency toward drinking problems. In other words, alcohol abusers exhibited more sex-role conflict within the conscious level than normal drinkers.

Also, at the *unconscious* level, there was a correlation between high drinking scores and masculine identity, inferred (perhaps questionably) from subjects drawing a male figure first on a drawing test. This seems to confirm Wilsnack's idea that alcohol abusers suffer from conflict between conscious femininity and unconscious masculinity, with the added twist that they exhibit conflict within the conscious level as well. Scida and Vannicelli claim that the magnitude of sex-role conflict, rather than the direction of it (or the levels of consciousness involved), may be the more crucial element. This conclusion implies that they found conflict in more than one direction, although they do not explicitly say so or provide detailed supporting data.

When the same women reported their conscious sexual images 'as if' they *had* been drinking, alcoholic women showed no more sex-role conflict than controls, either within the conscious level or between the conscious and unconscious levels. At first glance, these results seem consistent with the notion that drinking reduces sex-role conflict for women, thus supplying their motive for drinking. However, when we look at the changes from the not-drinking to the drinking state in more detail, the case is less clear.

When *not* drinking, 52 per cent of the alcoholic and 56 per cent of the problem drinkers had exhibited conscious level sex-role conflict, as opposed to only 38 per cent of the normals. (Note, though, that by no means all the alcohol abusers experienced this conflict — only about half the women were classified as alcohol abusers. Furthermore, the proportion of normals who showed sex-role conflict was substantial (38 per cent); if sex-role conflict is an important factor in the development of problem drinking, how do these women avoid becoming alcohol abusers?) However, in the women's reports for the 'as if' drinking state, differences between the three groups in the proportion exhibiting sex-role conflict became insignificant (alcoholics 43 per cent, problem drinkers 41 per cent, normal drinkers 46 per cent). So drinking did reduce conscious level sex-role conflict for a few women. But the proportions are not impressive; only 9 per cent of the alcoholics and 15 per cent of the problem drinkers showed less sex-role conflict for the 'drinking' than the non-drinking state. Therefore, even for alcohol abusers, this evidence does not strongly support the proposition that drinking reduces sex-role conflict and hence provides a motive for drinking.

The work of Scida and Vannicelli (1979) introduces a final complication. *General* identity conflict (measured by changes in responses to non-sexual words from the Bem Test) was greater in the 'as if' drinking than in the not-drinking state for all three drinking groups (the most for normals, the least for problem drinkers, and an intermediate but considerable amount for alcoholics).

The fact that identity conflict in general, as well as sex-role conflict, was related to the severity of drinking problems suggests the possibility that general discrepancies between ideal and real self may be an overall factor in women's alcohol abuse, of which sex-role conflict might be merely a special case.

Female alcohol abusers in treatment are slightly more likely than women without alcohol problems to be members of the workforce and to have attended college (Schuckit and Morrissey, 1976). If we assume that these activities are traditionally more male than female, we might infer that they could reflect or create sex-role conflict, which in turn could contribute to their problem-drinking. Probably non-traditional roles do subject women to forces which could increase their alcohol use and abuse, forces such as more exposure to drinking situations, competition, independence, and guilt over neglecting family duties. On the other hand, non-traditional roles could produce forces which actually lessen a woman's motivation to drink, such as greater opportunities, satisfaction with daily activities and self-esteem. Which of the opposing forces would be stronger? Or would they merely offset each other? Certainly, we all know women who have departed from traditional sex roles in occupation, education, etc., yet are leading happy, productive lives with no signs of sex-role conflict, alcohol abuse or any other form of deviance. Their example warns us against simplistic interpretations of sociological evidence to support the idea that sex-role conflict contributes to alcohol abuse.

A summary of the research on sex-role conflict is organised around the following central issues:

(1) Some form of sex-role conflict was positively correlated with degree of alcohol use and abuse in adult women in all the studies covered, though the case was less clear for younger women.

(2) The kind of sex-role conflict varied among the studies. Some found conflict between conscious femininity and unconscious masculinity; others identified the opposite form; some found conflict within the conscious level as well. Furthermore, such two-dimensional schemes do not exhaust the logical possibilities. Different combinations of masculinity versus femininity at multiple levels of consciousness could produce varying kinds and degrees of conflict within the woman and between the woman and society. Thus, it is likely that sex-role conflict is not just one thing, but many, which greatly complicates the task of identifying and measuring sex-role incongruence and its possible contribution to various patterns of alcohol use and abuse.

(3) It may be that the magnitude of sex-role conflict, rather than the direction, is the crucial element, since more than one kind is associated with alcohol abuse.

(4) The nature of the connection between sex-role conflict and female drinking remains to be identified. The idea that drinking makes women feel more womanly and thus provides a motive for drinking is belied by a number of research findings, which also suggest that motives are not necessarily the same for abusers as for normal drinkers, nor for young women as for older ones.

(5) Can sex-role conflict provide a general explanation for drinking? Some studies found that sex-role conflict was not exhibited by a majority of alcohol abusers, much less all of them, but *was* exhibited by a significant proportion of normal drinkers. Therefore, this concept alone certainly cannot explain female alcohol use and abuse. In addition, there are indications in the research that sex-role conflict may merely represent a special case of general identity conflict as an influence on drinking.

Sex Roles in the Power Theory

A prominent general theory of alcohol use and abuse can be interpreted as indirectly implicating sex-role conflict. As originally proposed and tested, the theory was intended to apply to men only. After a brief description of the pertinent work, we will turn to the implications of this theory for female drinking as well.

McClelland *et al.* (1972) proposed that men are motivated to drink by a need to feel more powerful. They found several sources of support for their theory. For one thing, they discovered that marked concern for impulsive power themes in a society's folk-tales predicted heavy drinking in that group. In addition, among individual men in contemporary US society, they found that a few drinks increase thoughts of social (altruistic) power, while more drinks shift thoughts to concern for personal (self-centered) power, as indicated by analyses of stories (Thematic Apperception Test) the men wrote before, during and after drinking in a variety of settings. High personal power scores before drinking also identified men with histories of heavy drinking. Furthermore, subjects' need for power predicted the level of intoxication in experimental drinking sessions, when drinking history was held constant (Boyatzis, 1976).

Sex roles enter the picture in the explanation offered for the male's need for power. McClelland *et al.* (1972) assume that most societies expect men to be powerful and that alcohol produces physical signs which men interpret as sensations of increased strength (burning in the throat, boosts in levels of adrenalin and energy). Thus, drinking provides one convenient and inexpensive means for men to satisfy their needs to feel powerful. Need for power leads to drinking which produces feelings of power.

However, results of another of their experiments seem to contradict the power theory of drinking. A number of guides and blindfolded persons walked through the streets to a bar, where the guides achieved higher power scores and also drank more than the blindfolded persons. Why would the person who already feels more powerful drink more than the one who felt weaker, if drinking is supposed to satisfy the need for power?

The power theory parsimoniously postulates the same motive for moderate and heavy drinkers. Differences are quantitative, not qualitative, and are accounted for by individual differences in personality, as moulded by experience, which results in varying degrees of need for power.

Furthermore, with some assumptions about sex roles, the power theory can account for men's tendency to drink more than women in most societies. Where men, but not women, are expected to be strong, independent, aggressive achievers, men reach for alcohol as a convenient instrument to enhance their feelings of power, while women have no need of it.

However, if the power theory is to account for female as well as male drinking it should assume that women interpret the physical sensations produced by alcohol as signs of enhanced power, in the same way men are said to do. But Wilsnack (1974) contends the opposite: women construe the physical effects of alcohol as a set of feelings, summarised as 'womanly', which are inconsistent with the feelings of power which McClelland *et al.* (1972) claim their men found via the bottle. In addition, among her young female social drinkers, Wilsnack found that drinking *decreased* personal power themes and had no effect on social power themes in experiments similar to those of McClelland *et al.* with men. However, like the men, Wilsnack's women who scored high on personal power concerns drank more than the women who scored lower. Thus, although personal power concerns predict heavier drinking in both men and women, alcohol affected their power fantasies in opposite ways. In any case, even if the desire for feelings of power were a general motive for drinking, the problem of accounting for the fact that some drinkers become abusers would remain.

One important puzzle is presented by the power theory: if 'need-for-power' scores are higher after drinking than before, how can it be proposed that people use alcohol to satisfy power needs? Our primary interest here is in the importance of sex roles in the assumptions and conclusions of the studies concerning the power theory, but these lose their significance if the overall validity of the power theory is in question.

This short summary of the power theory's sex-role implications is necessarily an oversimplification of the ten years' research and fancy semantic footwork on which it is based. The formulation will remain speculative pending more rigorous tests, particularly of the assumption that alcohol actually produces feelings of enhanced power in men, and possibly in women. (Wilsnack's findings that drinking reduces power feelings in women must of course be subjected to further scrutiny. Certainly it is conceivable that women could seek feelings of enhanced power, if alcohol actually can produce these; for example, during the menopause and other crisis times of impaired self-esteem, or merely in conjunction with women's efforts to compete directly for power with men during a period of sex-role change.)

Sex Roles in the Dependency Theory

Assumptions about sex roles are also intrinsic to the dependency conflict theory of drinking — a venerable formulation to which the power theory is a recent rival. Common to most of the various versions of the dependency theory (see reviews by Blane, 1968, Barry, 1976; Bacon, 1974) is the assumption that people drink to alleviate conflict between basic human needs for dependency and societies' responses to these needs, which vary across cultures.

Groups which frustrate dependent behaviour in infants, exert strong pressures for self-reliance and achievement among children and forbid dependent behaviour in adults create a conflict in their members between an inherent longing to be cared for and culturally instilled desires for independence. Alcohol is assumed to resolve temporarily such conflict by creating feelings of warmth, comfort, security, acceptance and infantile omnipotence which allow the drinker to escape for a while society's demands for self-reliance and to satisfy briefly yearnings to feel dependent.

The major support for the dependency conflict theory comes from clinical impressions and from cross-cultural evidence of an association between frequency of drinking/drunkenness and cultural practices which are inferred to create dependency conflict.

In modern Western societies, the open expression of dependent behaviour among men is assumed to be severely restricted to special situations, such as illness, old age and childhood. Thus, the male must hide his dependency needs. As Blane (1968, p. 14) says: 'Consequently, the tone, the early flavor of dependency remains throughout life, pushed underground or repressed from conscious awareness under the pressure of the male child's quick perception of society's disfavor . . . '

However, what is the direction of the postulated association between dependency conflict and the male sex role? McCord and McCord (1960) and others contend that males with the greatest dependency conflict adopt a 'hyper-masculine' facade to hide it. On the other hand it is possible that a pre-existing exaggerated commitment to traditional male roles leads to dependency conflict.

In corresponding life situations, it is assumed that women are allowed, and even encouraged, to be dependent. Thus they avoid conflict over dependency needs and have no motive to drink. Hence, like the power theory, the dependency theory fits the fact of lower rates of alcohol use and abuse among women than men. But note that while both theories supply a positive motive for male drinking, they assume a negative (i.e. absence of) motive to drink for women, which makes it difficult for either theory to account for the amounts of drinking and associated problems which do occur in females. However, if we replace absolute with relative differences in power or dependency needs between men and women, both theories could fit the fact of some alcohol use and abuse among women but at a lower rate than men's.

Although both the power theory and the dependency conflict theory sound plausible and can accommodate drinking differences between men and women, we must deal with the dilemma that the two formulations assume opposite effects for alcohol. One claims that alcohol makes people feel more powerful; the other holds that alcohol makes people feel less powerful (i.e. more dependent). It seems clear that the first order of business is to investigate which (if either) of the proposed effects of alcohol actually occurs.

The effects postulated by the dependency theory fit Wilsnack's (1974) self-reports for young female social drinkers (warmth, etc.). However, she specifically looked for changes in dependency in women after drinking and found none.

Even for men, there is little evidence to support the notion that alcohol enhances dependent feelings or, aside from clinical impressions, that more dependent subjects drink more than others (Williams, 1976). On the contrary, McClelland *et al.* (1972) looked for, but found no evidence of, dependency needs or conflict in folk-tales of heavy-drinking societies. Evidence is strong that alcohol abusers exhibit high perceptual field dependence, but there is little empirical basis for relating this trait to motivational dependency (Williams, 1976). In fact, such a relationship seems contraindicated, if there is any substance to the folk-wisdom that females are more dependent than males, by the fact that males are consistently more field-dependent than females.

To overcome the problem of pinpointing empirical referents for dependency, Lemert (1962) defined it in terms of attributes of inter-family relationships, an interactionist perspective more compatible with the assumptions of his own discipline (sociology) than a definition based on discrete personality traits, which have predominated in the studies (mainly by psychologists) discussed so far. He measured wife dominance in the family, economic dependence on the wife or parents and imputed (affectional) dependency. The occurrence of at least two of these attributes was interpreted as evidence of dependency. Note that this approach assumes a set of cultural norms for dependency which in turn incorporate strong assumptions about sex roles.

Men whose drinking problems developed before marriage showed a much higher incidence of these dependency attributes than those whose alcohol abuse was delayed until after marriage. This suggests that if dependency is related to drinking problems it is as a contributor to, rather than merely a result of, alcohol abuse.

Wives were dominant in about one-third of the families of subjects whose drinking problems appeared before marriage and in only one-sixth of those whose problems developed subsequently. Some form of economic dependency was present in nearly half the families; partial dependence on the wife was the most common form and complete dependence was rare. Affectional (imputed) dependency (sharing more time, attention, affection, or emotion with parents than wife, or making excessive demands therefore on the wife) occurred in about two-fifths of the cases. About half of these focused dependence on one parent, mostly the mother, about one-third on the wife, and about one-sixth on both parents or on the wife and both parents.

The case frequency of dependency attributes correlated with severity of drinking problems as estimated by having the wives compare their spouses' drinking to a case description of a severe spree alcohol abuser. Over three times as many men with 0-1 dependency traits were rated 'not as bad' as were rated 'worse' than the comparison case. Over three times as many men with three dependency attributes were rated 'worse' than men who were rated 'not as bad' as the sample comparison. However, no association was found between the kind and frequency of dependence and the severity of the drinking problem when measured by a set of 'drinking behaviours', such as morning drinking.

One of Lemert's findings seriously challenges the dependency theory as a general explanation of alcohol abuse. That is, only about two-fifths of the alcohol abusers exhibited two or more of the three dependency behaviours required to qualify for the study's definition of dependent. This suggests that dependency is neither a sufficient nor a necessary cause of drinking problems.

In general, the power theory's assumptions seem more compatible than the dependency theory's with the available evidence regarding both the effects of drinking on behaviour and the personality characteristics of males with high alcohol involvement. For example, the idea that alcohol creates power feelings fits straightforwardly with the bravado and hypermasculine facade often exhibited by male drinkers in experimental and natural settings, as well as in self-reports. The dependency theory, on the other hand, must account for such behaviour by assuming it compensates for or masks actual dependency yearnings. The positive motive for drinking postulated by the power theory can more plausibly accommodate both normal and problem-drinking (at least in males) than the dependency theory, and its advocates have argued that the power theory can include the dependency theory as a special case (McClelland *et al.*, 1972). Likewise, the power theory is supported (and the dependency theory challenged) by such findings as feelings of greater assertiveness and power after drinking among alcoholics and heavy drinkers (MacAndrew and Geertsma, 1963; McClelland *et al.*, 1972); of heightened activity, aggressiveness, impulsiveness and antisocial behaviour in young pre-alcoholics, heavy drinkers and problem drinkers (Williams, 1976); and of elevated independence (rather than dependence) in delinquents heavily involved in alcohol (Blane and Chafetz, 1971; McCord and McCord, 1960).

Blane (1968) deals with these apparent contradictions by proposing three different styles of coping with dependency: open expression thereof (the majority of problem drinkers, whose behaviour is straightforwardly dependent); counterdependence (a sizeable minority, who exhibit the exaggerated masculinity which inspired the 'power theory); and an intermediate residual group who fluctuate between the two responses (and who incidentally are supposed to have the best prognosis of the three, according to Blane). In other words, the power theory becomes a special subcase of the dependency theory. This formulation would be strengthened by accounting for an individual's choice among the three alternative responses to dependence. Blane (1968, p. 33) merely says it is 'influenced by society's negative attitude toward open avowals of dependency in men and by society's tendency to equate independence and masculinity' — presumably he means by the variation in relative amounts of each of these forces which an individual experiences.

Sex Roles in Other Pertinent Theories

Jessor *et al.*'s (1968) general theory of deviance, including alcohol abuse, incorporates assumptions about sex-role differences which are confirmed by some of the data generated in testing the theory. They treat deviance as learned, purposeful adaptive action. The choice of behaviour on a continuum between deviant and conformist is viewed as a product of the relative pressures toward deviance versus controls over deviance, resulting from a combined set of sociocultural, socialisation and personality influences experienced by persons or groups in a particular environment. Variation in rates of deviance between groups and among individuals within groups reflect the balance between pressures toward and controls over deviance.

They present evidence that females in the community exhibited less deviance, including alcohol abuse, than males. Consequently, their theory predicts, the women must have experienced to a lesser degree than the men the forces which encourage deviance. However, in fact the women experienced the same pressures towards deviance, including alcohol abuse, as the men, but these were offset by greater societal and personal controls over the women than the men.

Jessor *et al.* (1968) did not attempt to account for their findings of greater sociocultural and personal controls against female than male deviance in women, but sex-role differences could be implicated. The fact of greater sociocultural and personal control over deviance in women also fits Walter Clark's (1964) suggestion that women's sex roles require them to behave in a more conventional manner than men (i.e. to accept more readily and abide by 'official' standards of morality and propriety), which in turn accurately predicts his findings that more men than women will drink heavily, frequently, in public, with non-family members, as well as admit getting drunk and enjoying it.

Edwards *et al.* (1972) posed two questions which are pertinent here: the first, 'whether women drink less (and hence experience less trouble) because of constraints on drinking itself or because of prohibition imposed on problematic behaviour . . . '; the second, 'how far such constraints are a matter of external control and how far they are introjected and sensed as personal values.' The results of Jessor *et al.* (1968) and of Clark (1964) suggest, in answer to the first question, that constraints on drinking are merely a subclass of prohibitions on deviant behaviour in general for women. Toward answering the second question, the Jessor study indicated that both external and internal controls are important predictors of deviance, including alcohol abuse, but the predictive value was even higher when both systems were considered simultaneously.

When alcohol abusers are divided into those with no pre-existing major psychiatric disorder (primary alcoholics) and those whose alcoholism is incidental to other psychiatric problems (secondary alcoholics), differences between the sexes appear which could be pertinent to sex roles. The most common form of secondary alcoholism in women (25 per cent, compared to about 5 per cent in men) is affective disorder (which may be simply defined for our purposes here as severe depression). As compared to primary alcoholics, affective disorder alcoholics develop drinking problems at a later age, are hospitalised after fewer years of alcohol abuse and have higher rates of previous alcohol-related hospitalisations, fewer medical consequences of alcoholism, more suicide attempts, but a better prognosis overall. Male secondary alcoholics, on the other hand, more commonly (25 per cent, versus about 8 per cent in women) evidence sociopathic alcoholism. As compared to primary alcoholics, sociopathic alcoholics develop drinking problems and are hospitalised at an earlier age, evidence higher rates of antisocial behaviour prior to their drinking problems and have higher rates of personality disorders, marital difficulties and a poorer prognosis in general. Differences between male and female alcoholics (recently reviewed by Schuckit and Morrissey, 1976) on these factors are minimised when primary alcoholics are compared with each other and are maximised when secondary alcoholics are compared (Schuckit and Morrissey, 1976).

The differences between men and women implied by the labels 'sociopathic' versus 'depressive', fit the sex-role stereotype of a more active, instrumental approach to life in men compared to a more passive one in women. However, before we interpret this as evidence that sex roles influence drinking behaviour, we must remember that only a small proportion (one-quarter) of the total population of alcoholic subjects fit into these categories. Also, although Beckman divided her female alcoholic subjects into those with alcoholism secondary to affective disorder (17 per cent of the sample) and those with primary alcoholism (33 per cent), she mentions no association between these categories and the type of sex-role conflict displayed. (Unfortunately, she did not carry out the classification completely to identify sociopathic secondary alcoholic women, if any, in her sample.) Furthermore, Schuckit and Morrissey's (1976) three-way categorisation is far from universally accepted and incidentally failed to be confirmed in a later study by the same group.

Nevertheless, comparisons of the sex-role beliefs and behaviours of people of the same sex who exhibit different forms of secondary alcoholism might reveal some interesting leads in exploring the relevance of sex roles to problem-drinking. For example, if the males whose secondary alcoholism takes the form of affective disorder and the females whose secondary alcoholism manifests itself as sociopathy exhibit more departure from traditional sex roles (or a different form of departure) than their counterparts who adopt the kind of secondary alcoholism more common for their sex, this would encourage us to continue exploring the possible contribution of sex roles to this category of alcoholism. Also, perhaps the distinction between affective disorder and sociopathic secondary alcoholism is broader than that between early versus late onset, discussed earlier, and would better correlate with reported differences in the form of sex-role conflict among women (i.e. conscious femininity versus unconscious masculinity in contrast to conscious masculinity versus unconscious femininity).

Family Organisation and Sex Roles

The literature on family factors in the development of drinking problems contains elements which could be interpreted as implicating sex-role factors in alcohol abuse. For example, as documented in a review by Cotton (1979), alcoholism occurs more frequently in male relatives and depression in female relatives of alcoholics. Male relatives of women alcoholics, both primary and secondary to affective disorder, tend to be alcoholics, while their female relatives tend to have the same *primary* illness as the patient. It is tempting to dismiss this evidence as a mere artifact of higher rates of alcoholism among men than women, but it might also be viewed as strengthening our suspicions that sex-role differences could help to determine variation in manifestations of deviance in general, including alcohol abuse, between the sexes.

Alcohol problems tend to run in families. Winokur (1976) has reviewed evidence for a genetic component in the transmission of alcohol abuse across generations. In addition to heredity, the majority view holds that familial alcoholism reflects other factors as well. In our exploration of the possible contribution of sex roles to problem-drinking, it is of interest that women are even more vulnerable than men to the impact of alcoholism among relatives; female alcoholics are more likely than male to come from families in which other members exhibit pathological drinking, according to the balance of opinion in 39 studies reviewed by Cotton (1979). The nature of the part sex roles might play in this relationship remains obscure, however.

Wolin *et al.* (1979) found that the more a family's rituals (holidays, mealtimes, vacation, visitors, etc.) were disrupted by an alcoholic parent, the more likely it was that an alcohol problem would occur in the children's generation. They identified behaviours which differentiated 25 families with varying degrees of ritual disruption. Transmission of alcohol abuse to the children's generation was associated with the following: the alcoholic parent was usually present in the home, drinking and drunk, during family rituals and the parent's level of participation changed over time; the family passively accepted the intoxication and the change in participation; and there was overall change in the family rituals observed. A rejection of the alcoholic parent's intoxication by direct confrontation characterised most of the families in which alcohol problems were *not* transmitted to the children's generation. If the data had been analysed separately by sex of the alcoholic parent, this approach could have shed some light on the contribution of sex roles to the transmission of alcohol problems. If, as seem likely in modern Western societies, women take more responsibility than men for the perpetuation of family rituals, disruption (and transmission of alcohol abuse to children) should be greatest in the families where the female parent is alcoholic.

In many modern societies, more alcoholics are the last children to be born in their families than would be expected by chance. There were 126 last-born for every 100 first-born cases among 5,606 patients in 27 studies reviewed by Barry and Blane (1977). This is particularly true in large families. There were almost twice as many last-born as first-born cases for families with 5-10 children than for families with fewer children: the difference was progressively smaller the smaller the family (Barry and Blane, 1977). In terms of our focus here on sex roles, it is of interest that this pattern is more firmly established for men than for women. A Japanese study found the opposite results (more first-borns than last-borns in male alcoholics), which suggests that birth order in general may play a part in the development of alcohol abuse, but the particular form may be culture specific. In general, alcohol abusers tend to come from large families.

However, the nature of the relationship between birth order, family size and problem-drinking remains problematic. Younger children have the higher statistical probability of parental separation or loss. Children in large families may receive less parental attention per child (Schuckit and Morrissey, 1976). Both circumstances could interfere with sex-role learning and thus lead to sex-role confusion. However, birth order and family size also could encourage the development of drinking problems in other ways which have nothing to do with sex roles, e.g. by increasing the likelihood that the last-born child (regardless of sex) is unwanted, by maximising competition among siblings, especially the last-born, by encouraging dependency in the last-born, etc. Last-born children are not overly-susceptible to all types of psychopathology, but mainly to the choice of alcohol abuse as a symptom (Barry and Blane, 1977). The effect of birth order on problem-drinking varies with the sex of the child as well as the sexes of the other children in the family.

For example, among males in the third or later birth position, the child in the second earlier position was much more likely to be a sister than a brother, and in general older sisters, rather than older brothers, predominate in male alcoholics (Barry and Blane, 1977). This fact, too, raises the spectre of sex roles as a contributor to the apparent effects of birth order on drinking behaviour.

A review (Zucker, 1976) of major studies of parental influences on alcohol abusers, either as youths or as adults, presents a consistent connection between drinking problems in offspring and deficits in parental (1) group maintenance functions, particularly family affection and (2) socialisation (parental reward and modelling alternatives). Alcohol abusers have experienced:

> more parental absence, high family tension . . . open rejection and emotional distance . . . parent-child interaction [that] is low and . . . unresponsive to the child's needs . . . either antisocial activity or directly alcohol-related problem behavior by the parent . . . parent alienation and cynicism (pp. 226-7).

Such parental behaviours are more destructive in the lower social classes than in the higher ones. The same sorts of deficits that characterise the families of problem drinkers occur in even stronger form in families where the offspring's deviance takes a more antisocial form than alcohol abuse: 'heavy alcohol use, problem drinking, and antisocial activity are alternative pathways for expression of similar need systems' (Zucker, 1976, p. 233). Certainly it is possible that sex-role confusion or conflict could mediate between such parental actions and the offspring's deviance, including alcohol abuse, but this possibility was not specifically examined in the studies reviewed.

Often it is assumed that separation from parents during childhood could encourage later problem-drinking, for example through relative deprivation (emotional and/or economic), or consequent inconsistency in learning behavioural norms. However, Cahalan *et al.* (1969) found little difference in levels of drinking between persons who lived with both parents to age 16 and those who did not — none for women and only a slight excess of heavy drinkers in the men. However, when age and social status were controlled, older men of both high and low social status who had been deprived of parents as children exhibited a heavy drinking rate nearly twice that of the men who had been raised by both parents. There was a bit more drinking (primarily moderate) among older women not reared by both parents, especially those in the upper social status, than among their age peers who lived with parents in their youth. Cahalan *et al.* (1969) say this suggests that deprivation of parents in youth may be associated mainly with the development of drinking after age 45 (heavier in men than women), but pronounce the possible causes to be 'obscure'. Possible sex-role implications seem equally obscure. It is hard to imagine, if interference with sex-role learning were to be implicated, why this should take so long to manifest itself in heightened alcohol involvement in later years. In fact, such a diachronic inference is not justified on the basis of the synchronic evidence from the national survey.

Contrary to the heavy drinkers in Cahalan *et al.* (1969), Gomberg (1979) concludes from her review of 18 pertinent studies (1937-76) that women alcoholics do exhibit more early deprivation of parents than their male counterparts (as well as additional indicators of early family disruption: more parents who are psychiatrically ill and more alcoholism/problem-drinking in the family of origin). She does not attempt to account for the greater vulnerability to disruption among women than men in the studies she reviews, either in sex-role terms or any other.

Moving from the parental family to the conjugal one, there is a strong relationship between heavy drinking and 'marital failure' (a term used here for convenience as a label for adults who are single, separated or divorced), as noted in an early study by Bacon (1945) and subsequently confirmed with great consistency. Some aspects of the relationship between alcohol abuse and marital instability vary decidedly between men and women. Could sex roles contribute to this difference?

In a survey of American drinking practices in the mid-1960s (Cahalan *et al.*, 1969), marital failures are distributed about equally between men and women in the total sample (comprised of drinkers and non-drinkers). For both sexes combined, this marital failure rate is 14 per cent: 13 per cent for men and 15 per cent for women. Among drinkers the proportion of marital failure is similar. Among *heavy drinkers*, however, the proportion of marital failures is higher − 21 per cent when both sexes are combined. The sexes contribute unequally to this higher rate, however. Only 17 per cent of the male heavy drinkers are unsuccessful at marriage (a failure rate only slightly higher than that for drinkers and for the total sample), while 32 per cent of the female heavy drinkers experience such failure. Thus heavy drinkers exhibited about 55 per cent more marital instability than would be expected on the basis of their proportion of the total sample, but females contributed much more to this total than males; 125 per cent over expected rates compared to 29 per cent for males.

When we compare the proportion of marital failures among heavy drinkers to that experienced by the *drinkers* in the sample, the heavy drinkers again account for more than their share of marital failures — about 41 per cent more than would be expected on the basis of their proportion of that sample. But, again, female heavy drinkers exhibit a much higher rate of excess marital instability (86 per cent) than the male heavy drinkers (21 per cent) — a ratio of about 4:1 when compared to the sample of drinkers. The disparity in marital failure rates between men and women heavy drinkers could reflect greater economic dependence of wives on husbands than vice versa, or a double standard which condemns female heavy drinkers more severely than male (e.g. Knupfer, 1964). Either situation seems to implicate role differences between the sexes as contributing to the greater impact of heavy drinking on marriage among women than men.

Summary and Conclusions

It seems appropriate to combine the foregoing material to see what perspective it provides about the process by which sex roles might influence drinking behaviour.

Four interacting systems may contribute to general sex-role differences. One of these is physical. Zealots to the contrary, it seems highly likely that *physical* differences between the sexes, such as strength, child-bearing capacity and hormonal make-up, contributed to the original differentiation of roles between the sexes. These role differences persist long after technology has diminished the functional significance of sex-linked physical differences and there is recent rekindled interest in their implications for sex differences in alcohol use. However, I leave that discussion to specialists and concentrate here on the remaining three interacting systems which may provide the impetus for sex role differences: the cultural, the social and the psychological.

In the *cultural system,* norms somehow evolve to govern the general differential responsibilities and prerogatives of the sexes. These general sex-role norms in turn shape the subset of drinking behaviour norms. The magnitude of the sex differences in the two sets of norms should be directly correlated, as some cross-cultural studies already suggest. The family provides the primary mechanism by which individuals are induced to internalise these norms and the context in which much of the resulting behaviour occurs.

In looking at the possible relationships between sex roles and drinking, we are handicapped by ignorance of the actual content of current sex-role norms. The assumptions about how women do and should behave reflected in tests of sex-role conflict have little or no empirical foundation, beyond having distinguished male from female subjects in past tests, and may merely reflect folk-notions peculiar to the test devisor's own cultural, subcultural (sociodemographic characteristics, ethnicity, etc.), familial and individual experience. Alcohol studies could draw more than they have from the large, recent international literature on this subject. However, so far such work has revealed few marked contrasts in the capacities of the two sexes: greater spatial-visual acuity, complex mathematical ability and aggressiveness in males; stronger verbal ability in females. The alcohol abuse implications of none of these is obvious, much less compelling. Nor have we succeeded in identifying a set of traits which are accepted as characterising current sex roles, even for the US and Europe (the targets of most of this research). We need to break down 'sex roles' into specific behaviours and expectations to investigate their differential incidence in various cultures and subcultures. Actual sex-role norms must be discovered before sex-role conflict can be successfully identified.

Since women's responsibilities and privileges are thought to be changing rapidly in many Western countries, this situation could be used as a natural experiment, providing opportunities for comparisons among groups. If sex roles play an important part in the development of drinking problems, then as the roles of men and women converge, differences in rates of alcohol abuse between the sexes should decrease. It is generally assumed that both these conditions characterise the present situation in modern Western society, particularly the US. Family organisation, too, seems to be changing. How, if at all, will this affect sex roles and drinking norms?

A second cultural system, the *symbolic* may seize on sex differences in drinking behavior to represent the more general differences in sex roles. Drinking behaviour could become an instrument for validating (or rejecting) the role assigned to one's own sex. If norms allow or require men to drink more than women, or in a different way, then drinking may become a positive sign of maleness, either directly (the power theory) or indirectly, as compensation for uncertain masculinity (the dependency theory). Males would symbolise rejection of their male role by *not* drinking, but, this is rare, probably because males usually enjoy more prestige than females. For men, then, not drinking may merely represent omission of this particular positive claim to the male role, rather than rebellion against it.

Women, too, could use drinking as a positive sex-role symbol, if the 'womanliness' theory is confirmed by more data. However, again assuming relatively lower prestige for females and identification of drinking with the male role, women may use alcohol as a negative symbol, to express rejection or dissatisfaction with their performance of the female role. In other words, women may employ alcohol to negate, rather than reinforce the female role, leaving themselves roleless.

To investigate the possible use of alcohol to symbolise sex roles, we need to know more about the actual effects alcohol has on the sex-role self-perceptions of each sex. Another high priority is to look further at differential symbolic use of drinking in terms of timing of onset of problems, and variation in family factors. For both sexes, the symbolic system could in turn reinforce the culture's sex-role norms (including those for drinking) which have shaped the symbols in the first place.

Sex-role norms also could operate on the *social system* by creating different numbers and kinds of opportunities for each sex to use alcohol. Drinking occurs in more situations (Harford, 1978) and is subjected to fewer restraining influences (Clark, 1964) for men than for women. Sex roles can mediate between drinking and factors in the family environment as well as in wider social contexts.

In addition, sex-role norms can affect the *psychological system* by arousing different needs (e.g. power, dependency, womanliness, access to goals) and conflicts concerning these for each sex. The resulting personality traits in turn may influence the relative appeal of alcohol, although the mechanism remains unknown. Conflicts may take the form of discrepancies between sex-role dispositions within the personality (perhaps at different levels of consciousness, as several investigators have suggested). Alternatively (and perhaps additionally), the conflict may occur between internalised sex-role dispositions and contrary demands of the cultural situation (e.g. a woman may be expected to perform the role of wife and mother in traditional style, but to compete with men on their own terms in her occupation); this process has received little research attention so far.

To simplify the exposition, the various processes by which sex roles could be related to drinking have been depicted so far as a series of two-way interactions between (1) sex-role norms and (2) symbols, (3) situations and (4) personality. Reflecting my own presuppositions as an anthropologist, the scheme presents norms as pivotal. However, none of these factors is necessarily more central than the others — that is a matter to be discovered, not assumed — and each of these systems can interact with the others. In addition, the formulation could include the physical system, increasing the number of possible interactions still further. If the physical (or other systems) were further divided into subsystems, such as genetics and physiology, the number of interactions would increase further. Note that such a set of interactions does not distinguish between cause and effect (for example, does sex-role disturbance cause problem-drinking or does alcohol abuse interfere with sex-role learning and performances?) The foregoing scheme simultaneously simplifies and elaborates the formulation of Wilsnack and Wilsnack (in press), by which it was inspired.

It seems clear that sex roles are only one of many likely contributors to the way individuals and groups handle alcohol. In fact, none of the studies covered herein has seriously proposed that sex roles, alone, can explain drinking. If my summary has given that impression, it is an inadvertent artifact of simplifying discussion of complex concepts. On the contrary, some of the authors have explicitly warned against the notion that sex roles hold *the* key to understanding alcohol use, which Sharon Wilsnack (personal communication) has aptly called 'a straw (wo)man'.

6 THE IMPACT ON SPOUSES AND HOW THEY COPE

Theodore Jacob and Ruth Ann Seilhamer

In addition to the adverse impact that excessive drinking exerts on the alcoholic's psychological and physical functioning, the destructive effects of alcoholism on social relationships in general and marital interactions in particular are of major proportions. Forty per cent of all problems brought to family court in the United States, for example, involve alcoholism in some way, whereas approximately one-third of problem drinkers report marital discord to be a major problem associated with their drinking (Cahalan, 1970); others suggest an even higher incidence of marital disturbance among problem drinkers (McClelland et al., 1972). In addition, a higher proportion of alcoholics have broken marriages than do non-alcoholics, although both groups marry at the same rate (Bailey et al., 1962). Clearly, the impact of alcoholism on marital functioning and the influence of marital relationships on the development and maintenance of alcoholism represent enormously challenging problems for theorists, researchers, and clinicians alike.

The vast majority of studies concerned with alcoholism and marital relationships has focused on the alcoholic's spouse rather than the relationship per se; it has emphasised individually-oriented perspectives in which personality traits and characteristics are assessed and has been more concerned with wives of male alcoholics than with husbands of female alcoholics. In the present chapter, a summary and evaluation of the extant literature on alcoholics' spouses will be presented first and then followed by a brief introduction to more recent research directions which have emphasised interactional variables by means of direct observation procedures. The interested reader can obtain detailed descriptions, evaluations, and references to this area in several recent and excellent critical reviews (Edwards et al., 1973; Jacob et al., 1978; Orford, 1975; Paolino and McCrady, 1977).

Wives of Alcoholics

Investigations of the alcoholic's wife during the past 40 years have been directed towards the assessment of two major propositions.

114

First, that women with certain types of personalities tend to select alcoholics or potential alcoholics as mates in order to satisfy unconscious needs of their own, and these needs foster the continued drinking of the husband. In the literature supporting this hypothesis, evidence is cited that the wife of the alcoholic exhibits psychosocial problems, psychological decompensation such as depression, anxiety or phobias, somatic disorders (Kalashian, 1959), or attempts to sabotage improvement when her husband shows signs of controlling his excessive drinking. In their thoughtful review of the literature concerned with wives of alcoholics, Edwards *et al.*, (1973) called descriptions of the above hypothesis 'the disturbed personality theories'.

Secondly, that women undergoing experiences of stress as a consequence of living with an alcoholic spouse will, as a result, manifest neurotic traits of psychosocial disturbances. In the literature supporting this second hypothesis, the wife's unco-operative or dominant behaviour is explained as a necessary coping mechanism developed to maintain family functioning and stability. That is, the wife would tend to minimise changes in her husband's drinking patterns on the basis of past experience, viewing a period of abstinence as merely a temporary dry spell rather than an actual step toward recovery. That the alcoholic's wife may disparage improvement in her husband's behaviour is not a result of her pathological needs but only a realistic recognition of his undependability. Edwards *et al.* (1973) categorised literature in support of this hypothesis as 'the stress theories'.

The 'disturbed personality' theories, the first to be formulated, were based on clinical impressions and case studies of social workers and psychiatrists. These theories were developed within a psychodynamic frame of reference which was the predominant ideology at the time. As environmental perspectives gained greater emphasis, the wife of the alcoholic was reconceptualised in the context of the stressful components of her life.

Disturbed Personality Theories

As noted above, the early literature concerned with the marriages of alcoholics focused on the alcoholic's wife as a psychologically disturbed individual. Although several different characterisations of the wife's 'disturbed personality' appeared, most of this literature described the wife as an aggressive, domineering woman who married in order to mother or control a man, and who was largely responsible for the continuation of his excessive drinking. Lewis (1937), for example, pictured the alcoholic's wife as a woman who found an outlet in her marriage for her aggressive impulses, directed these impulses towards a man who was dependent, and created situations that enabled her to punish him. Similar psychodynamically-based conclusions were reported by Futterman (1953) and Price (1945).

Subsequent to these early reports, a number of studies attempted to assess the 'disturbed wife' theory in a more careful and systematic manner. In six separate studies, for example, scores of the wives of alcoholics on the Minnesota Multiphasic Personality Inventory were reported and in none of these investigations was the 'disturbed wife' perspective clearly supported. A second research direction that can be noted among the more recent literature involves several attempts to categorise wives into more homogeneous subgroups — for example, Deniker *et al*.'s (1964) comparison of wives married to 'psychiatric alcoholics' versus 'digestive alcoholics' (those with chronic hepatodigestive disorders); and Rae and Forbes' (1966) distinction between wives with and without high psychopathic deviate (Pd) scores on the MMPI. (High scores on Pd purportedly indicate shallowness of emotion, egocentricity and limited capacity for deep relationships.)

In overview, it must be noted that much of the 'disturbed wife' literature has been based on clinical observations and anecdotal reports in which the husband's alcoholism had existed for a long period of time. As a result, it cannot be determined whether these wives exhibited the described behaviour characteristics and personality disturbances prior to the marriage or to the husband's alcoholism. In addition, most of this literature failed to recognise that there may be significant stages in the development of alcoholism and that an alcoholic and his spouse may exhibit different behavioural patterns based on stages of adjustment (Jackson, 1954). Finally, serious methodological weaknesses characterise most of this literature, notwithstanding recent reports based upon more adequate data collection procedures and experimental designs.

Stress Theories

As suggested, most of the 'disturbed wife' literature has assessed wives of alcoholics after husbands have reached an advanced stage of alcoholism, and has presumed that these traits would have been found prior to the onset of the husband's drinking. Given the correlational nature of such studies, however, it is certainly possible that disturbance observed in wives (if present at all) may be a consequence of coping with an extremely stressful situation. Specifically, the behaviour and personality traits of the alcoholic's wife may be viewed as a reaction to cumulative marital and family crises in which the wife experiences progressively more stress associated with her husband's alcoholism.

Initially, this position was presented by Jackson (1954) who focused on how the family as a total unit adjusted to the stress of alcoholism over time. Briefly, Jackson theorised that in their attempts to cope with the problems presented by the alcoholic, family members become guilty and ashamed, become isolated from social supports, and experience feelings of inadequacy and failure. In support of this position, wives of alcoholics who belonged to Al-Anon were studied over a three-year period, and from verbatim recordings made during this time, Jackson formulated a description of the stages of stress that an alcoholic father-husband brings to a family. The seven postulated stages of adjustment were as follows (Jackson, 1954):

(1) Attempts to avoid and deny the problem.
(2) Attempts to eliminate the problems; increased social withdrawal.
(3) Family disorganisation.
(4) Attempts to reorganise with the wife taking control.
(5) Efforts to escape the problems; possible separation.
(6) Wife and children reorganise without the husband.
(7) Recovery and reorganisation of the family with sober father.

Jackson's contribution was in recognising that the wife's behaviour may be viewed as a response to circumstances and not solely as a consequence of a disturbed personality. Although subsequent studies have generally supported the stress hypothesis as initially posited by Jackson, there were some three areas of obvious weakness in her study which Jackson herself acknowledged. (1) Sample bias: the study involved families who sought outside help, mainly families of Al-Anon members. (2) Sex/sex-role bias: the study did not include spouses of female alcoholics. (3) Family role bias: only the wife's accounts were considered, with no input from other family members.

That such sample characteristics could limit the possibility of generalising from Jackson's work is underscored by the studies of several investigators. Bailey (1965), for example, compared Al-Anon members with non-member wives of alcoholics, and found that the former were more motivated, educated, less moralistic and more apt to regard alcoholism as a sickness than were the latter. In addition to issues related to sample characteristics, Jackson's hypothesis regarding a distinct seven-stage progression has not been replicated by others. Specifically, Lemert's (1960) study did not reveal well-defined stages in wives' adjustment to the crises of alcoholism; instead, wives' behaviours were found to cluster into early, middle and late phases of adjustment of coping with their husband's alcoholism.

Notwithstanding these limitations, Jackson's work did stimulate important efforts in the area, as well as providing a highly descriptive, clinically rich account of typical stresses with which wives of alcoholics must cope. Generally, those stresses may be grouped as follows.

(a) Social Isolation. Initial embarrassment and sensitivity to social stigma leads the family to withdraw from social participation. Fewer invitations are extended and accepted. Fear of discovery accelerates as drinking bouts become more frequent, and cover-up attempts are increased. The family becomes increasingly insular and cut off from social supports in their extended family and community. Their isolation leads to diminished objectivity, and the family centers more and more on the alcoholism.

(b) Problems with Children. The wife must deal with children's questions and confusion. She may initially try to shield them, evading questions and explaining the father as 'sick' in attempts to maintain her alcoholic husband in the father role. The wife may become over-involved with the children, seeking from them the emotional support she does not get from her husband. Emotional disturbances and behavioural problems may erupt. Kalashian (1959) reports that wives may 'feel able to be supportive of younger children, but inadequate in coping with overt hostility of the adolescent toward the drinking father.' To avoid tension, older children may be absent from the home more frequently. As Kalashian further notes, if recovery should occur and the father reassumes his paternal role, there may be some adjustment problems with an adolescent son 'who had been enjoying some measure of importance as the responsible male in the home'.

(c) Economic Problems. Not only is there the expense of alcohol consumption, but the husband's absence from work or loss of employment may contribute to mounting debts and depletion of economic resources. The wife may have to assume management of family finances and sole responsibility for monetary decisions, a function which may be new to her. Jackson notes that the wife may also have to resort to techniques to gain control of the husband's paycheck, if there is one.

(d) Sexual Problems. Increased emotional distance may lead the wife to

avoid sexual contact, especially when her husband is drinking. Additionally, there is the effect of alcohol on the sexual performance and behaviour of the husband.

(e) Violence. As Jackson notes, hostility and frustration may erupt in violent expression, and reports abound which point to the high frequency of alcoholism in child abuse and wife battering (Freeman, 1979). According to Gelles and Straus (1979), however, the highly correlational nature of these accounts has fostered a 'folk theory' of the relationship of alcohol and violence − a perspective which suggests that alcohol is a disinhibitor which releases aggressive tendencies that are supposedly an inherent characteristic of human nature. There is little empirical support, however, for this causal hypothesis and on the basis of their own examination of this literature Gelles and Straus suggest an alternative viewpoint: alcohol provides the drunken husband-father with an excuse for his abusive behaviour whereby his violence is attributed to a loss of memory or loss of control brought on by alcohol. If the wife accepts this rationale, she may believe that if the alcoholism were controlled, then the abuse would cease.

Although additional research will be necessary to specify the direction-of-effect in the admittedly complex relationship between alcohol and violence, there is little doubt that when alcoholism and violence overlap, the stresses upon the wife and children are seriously intensified.

(f) Cultural Attitudes and Stereotypes. Prevailing cultural attitudes about drinking and about family self-sufficiency may contribute to the wife's frustration. As Jackson notes, 'the wife . . . finds herself blocked by the sacredness of drinking behavior to men in America. Drinking is a private matter and not any business of the wife's.' Changing sex roles in the United States may have relaxed this stereotype since Jackson's 1954 observation, but to the extent that the wife still accepts this cultural definition, it may be a source of stress for her. Other cultural dictates that uphold family self-reliance and privacy contribute to family isolation. Seeking outside help may mean a breach of loyalty to her husband and an admission that the family as a self-sustaining unit has failed.

Additionally, if the wife accepts the disease model of alcoholism, she may feel guilty for failing to support or sympathise with a 'sick' husband. Cultural attitudes which imply that the quality of family functioning is dependent upon the nurturant behaviour of the wife-mother may induce feelings of inadequacy and low self-esteem.

This list of sources of stress is not comprehensive, and it should be noted that the constellation of stresses may vary considerably across samples of wives of alcoholics, depending on such variables as family developmental stage, family size, or socioeconomic level. For instance, in a standard interview procedure, Lemert (1960) found a differential response to items 'indicative of fear' (i.e. violent acts) between welfare wives and Al-Anon wives, suggesting that there may be a greater tolerance of violence in family relationships in low economic classes.

Not only do the *types of stresses* differ with stages of alcoholism, but *styles of coping* in response to these stresses have also be categorised and differentiated. Coping, as an adaptive response to stress, is often dichotomised in the broader psychological literature into defensive coping and direct coping. Defensive coping is a form of self-deception, an attempt to ignore a problem when the person is unable to deal with the source of frustration directly. Direct coping refers to action taken to alter a situation in order to reduce or eliminate frustration or conflict. As will be suggested below, wives of alcoholics use both defensive and direct coping in efforts to deal with their husband's drinking.

In an attempt to integrate Jackson's stages of family adjustment with Orford and Guthrie's (1976) five styles of coping behaviour, James and Goldman (1971) assessed the behaviour of the wives in different stages of their husbands' alcoholism. Specifically, Orford and Guthrie's factor analysis of the respo ses of wives of alcoholics to 50 questions yielded five reasonably distinct and persistent styles of coping behaviour: safeguarding family interest; withdrawal within marriage; attacking; acting out; and protecting the alcoholic husband. Subsequently, James and Goldman administered a questionnaire to 85 wives of alcoholics asking them to recall the consequences of their husband's drinking and their own coping behaviour at various times during their marriage. Overall, coping styles of wives were reported to change as the husband's drinking pattern changed. As drinking progressed, there was a steady rise in behaviours associated with all five coping styles, although more markedly in withdrawal, protection and attack behavioural categories. Together with the finding that all wives used more than one style of coping behaviour, the authors suggest that wives cope in response to the intensity or frequency of the alcoholic episodes.

Examples of defensive coping can be found in Jackson's early stages of denial where both husband and wife make excuses for the drinking episodes or avoid talking about them at all. Likewise, in the withdrawal-within-marriage style which Orford and Guthrie posit, the wife avoids the husband and her feelings of anger and helplessness. More direct coping behaviour can be found in the safeguarding-family-interest style where the wife assumes financial responsibility, keeps children out of the husband's way, and hides family valuables so her husband can't sell them. Characteristic of the acting-out style are efforts to stop the husband's drinking by getting drunk herself, making him jealous or ridiculing him. The attack style includes locking him out of the house or seeking a separation. Divorce may be thought of as an ultimate 'attack' coping strategy, and statistics indicate that it is a high frequency response. Paolino and McCrady (1977) list several analyses from 1912 to 1974 which confirm the high proportion of alcoholics who are divorced or separated.

Additional support for the 'stressed' wife perspective was found in the work of Bailey *et al.* (1962), Haberman (1964), and Clifford (1960), although Orford's (1976) recent, well-designed study of personality characteristics of alcoholics and their wives failed to support the 'stressed wife' position. Specially, wives' neuroticism scores on the Eysenck Personality Inventory did not decrease over a 12-month intake-treatment-follow-up period. In fact, there was a tendency for these scores to increase between intake and follow-up, a tendency (not statistically significant) which was greater for wives whose husbands received 'good' treatment outcome ratings. As noted by Orford (1976, p. 543), 'these results are quite contrary to those that would be expected on the basis of a stress reaction hypothesis'. Also at variance with a stress hypothesis, was a negative correlation between duration of marriage and wives' neuroticism scores. 'The argument is not foolproof, but one would, on the face of it, expect wives whose marriages are of the shortest duration to have had the least to react to' (Orford, 1976, p. 542).

Conclusions

From the foregoing review of the 'disturbed wife' and 'stressed wife' literatures, the following conclusions can be drawn:

(1) Viewing wives of alcoholics as a unitary, single case is unwarranted by the existing data.

(2) With the exception of Orford's (1976) data, more recent studies (especially those involving MMPI data as the primary dependent variable) provide little support for the contention that most wives of alcoholics reflect significant psychological disturbance.

(3) The 'stressed wife' position has received modest support (again, with the exception of Orford's recent data) from a limited

number of studies, although identification of cause-effect relationships remains highly problematic.
(4) Although more recent studies (i.e. from 1960 to the present)
reflect more adequate methodologies than did earlier reports,
this literature is still characterised by a general lack of reliable
measures, appropriate control groups, and sophisticated analyses,
and almost without exception, has relied on self-reports of
current and past events as the primary data collection procedure.
In addition, data have been limited to wives' reports and perceptions of what transpired in these marriages; samples have been
restricted to wives involved in treatment or married to alcoholics
involved with social or legal institutions; and subject pools have
been small and unrepresentative.
(5) Finally, the dominant theoretical-conceptual framework associated with most of these studies suggests a one-sided perspective in
both the 'disturbed wife' and 'stressed wife' literatures; that is,
one marital partner is viewed as the victim and the other as the
villain. In her classic review, Bailey commented on the problem
in the following manner: 'Research on alcoholism and the family
has suffered from several serious defects, not the least of which
has been failure to achieve an integrated psychosocial approach.
The psychiatric focus on neurotic interaction and the sociological approach through stress theory have proceeded with a minimum of cross-fertilization' (Bailey, 1961, p. 91).

Husbands of Alcoholics

Notwithstanding the conservative estimate of 900,000 female alcoholics
in the USA (Beckman, 1975), well-controlled studies of husbands of
alcoholics have been extremely limited. For the most part, reports
concerning alcoholics' husbands have been based on wives' reports,
clinical impressions or unspecified sources and have suggested a variety
of general and often conflicting characterisations. For example, Flintoff
(1972), Myerson (1966), and Wood and Duffy (1966) report that
alcoholic women tend to marry domineering husbands whereas Busch
and Feuerlein (1975) and Rieth (1974) suggest that husbands of alcoholic women have feminine and passive personalities. Other characteristics attributed to alcoholics' husbands include emotional inaccessibility
(Wood and Duffy, 1966), lower sociability and lower extraversion than
normal controls (Busch *et al.*, 1973), and rigidity (Flintoff, 1972). An

often cited classification of husbands of alcoholics is Fox's (1956) five category schema: (1) the long-suffering martyr who spoils his child-wife, (2) the unforgiving and self-righteous husband, (3) the punishing sadistic husband, (4) the dependent husband, disappointed to find his formerly self-confident wife now dependent on him due to her alcoholism, and (5) the normal man, dismayed to find himself married to an alcoholic. Fox makes no reference to empirical data or case studies to support her categorisation; it remains for future research to validate any such typology.

In only a few studies have investigators obtained information directly from husbands of female alcoholics. First, Rimmer (1974) interviewed 25 husbands whose alcoholic wives had been admitted to a private psychiatric hospital and reported that 20 per cent of these husbands were alcoholics, an additional 16 per cent were excessive drinkers (undefined criteria), and 40 per cent evidenced other types of psychiatric disturbance, generally depression. Although Rimmer provided no reasons for his statement that his sample was not representative of alcoholics' husbands, one can speculate that they were younger than average and probably more affluent. Secondly, Busch *et al.*, (1973) reported on a Bavarian sample of 19 husbands of alcoholics in treatment and 19 control husbands matched on age and social class. Interviews focused on dominance patterns and quality of marriage, husbands' professional status, and personal and family history of alcoholism and drug addiction; both groups consisted of lower, lower-middle, and upper-middle-class subjects. No differences emerged between the groups on the variables studied, except that the quality of marriage in the female-alcoholic families deteriorated significantly over the years and the husbands became more dominant during the marriage. In early years of marriage, the alcoholic wives had more often been the dominant spouse, unlike the control couples who showed a husband-dominant pattern throughout marriage. Finally, Paolino *et al.*, (1976) administered Lanyon's Psychological Screening Inventory (PSI) to 15 husbands of hospitalised alcoholics. Comparison between husbands' scores and Lanyon's normative male sample revealed no significant differences on the Discomfort scale, whereas scores on the Defensiveness scale were significantly higher than that of the normative male group. For the Alienation scale, the mean score for husbands was significantly lower than that of the normative sample, although all scores still fell within the normal range as defined by Lanyon.

Conclusions

Based on the limited amount of research concerning husbands of alcoholics, the only result that emerges consistently is the high prevalence
of alcohol abuse or alcoholism among such men — data which strongly
support the hypothesis of assortative mating of female alcoholics
(Rimmer and Winokur, 1972).

In general, hypotheses regarding marital selection found in the
broader sociological literature are more congruent with the 'disturbed
personality' perspective of women who marry alcoholic men. The
'parental image' (Clayton, 1975) hypothesis, for example, claims that
men and women seek mates who are substitutes for opposite-sex
parents. To the extent that wives of alcoholics often have alcoholic
fathers and/or siblings (Futterman, 1953), the 'parental image' perspective would suggest that the wife of the alcoholic seeks to replicate
the family situation of her childhood. Another perspective, the 'value
hypothesis' (Clayton, 1975), postulates that similarity of values and
beliefs are deciding factors in choosing a marital partner. According to
this position, the tendency of alcoholic women to marry alcoholic-
prone men may be construed as a reflection of similar attitudes toward
alcohol and its consumption. Finally, the 'complementary needs'
theory (Winch, 1967) states that mates are selected from a field of
eligibles who offer the best possibility of gratifying each other's needs.
This perspective, as noted above, is a principal tenet of the 'disturbed
personality' theory.

Aside from this marital selection bias, however, evidence concerning
other psychopathology and personality traits of husbands of alcoholics
is mixed and is based on an extremely limited source of empirical data.
Even more so than the previously reviewed research on alcoholics'
wives, existing studies concerned with husbands of alcoholics reflect
severe methodological inadequacies and limited theoretical/conceptual
frameworks.

Conclusions and Future Directions

As suggested throughout this review, much of the empirical literature
on the alcoholic's spouse has been characterised by inadequacies of
methodology and experimental design. These deficiencies include:
vaguely described criteria by which alcoholism is defined; small, unrepresentative samples of alcoholics; control groups which are not
demographically comparable to the experimental group; inappropriate

and unsophisticated statistical analyses; and measurement procedures having inadequate reliability and validity characteristics. In addition, and of particular importance, the vast majority of studies in this litera- ture has been based on indirect, self-report procedures (questionnaires, individual interviews, and standardised or unstandardised tests) — procedures which have been described as methodologically weak and vulnerable to major interpretative difficulties (Jacob, 1975). Specifically, the validity of such procedures assumes that people are able and/or willing accurately to report events and feelings of the past and present and that such reports are minimally affected by forgetting, defensive distortion, or inaccurate elaboration as a justification of actions. Given the frequent lack of congruence between reported and actual behaviour, however, such assumptions would usually be very difficult to defend (Jacob, 1975). Hopefully, future investigations will be characterised by more rigorous experimental designs and by greater concern for the methodological base from which substantive findings are ultimately interpreted.

In addition to methodological weaknesses characterising investiga- tions of alcoholics' spouses, most research in this domain has been guided by individually-focused, psychodynamically-based conceptual frameworks. As a result, the range of theoretical concepts (as well as experimental strategies) incorporated into this area has been quite restricted, with most investigators having focused on individual descrip- tions and analyses. In the light of this situation, Orford (1975) argues that the 'specialised' interests of the 'alcoholism and marriage' literature must be related to and integrated with broader and more general con- ceptual frameworks in order for significant gains to be achieved. He suggests that 'the wider social-psychological and sociological literature in marriage, as well as testifying to non-uniqueness of the alcoholism- complicated marriage, provides the guidelines for the development of a more truly social-psychological theory of alcoholism and marriage.' Reviewing a variety of literatures (e.g. marital role expectations and enactments, marital satisfaction and its correlates, interpersonal percep- tion and marriage, mate selection and marital dissolution), Orford makes a strong argument that 'concepts employed in the more special- ised alcoholism literature have been oversimple . . . [and that] . . . parallels between events occurring in alcoholism-complicated marriages, and other marriages, have been neglected.' Efforts to incorporate such psychosocial perspectives into studies of alcoholics' spouses and marriages include Drewery and Rae's (1969) use of the Interpersonal Perception Technique with alcoholic and control couples, and Hanson *et al.*'s (1968) data regarding spouse's prediction of partner's perceptions. In addition to finding that communication between spouses was unidirectional — with the wife disclosing more opinions and feelings than the husband — Hanson *et al.* found that the wife perceived more incongruence between herself and her husband (1) the more both spouses differed in their ratings of the husband, and (2) the more negatively the wife saw her husband. Drewery and Rae's data support Hanson *et al.* in that they found less husband-wife agreement on ratings of husbands within alcoholic couples than within control couples.

In addition to the potential value of incorporating such social-psychological perspectives into future studies of alcoholic marriages, family researchers of the past decade have directed increasing attention toward identifying/describing the alcoholics' marital/family interactions. Being significantly influenced by the gradual integration of systems theory and family theory, family interaction investigators have begun to focus attention on the interacting dyad containing an alcoholic member, and in so doing, have attempted to identify processes and patterns that characterise the alcoholic marriage and that differentiate it from non-alcoholic marriages. In addition, experimental drinking sessions have been introduced and emergent interactions within these periods have been compared with marital interactions that occur when alcohol is not available. Hopefully, such data will suggest marital interactions that are associated with and seem to foster problem drinking. Finally, the nature of various communication patterns has been explored in several recent studies, directing attention to problem-solving interchanges as well as affective communications that characterise alcoholic-spouse relationships. As detailed in the next chapter, these early exploratory efforts would appear to represent an extremely promising approach to the study of alcoholism and marriage.

7 THE ROLES OF ALCOHOL IN FAMILY SYSTEMS

Peter Steinglass

The previous chapters in this book have addressed a wide-ranging series of family factors associated with alcoholism. The family's ethnic background, its relationship to its social community and social history, its style of distributing roles and its way of adapting to the presence of an alcoholic in its midst have all been addressed at great length. In discussing each of these issues, however, an implicit assumption has been made about the nature of the drinking behaviour itself. Although it has been pointed out that drinking appears sensitive to social and cultural influences and has clear-cut secondary implications for family members who have to live with an alcoholic, the alcoholism itself (that is, alcoholism as a disease process), has rested squarely on the shoulders of the person doing the drinking. It has not been the primary thrust of the previous chapters to suggest that society or a particular cultural group or even historical determinants might be the actual *site* of alcoholism.

In this chapter we will be taking a conceptual leap. We will be leaving the individually-oriented 'disease model' of alcoholism behind us and moving instead into the world of systems theory. In this world, alcoholism is described as both a product of and an impacting agent on the family system itself. The person who happens to be consuming the alcohol in excessive amounts is called the 'identified alcoholic', meaning that this person is behaviourally expressing what is in fact a systems level property. For theoreticians and family clinicians operating within this conceptual framework the subject at issue is not the family with an alcoholic member (the focus of the previous chapters), but the 'alcoholic family'.

Because family systems theory may be unfamiliar to the reader, a condensed version of its historical roots and basic concepts will be introduced at this point. After presenting these basic concepts, we will present a descriptive review of a series of clinical models derived from an application of family systems theory to clinical data about alcoholism and the family.

Basic Principles Of Family Systems Theory

Although there are currently many versions of family systems theory, each with its own following, all versions have their conceptual roots in General Systems Theory. General Systems Theory is a term applied by the biologist Ludwig von Bertalanffy (1968) to a series of concepts collectively intended to stress organismic rather than reductionistic approaches to biological problems. Historically, these concepts were developed in response to major dilemmas that had been arising in the biological sciences, dilemmas which von Bertalanffy felt were related to limitations imposed on scientific explanation by the reductionistic/ mechanistic tradition in science. This tradition gave rise to explanatory theories composed of series of linearly related, cause and effect hypotheses, customarily linked in an A → B → C → D fashion. (In alcoholism, this approach is embodied in behaviouristic learning explanations of why people drink, in the search for personality factors that provide the fertile substrate for the development of alcoholism, or in the search for genetic predisposition to alcoholism.) In the systems approach, on the other hand, the emphasis is on:

> Looking into those organismic features of life, behavior, society; taking them seriously and not bypassing or denying them; finding conceptual tools to handle them; developing models to represent them in conceptual constructs . . . and so come to better understanding, explanation, prediction, control of what makes an organism, a psyche, or a society function (von Bertalanffy in Gray *et al.*, 1969, p. 36).

In the field of human behaviour, systems theory has had an uneven reception being embraced to a greater or lesser extent depending upon the primary interests in question. Systems theory has been attractive to theorists whose interests are directed towards relationships among individuals or groups of individuals (sociologists, social psychologists, family therapists [see Buckley, 1967; Gray *et al.*, 1969]), and less attractive to those primarily interested in individual behaviour (experimental psychologists, psychoanalysts, behaviour therapists). In the alcoholism field, interest in systems approaches has increased as emphasis has shifted from an almost exclusive interest in the alcoholic individual to an appreciation of the role of the family both in the etiology and maintenance of chronic alcoholism.

Although family systems theory is at present much more a shared philosophical viewpoint attached to a heterogeneous group of middle-range theories about family organisation and functioning than it is a unified body of theory, it is possible to identify a series of core concepts subscribed to by each of these theorists. It is because the theoretical and conceptual field is still so heterogeneous that treatment techniques employed by family therapists also have such a varied quality to them. In fact, the diversity in form and structure of the family therapy field led the GAP Committee on the Family (1970) to conclude that family therapy is 'not a treatment method in the usual sense'. Pointing out that there is 'no generally agreed upon set of procedures followed by practitioners who consider themselves family therapists', they conclude that the shared base is the common conviction about the relationship between individual and family psychopathology, at least in the therapeutic benefits of seeing the family together. These shared convictions can be summarised by describing five core concepts that distinguish family systems from other theories of human behaviour and psychopathology.

The Family as a System

The most important conceptual premise is the proposal that the family can be viewed as an operational system. A system is customarily defined as a set of units or elements standing in some consistent relationship or interactional stance with each other. Clearly the nuclear family fits such a definition. For the family systems theorist, therefore, the family is treated as the primary organisational unit. Although individuals within the family might also be viewed as systems of their own (for example, from a biological perspective), in the family systems approach individuals are conceptualised as component subsystems of the primary organisational unit, the family.

This definition of a system places primary emphasis on the organisation of the component elements within the system and the notion that this organisation is defined by the nature of the consistent relationships between these elements. Hence the focus on interactional behaviour, structural patterning within the family, and the balance or stability of the system as a whole. We will see, in our later discussion, how this conceptual approach has been used in the analysis of the role of the family in contributing to the maintenance of chronic alcoholic behaviour and the interpretation of the function alcohol might play for specific systems needs within the family.

The Concept of Homeostasis

First introduced by Don Jackson (1957, 1965), one of the pioneers in family systems theory, this concept points to a tendency within families to establish a sense of balance or stability and to resist any change from this predetermined level of stability. The term homeostasis was originally applied to physiological mechanisms utilised by organisms to regulate their internal environment. Jackson's notion of family homeostasis implies that the family also has an internal environment which it carefully regulates in order to maintain overall stability. This stability does not necessarily imply a healthy state of affairs. The family might, for example, include as part of this stabilisation pattern a piece of chronic psychopathology, such as chronic alcohol abuse. But regardless of the quality of stabilisation, there are strong forces within families that operate according to homeostatic principles and appear parenthetically to resist changes in family level behaviour.

The negative feedback loop is the primary mechanism for the maintenance of homeostasis. In family systems terms, the negative feedback loop is composed characteristically of two interrelated aspects of behaviour, usually carried out by two or more individuals in the family. The behaviours are in conflict in that they tend to inhibit each other. When they occur sequentially the end result is a tendency to return to a prior level of functioning (the homeostatic level) of the family. A clinical example of such a negative feedback group is the spouse who encourages socialising or brings alcohol into the home or demands to be taken to a restaurant where drinks are ordered, every time the alcoholic member of the family makes a try at abstinence.

Positive feedback loops are also thought to occur in family systems. Although it was originally thought that such patterns of behaviour, when they occurred, tended to produce explosive, destructive outcomes for family life, family systems theorists have more recently adopted the view that the positive feedback loop is one of a series of behaviours that contribute to growth forces within the family system. These behaviours have been referred to as the morphogenetic properties of families, as opposed to the morphostatic properties associated with homeostasis (Speer, 1970). This shift in thinking has important philosophical and treatment implications. The earlier emphasis on homeostatic mechanisms within families left the impression that families tend to opt for the familiar and in this sense are a force for maintaining the status quo. When the status quo comes to include a chronic illness such as alcoholism, the family is inevitably perceived as a negative force and treatment programmes urge that the alcoholic be removed from this destructive family atmosphere and treated instead in a community of his/her peers, that is, other alcoholics. The growing interest in morphogenetic properties of families has spurred an increased interest in the family as a force for change. Thus we see a dramatic increase in interest in family coping mechanisms, in the nuclear family as a force for health, and in the active involvement of the family in alcoholism treatment programmes.

The Concept of the 'Identified Patient'

Perhaps the most revolutionary impact of family systems theory on mental health issues has been the redefinition of psychopathology in family terms. The schizophrenic individual becomes the 'schizophrenic family'. The alcoholic individual becomes the 'alcoholic family'. In this process the symptomatic member of the family is termed the 'identified patient'. According to this concept, the family member, rather than being viewed as a disturbed individual who would be clearly symptomatic regardless of the behavioural setting, is instead a labelled or identified patient, selected by the family system to express for the entire family the particular piece of disturbance represented by the symptom selected. For example, the schizophrenic individual is seen as manifesting the stresses and strains created by the psychotic pattern of interaction within the family as a whole. The antisocial adolescent is viewed as acting out antisocial fantasies shared by all family members.

It is also felt that the selected individual might in many cases be protecting or stabilising a level of functioning of other family members by manifesting such clearly identifiable pathological behaviour. For example, the alcoholic member of the family might, through his or her drinking, be protecting the family from overwhelming depression or intolerable levels of aggression. Such a model would be used to explain, for example, the clinical appearance of significant depression in a non-alcoholic spouse when the alcoholic stops drinking. The metaphor of the 'scapegoat' (Bermann, 1973) has been frequently mentioned when such a phenomenon is described in family life.

Most family systems theorists acknowledge that the concept of the identified patient should not be used to preclude the simultaneous existence of predisposing factors such as biological determinants or personality variables that contribute to both the initial appearance of the symptomatic behaviour and help answer the question of why a particular individual in a family system turns out to be symptomatic. However, the concept of the identified patient is quite helpful in describing the family forces that tend to exaggerate and concretise the frequency pattern and direction of symptomatic behaviour being expressed.

Communication Patterns

Information is a critical commodity in any behaviour system. Information reduces uncertainty and leads to the establishment of the patterned interrelationships that form the organisational matrix of the system in general. In human behavioural systems, information exchange is synonomous with communication. Communications, both verbal and non-verbal, are viewed as reflecting the basic structural and interactional patterns governing the family's behaviour, and therefore frequently become a primary focus of attention for clinicians operating from a family systems orientation. Some family systems theorists even contend that healthy channels of communication within the family are the sole prerequisite for adequate problem-solving and growth.

In alcoholism, interest in communication has focused on the nature of communicational patterns during intoxication. An appreciation of the contrast between sober and intoxicated interaction of the entire family has been viewed by some family theorists as critical to an understanding of the dynamics of the alcoholic family.

Boundaries

Because family systems theorists are interested in interactional *fields*, they must also pay attention to the quality of the boundaries separating participants in the field, and the boundary surrounding or separating the entire field from the outside world. Rigid and impermeable boundaries between the family and the outside world tend to isolate the family, preventing it from utilising extra-family resources to benefit individuals within the family. Excessively permeable boundaries, on the other hand, destroy the family's sense of group integrity and connectedness, often preventing it from behaving as an effective unit. Alcoholic families have often been characterised as having extremely rigid boundaries, leading to a characteristic sense of isolation within the community. Alcoholic behaviour itself often contributes to this sense of isolation and makes such families less available to interventions from the treatment community.

The Application of Family Systems Principles to the Problem of Alcoholism

As early as 1937, a clinician was struggling with the issues that ultimately have made the systems approach so attractive to family therapists:

> Why should these families of alcoholics hang together at all? What sort of people are these men and women who over and over are ready to fly apart and yet who remain inescapably bound? . . . so close is the interlocking between strengths and weaknesses that we should perhaps speak of the 'alcoholic marriage' rather than the 'alcoholic man' (Lewis, 1937 in Paolino and McCrady, 1977).

For the family systems theorist, the challenge of alcoholism is the attempt to understand the unique relationship that comes to exist between abusive consumption of alcohol and patterns of interactional behaviour within the family. Of the many aspects of alcoholism that make it a fascinating and puzzling condition for the behavioural scientist, the distinctive features that have captured the interests of family systems thinkers are:

Its Chronicity. Because alcoholism is so clearly a chronic disease process, interest logically focuses not only on factors that contribute to the onset of the condition (etiology) but also factors that tend to maintain chronic alcoholic behaviour once it has started. Patterns of family behaviour may be one such factor.

The Use of a Psychobiologically Active Drug. The psychopharmacological properties of alcohol, particularly its depressant qualities and the disturbances it produces in memory function, interfere with both cognition and verbal interactional behaviour. Communication must operate along channels other than verbal channels when alcohol is introduced into family systems. Investigations of non-verbal physical communication, affective feeling tone in families, etc., therefore become important in understanding the impact of alcoholism on the family system.

The Dual-state Pattern of Behaviour (Off-on Cycling). Most alcoholic drinking patterns are cyclical in nature. Periods of intoxication ranging from several hours to several days are interspersed with periods of sobriety. The often sharp contrast between intoxicated and sober behaviour is as striking in dealing with the individual alcoholic as the manic-depressive cycling of bipolar affective psychosis. Is there a comparable duality of cycling of interactional patterns for the alcoholic family?

The Predictability of Behavioural Responses to the Drug. Individual alcoholics have been found to have remarkably consistent patterns of behaviour during periods of intoxication. Behaviour during one drinking binge can be predicted from a knowledge of prior responses to alcohol. Predictability of behaviour implies a high degree of patterning, a process system theorists feel occurs with increasing frequency in complex behavioural systems such as families. What is the relationship between alcohol use and this patterning of behaviour for the alcoholic family?

The first serious attempt to apply family systems concepts to problems of alcoholism was a theoretical article by Ewing and Fox (1968) which adapted Jackson's notion of family homeostasis to this issue. In the alcholic marriage, they wrote, specific mechanisms have been developed 'to resist change over long periods of time. The behavior of each spouse is rigidly controlled by the other. As a result, an effort by one person to alter his typical role behavior threatens the family equilibrium and provokes renewed efforts by the spouse to maintain the status quo.'

Such a marital 'quid pro quo', to use Jackson's (1965) terminology, occurs to some extent in all marriages. But Ewing and Fox proposed that in the alcoholic marriage, the bargain struck would take on a particular cast. Discussing marriages between male alcoholics and their wives, they proposed that the male alcoholic's passive dependency implicitly encouraged his wife's protective nurturing needs. In the process a sexual bargain is also struck engaging an undemanding alcoholic husband in a behavioural pattern which complements the behaviour of the sexually unresponsive wife. Both of these interactional pacts are played out within the context of a cyclical system in which the alcoholic marriage alternates between periods of sobriety and periods of intoxication. 'By alternating between suppression of impulses and direct expression of them, he (the identified alcoholic) can maintain the conflict around impulse gratification for a life time.' One can clearly see in this early model, an attempt by a systems theorist to address those aspects of alcoholism we have listed above — chronicity, behavioural cycling, predictability of behaviour, etc.

Our own interest in the application of family systems theory to the problem of alcoholism was first stimulated by an opportunity to observe, first-hand, patterns of interactional behaviour manifested by family members during periods of intoxication as well as sobriety. The Laboratory of Alcohol Research of the National Institute on Alcohol Abuse and Alcoholism had for a number of years been carrying out a series of biomedical and behavioural studies using the 'experimentally induced intoxication' paradigm. This paradigm, as originally conceptualised, afforded the biomedical researcher an opportunity to study directly the effects of chronic alcohol ingestion.

The basic experimental model involved using the subject as his own control and comparing findings during baseline periods of sobriety with findings during extended periods of intoxication. A major finding stemming from these early studies was the remarkable inaccuracy of alcoholic subjects in predicting their intoxicated behaviour when questioned during baseline periods of sobriety (Tamerin *et al.*, 1970). This was particularly true regarding the affective components of intoxicated behaviour. These findings were considered unusual in so far as the subjects had been drinking at alcoholic levels for many years and seemingly would have had ample opportunity for feedback from drinking colleagues about the nature of their behaviour.

One possible extrapolation of these findings was the suggestion that clinical data in the family field about the nature of marital or family interaction associated with drinking, which at that time was based almost entirely on retrospective self-report, might be largely inaccurate. This suspicion was buttressed by a series of clinical reports coming from the same laboratory that dealt for the first time with direct clinical observations of interactional behaviour between family members observed during periods of experimentally-induced intoxication (Weiner *et al.*, 1971; Steinglass *et al.*, 1971). The family members included a father and son and two pairs of brothers, all chronic alcoholics.

The clinical setting for these observations was as follows. Subjects were admitted for a four-week period to a closed research ward. The environment was organised as a token economy in which subjects performed behavioural tasks to earn tokens that could be used to purchase a variety of commodities, including alcohol. The four-week stay was divided into a baseline period (when alcohol was not available), a drinking period (of ten to fourteen days), and a withdrawal period. Alcohol was purchased from a dispensing machine; staff were available to provide necessary medical backup and supportive controls, but did not interfere with decisions by subjects about the purchase of alcohol.

Clinical observations reported of these familial dyads in this setting revealed the anticipated dramatic changes in patterns of interactional behaviour during intoxication as contrasted with sobriety, but of particular interest was the unexpected directions that this behaviour took. For example, a father and son who had been distant and highly critical of each other whilst sober expressed warmth, tenderness and closeness while drinking. A pair of brothers whose past histories seemed liberally sprinkled with episodes of intrafamilial violence and psychosocial chaos alternated their drinking patterns so that one brother always remained sober while the other brother drank, and the sober brother exercised a controlling influence on his manifestly drunken sibling. The intensity and psychodynamic content of interactional behaviour during intoxication was also quite striking. The following vignette, taken from a report of a conjoint interview carried out with a pair of brothers during the third day of drinking illustrates the dramatic quality of these interactions:

> Bill was extremely drunk, displaying dysarthria, ataxia, confusion and short-term memory difficulties. His speech and thoughts seemed constricted; when asked a question he tended to repeat one of two phrases, either, 'That's my brother right there', pointing to John, or, 'We don't give a damn, do we John?' John, for his part, seemed tense yet excited, talked with great affect, and superficially appeared angry and disgusted by Bill. He repeatedly insisted that the interviewer see Bill as an instigator of violence on the ward, a villain, a bad actor, etc. He would cut Bill off whenever the latter tried to speak, would threaten him, bully him, accuse him so often that Bill became increasingly confused. Note the following typical exchange:

> John: 'William, you've drunk enough liquor in the past two years to the point where it's obliterating your brain.'
> Bill: 'Are you trying to make me nuts or something?'
> John: 'I don't have to make you nuts because I think you are already. If you could see yourself, you'd know it too.'
> Bill: 'I ain't mad at you John.'
> John: 'You ain't capable of being anything except what you are William, a Goddamn drunk, and a worthless nothing.'

When by himself, John had previously related tales of his own drinking episodes with fervor and gusto, seemingly proud of some of his more outrageous stunts and of the extent to which he was willing to drink anything to get an effect. But in this situation with Bill, he took on a very different color, constantly berating Bill for behavior in no way dissimilar from his own previous behavior, accusing Bill of being amongst the lowest of the low, blasting Bill no matter what he said and doing it with tremendous effect.

Immediately following the interview noted above, John left the room with Bill, walked him over to the alcohol dispensing machine, made a four ounce purchase of alcohol for him, and helped him to drink it, holding the cup to his mouth when he stopped.

Observations such as these could not help but stimulate a profound respect for the intricate and at times baffling relationships between alcohol use, intoxicated behaviour, and family interaction patterns. Individual psychodynamic models of behaviour might have dealt with such observations by emphasising the unconscious needs satisfied in the alcoholic individual by the reliance on alcohol. Sociological stress theory might have attempted to explain the actions of the non-drinking brother as an attempt to cope with the stresses he was experiencing as a result of his brother's drinking. To the family systems theorist, however, the critical issue, as we had already noted, is the organisational relationship between the component parts in this behavioural system. At least four component parts can be identified: the two brothers, alcohol, and the drinking society that had been established in the laboratory setting. The unique component, of course, is alcohol.

A clinical model was therefore proposed, the central feature of which was the notion of the 'alcoholic system'. The model proposed that in intact families and stable interactional groups of chronic alcoholics, such as skid-row communities, the expression of abusive drinking might serve one of two very different functions. The first function would be as a signal or sign of stress within the system. This hypothesis would be most applicable to an understanding of behaviour during the early phase of alcoholism.

A second function, applicable primarily during the chronic phase of alcoholism, would be an emphasis on the role played by alcohol in systems maintenance. It was proposed that alcohol, by dint of its profound behavioural, cultural, societal and physical consequences might assume such a central position in the life of some families as to become an organising principle for interactional life within these families. A critical distinction would therefore be made between those families in which the main issue at hand was coping with a deviant alcoholic member, versus those situations in which alcohol use and intoxicated behaviour had come to play such a critical role in day-to-day behaviour as to be a major determinant of patterns of interaction between family members and between the family and its surrounding community.

In proposing a role for alcohol use in systems maintenance, this clinical model was emphasising the concept of homeostasis, as it has been previously described. (Remember, Ewing and Fox also stressed the homeostatic properties of alcohol use within marriages.) This notion, of course, represented a radical departure from the customary view of alcohol use as a disruptive force in family life. The model suggested, quite contrarily, that in certain families alcohol might actually be serving a stabilising function, contributing to maintenance not only of family life, but obviously in turn to maintenance of the drinking behaviour itself. Although it was also clear that the family often had to pay a costly price for this stability, the model helped explain the resistance to change that many clinicians had experienced in attempting to work with families dealing with alcoholism problems. In fact, the specific suggestion was made that the therapist should first develop a sophisticated notion of the patterns of interactional behaviour related to intoxication and their role in ongoing family life, before attempting to *disrupt* the family by returning it to a 'dry' state.

A second study carried out by the author and his colleagues added substance to these initial speculations and further clarified the role alcohol was playing in intact families (Steinglass *et al.*, 1977). This study, which was built around an experimental treatment programme for married couples, included a ten-day in-patient phase, during which time three couples were simultaneously admitted to an in-patient facility at the Laboratory of Alcohol Research. This period of hospitalisation was designed to permit simulation of home behaviour. The in-patient facility was redesigned to provide a home-like atmosphere, and alcohol was made freely available during the first seven days of hospitalisation. Although the artificial nature of the hospital ward was acknowledged, subjects were nevertheless asked to reproduce as closely as possible their usual interactional behaviour and drinking patterns.

A specific rationale for the use of alcohol in the programme was explained to the couples both before and at the start of the in-patient week. It was emphasised that this drinking experience was not intended to be inherently therapeutic but was based on the assumption that the therapist, by being able to observe directly intoxicated behaviour, could gain a better understanding of the role of alcohol consumption was playing in the couples' lives. This information was then to be used in the formulation of a treatment plan.

Once again, it was found that couples engaged in two very different sets of interactional behaviours, one associated with sobriety and another associated with intoxication. As had been true in the earlier study, these couples were also unable to predict accurately the nature of their behaviour during intoxication. In particular, it was again noted that many couples seemed more assertive in their dealings as a couple with their surrounding community than was the case during periods of sobriety. The homeostatic function related to alcohol use therefore seemed to be moving into sharper focus. In so far as behaviours manifested by couples during intoxication served an 'adaptive' or problem-solving function for the couple, the repetitive cycling between sober and intoxicated interactional states tended to keep the family system on course (Davis *et al.*, 1974). A couple who predicted they would experience disgust during intoxication was noted instead to be more affectionate. A couple who predicted an increased tendency toward depression during drinking instead became angry and affectively changed. A couple who described their alcohol symptom as increasing their ability to relate to strangers were noted to become more distant and appear to wall themselves off from other couples once drinking began.

Observations made of the familial dyads reported earlier had also emphasised the highly structured and repetitive flavour of interactional behaviour during intoxication. This observation seemed valid for the data obtained from the conjoint hospitalisation study as well. The ability to observe repetitive patterns in the interactional behaviour of married couples is an accepted finding in the family clinical literature. Yet, the intramarital interactional behaviour associated with intoxication was, if anything, even more non-random, and in this sense even more highly patterned than behaviour observed during states of sobriety.

Figure 7.1 illustrates the model that was suggested by our clinical observations. The role of alcohol in systems maintenance was conceptualised in terms of problem solving. These couples were thought to face repetitive and chronic problems that threatened the stability of the marital system, and alcohol offered a solution. The solution was inherent in the nature of intoxicated interactional behaviour. The solution, however, was only a temporary one, and hence a cycling effect would be established in which long-term stability of the family system was dependent on the presence of both sober and intoxicated interactional behaviour.

Based on the types of problems observed in the couples admitted to this study, it was proposed that alcoholism might serve an adaptive role related to three categories of problems. The first was an adaptive response by the couple to a psychological disarray in a single member. Although the 'infectious agent' could be identified with one individual within the family, the solution was a family-level solution. A second category was a serious impact arising between two or more

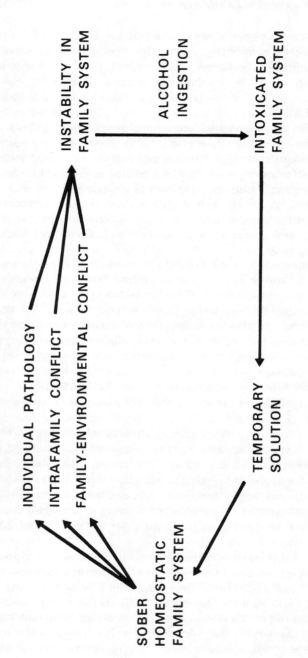

Figure 7.1: Family Systems Model of Alcoholism Maintenance

SOBER
HOMEOSTATIC
FAMILY SYSTEM

INDIVIDUAL PATHOLOGY

INTRAFAMILY CONFLICT

FAMILY-ENVIRONMENTAL CONFLICT

INSTABILITY IN
FAMILY SYSTEM

ALCOHOL
INGESTION

INTOXICATED
FAMILY SYSTEM

TEMPORARY
SOLUTION

family members that could not be attributed to disarray in a single member. The third was a response to serious difficulties the family faced in making an adjustment to its immediate social environment. In other words, it was being proposed that the presenting problems might arise at an individual level, an intra-family level, or a family/environment level. In all three cases, however, the response was a family-level response and incorporated intoxicated interactional behaviour as a critical component of the problem-solving strategy.

The concept of repetitive and predictable patterns of interactional behaviour between family members is also a central concept in a related theoretical approach, the transactional analysis model of alcoholism. Based on an application of principles originally developed by Berne (1961) and his colleages, Transactional Analysis (TA) attempts to extend psychoanalytic principles to transactional fields. Unmet psychological needs during childhood create conflicts around specific developmental issues creating personality fixations attached to these issues. These unresolved conflicts in turn cause the individual, in adult life, to engage important friends and family members in repetitive patterns of behaviours which have specific transactional goals. A 'game' analogy is used to describe these transactions, implying that the interactions engaged in follow a carefully prescribed set of rules. The games themselves are given pithy titles, usually derived from the perceived end point or goal of the game. The theory also proposes that individuals develop life 'scripts', highly repetitive series of interactions which are then played out in this almost programmed or game-like fashion.

Steiner, a colleague of Berne, has done the most extensive work in applying transactional analysis to the problem of alcoholism. Using the game analogy, he has described a series of repetitive interactional sequences characteristic of the alcoholic. For Steiner, 'the transactional view considers alcoholism the end result, or effect, of "alcoholic" behaviour' and therefore 'the addiction will subside if the alcoholic can no longer elicit certain necessary transactional responses from others' (1969, p. 921).

Although the colloquial names given to the names are selected primarily to engage the patient in an analysis of the scripts involved, their pithy quality (e.g. 'Drunk and Proud' or 'Lush') suggests that the TA approach tends to be quite judgmental in nature. In his description of these scripts, Steiner depicts the alcoholic as an unsavoury character, attempting to entrap his or her spouse, friends, or therapist in a series of quite nasty games, made particularly so because of their relatively infantile nature. Also, the focus is very much on the individual, although the data that are felt to be particularly important are the transactions between the individual and significant others (rather than, for example, symptoms, affects, or fantasies).

The TA approach therefore is more judgmental and interpretative than the systems approach we have been describing above. Systems theory tends to be more descriptive than it is interpretative. It is assumed that individuals act in particular ways because of the structural balances and imbalances within the behavioural system, rather than for personal gain. The games described by Steiner, on the other hand, clearly have a 'payoff' for the individual involved. Nevertheless, we can see in Steiner's work the description of a series of interactional patterns, often occurring at a marital level, which bear striking resemblance to the observations of interactional behaviour we made during our 'conjoint hospitalisation' study.

Up to this point, the emphasis in these studies has been on day-to-day behaviour in the alcoholic family. Evidence has been presented suggesting that in intact families chronic alcoholism can play a stabilising role within this day-to-day time frame by becoming an organising focus for interactional behaviour and by dint of the relatively stereotyped, predictable patterns of behaviour that come to be established by family members when the identified alcoholic in the family is actively drinking.

Although the chronic nature of alcoholism as a clinical condition has been acknowledged, the long-range development implications for the family of having to live side by side with such a condition have not been addressed. Yet we know that in addition to the day-to-day cycling of sober and intoxicated interactional states, these families also go through a series of more macroscopic phases, alternating this time not so much between physiological intoxication and sobriety, as between phases encompassing months or even years characterised by active drinking or total sobriety. Some families live through only one major transition from an active drinking period to a period of permanent abstinence. Most families however, experience multiple transitions between wet and dry phases. In this sense, there is a macroscopic wet-dry-wet cycling that compliments and incorporates the microscopic cycling between sober and intoxicated behaviour that we have already discussed at some length. However, whereas it was most useful to discuss the microscopic behaviour in terms of its homeostatic function for the family system, the more macroscopic pattern of cycling is best discussed in terms of its implications for family development.

The developmental approach, first introduced by sociologists as a research model, has subsequently gained wide popularity both as a conceptual framework for family life education and as a model for clinical intervention. According to this approach, the family is presumed to have a life cycle or life history that can be divided into a series of recognisable stages, each stage in turn associated with a series of developmental tasks. The sociologist uses the developmental approach as a framework for gathering information about such aspects of family life as role behaviour or changing value orientations. The clinician, on the other hand, tends to focus on those aspects of family life that seem either to promote or interfere with normal growth and development.

Although not exclusively so, clinical problems seem to emerge most frequently during periods of transition between life stages when new demands are being placed on the family and existing resources or patterns of behaviour are inadequate to meet these demands. Clinicians have therefore been particularly interested in family behaviour during these periods of transition. Insofar as developmental transitions are customarily stressful for the family, these time periods call forth a series of strategic behaviours on the part of the family that we label coping behaviour.

The use of a developmental model in the study of the alcoholic family has thus far been relatively limited. As has been discussed in Chapter 6, coping behaviour of non-alcoholic spouses has received considerable attention and from the beginning has been described within a developmental framework. Jackson's (1954) classical paper on the adjustment of the family to alcoholism, for example, proposed that the family goes through a series of recognisable stages, clearly a developmental hypothesis. But a focus on the family life cycle as it applies to the alcoholic family has clearly been missing. Yet this approach, when the issue at hand is the consequence for the family of having to manage a *chronic* illness, offers the clinician a particular advantage. A careful review of the life history of the alcoholic family would bring to light potential *distortions* in the customary life cycle introduced by the organisation of family life around the alcoholic condition (the definition we have been using of the 'alcoholic system').

My own attempt at formulating such a 'life history' model is shown in Figure 7.2. As can be seen, the model proposes that the alcoholic family goes through a series of developmental stages identified by two criteria: (1) the drinking status of the identified alcoholic; and (2) the relative stability or instability of the phase. In addition, the alcoholic family is differentiated from a non-alcoholic family counterpart. Our

Figure 7.2: Life History of the Alcoholic Family

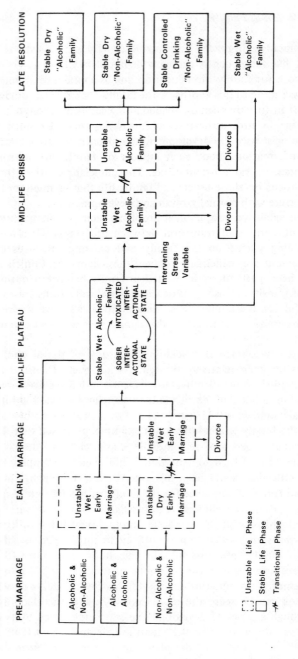

earlier model (Figure 7.1) has been incorporated in this new model as one life phase in the history of the alcoholic family, labelled the 'Stable-Wet' phase. This phase, however, is now placed in a historical perspective. What is our understanding of the customary sequences of this historical perspective, this life history of the alcoholic family?

For many alcoholic families the Stable-Wet alcohol phase becomes a way of life, proceeding year after year with remarkably little change in patterns of alcohol consumption, family attitudes or family behaviour. For other families, however, intervening stress variables arise that disrupt the homeostatic properties of the Stable-Wet phase. If the response to this challenge to family stability is merely increased alcohol consumption, that is if the solution is simply 'more of the same', than this now *Wet-Unstable* alcoholic family may dissolve under the continuing pressures brought to bear by its inability to deal successfully with the superimposed stress. A second alternative is possible, however, and many families appear to opt for this other course. This second alternative is an actual cessation of drinking – going 'on the wagon'. If the transition from wet to dry state is successfully managed, then the family enters a 'Dry-Stable' alcohol phase.

For some alcoholic families the transition from the wet to the dry state is a dramatic one that occurs only once in its life-time. For many families, however, the mid-life period is characterised by cycling between periods of wetness and dryness, each of which might encompass periods of months or years. The mid-life period in such instances might be diagrammed as a linear chain of Stable-Wet phase → Transitional phase → Stable-Dry phase → Transitional phase → Stable-Dry phase, etc.

In the model, four distinct late resolution patterns have also been identified that appear to represent different family level solutions to the problem of alcoholism. The first, the Stable-Wet Alcoholic Family appears to be merely a continuation of the steady-state solution established by the family during its mid-life period. Such families have continued year after year with remarkably little change in their lives. They remain alcoholic systems; they remain remarkably stable; but they also have an unchanging quality, a sense of being 'locked in concrete'.

The second resolution, the Stable-Dry Alcoholic Family, represents a successful conversion to the dry state. However, despite the fact that its alcoholic member is no longer drinking, the family's life continues to a remarkable degree to be organised around alcohol. Family members are active participants in AA, Al-Anon, and Al-Ateen groups. Individuals within the family have made career changes that incorporate alcoholism as a work focus (e.g. alcoholism counsellors and alcoholism lobbyists). In other words, family life is organised to maximise the prevention of regression to a wet state.

The third solution, the Stable-Dry Non-alcoholic family, differs from the second group in the single parameter that the family can no longer be thought of as an alcoholic system. Alcohol has been eliminated not only in a physical sense, but in a subjective and emotional sense as well.

The fourth resolution is the Stable-Controlled Drinking Non-alcoholic Family. The ability of chronic alcoholic individuals to return successfully to a controlled drinking or social drinking pattern is a highly controversial topic in the alcoholism field. However, a growing series of reports tend to support such a possibility. Therefore, although apparently occurring infrequently, this late resolution possibility should be included in a developmental model.

From a systems perspective, the life history model suggests that family behaviour within a particular family alcohol phase should have distinctive characteristics. In particular, those aspects of behaviour that seem to serve a regulatory function and incorporate alcoholism as an aspect of their regulatory process should be sensitive to (that is, change in response to) the current developmental stage of the family vis-à-vis chronic alcoholism. The three most interesting life phases from this point of view are the Stable-Wet phase, the Stable-Dry phase, and the Transitional phase. (Remember, according to the model, the family exhibits transitional behaviour whenever they shift either from Stable-Wet to Stable-Dry *or* from Stable-Dry to Stable-Wet phases.) We would therefore expect that families in the same alcohol life phase would share in common characteristic patterns of interactional behaviour. If such is the case, then the life history model can be used to develop a typology of alcoholic families based primarily on developmental staging.

Our attempts to investigate the relationship between these three family alcohol phases and patterns of interactional behaviour have thus far been encouraging in that they have provided strong support for the model. The most ambitious study to date is a longitudinal study of a cohort of alcoholic families who were systematically observed in three different interactional settings: their own homes; multiple family discussion groups; and a family interaction laboratory. As the study was conceptualised, the home setting afforded the researcher an opportunity to observe the mechanisms the family used in regulating its internal environment; the multiple   family discussion group provided an opportunity to study the family as it interacted with its surrounding community (in this case represented by other alcoholic families);

and the family interaction laboratory provided an opportunity to observe the family in a highly structured, novel social environment. In this particular study, the emphasis in all three settings was on the collection of direct observational data, especially regarding structural aspects of family behaviour.

A closer look at the home observation data should provide a good flavour of the findings that have been emerging from this work. The home observations were carried out using an observational technique that entailed placing two behavioural observers in the home for extended periods of time ranging up to four hours. Each observer 'attached' himself or herself to either the husband or wife in the family and, using a formal coding system, noted behaviour occurring between that subject and other people in the home.

Interactional data collected via this method were used to determine how the family behaved along five regulatory dimensions (Figure 7.3), which can be described as follows:

(1) Intrafamily engagement: a dimension measuring the frequency with which family members interact with each other while at the same time tending to ignore the presence of the behavioural observers.

(2) Distance regulation: a complex dimension combining the family's use of its space at home, the distance at which family members interact with each other and the comfort shown by family members in remaining together in the same location at home. Some families interacted at considerable distance one from another; other families tended to 'huddle' together in the home, rarely leaving each other's sight for independent projects.

(3) Extra-family engagement: a measure of the presence of extra-family members in the home during observation times. Some families were clearly more tolerant than others of welcoming friends in the home during observation sessions.

(4) Structural variability: a measure of the variability of interactional behaviour and physical movement from one coding session to another. Families scoring low on this factor most likely have a highly patterned and fixed style of interaction.

(5) Content variability: a measure of the variability not only of the content of verbal interaction between family members but also of the affective expression associated with these interactions.

The dimensions of intra- and extra-family engagement seemed to

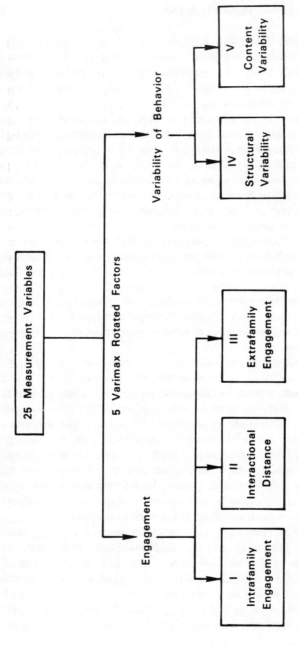

Figure 7.3: Home Factor Analysis

measure the activity level of the family. The other dimensions measure qualitative patterns adopted by the family in regulating its home environment. Statistical analyses of the data obtained from a sample of 31 families observed on multiple occasions over a six-month time frame indicated that home behaviour for the three family alcohol life phases being studied — Stable-Wet, Stable-Dry, and Transitional — was clearly different (Steinglass, 1981). A multivariate statistical procedure, discriminate function analysis, when applied to the data, suggested that the three alcohol groups could be clearly distinguished by plotting their scores for two separate functions.

A second set of analyses, examining differences between the three groups for each of the five behavioural dimensions, indicated that not all of these dimensions changed in relation to the family's current alcohol phase. The major alcohol-sensitive dimensions proved to be Distance Regulation and Content Variability. Therefore, if we suggest that what we are measuring here is the sensitivity of home behaviour to developmental issues related to chronic alcoholism, then the clear-cut finding is that the impact of alcohol on interactional behaviour is a selective one. It appears not to be the case that life in the families we studied is overwhelmed or totally distorted by the presence of chronic alcoholism. On the contrary, the picture one gets is of a far more complex interrelationship between symptom and interactional behaviour.

The dimensions of interactional behaviour that appeared to be alcohol sensitive, Distance Regulation and Content Variability, are both factors reflecting *patterns* of interactional behaviour, not activity levels of behaviour. The interaction *rate* between alcoholic and other family members does not, for example, differ in wet, dry, and transitional phases, but behaviour does take on a different stylistic cast.

These findings are of particular importance to us because the dimensions of behaviour being reported represent family-level properties. They are statements about the patterns of behaviour which the *entire family* manifests; they are not merely coping styles used by non-alcoholic family members in dealing with their identified alcoholic. Since the core concept of our systems approach has been the notion that the family comes to organise its life around chronic alcoholism, findings indicating that different patterns of behaviour can be clearly identified based on the alcohol life phase of the family are of obvious relevance. Furthermore, the fact that these differences concern the manner in which the family behaves at home during routine times of daily living, also seems consistent with the picture of the 'alcoholic family' as one that has come to manage its day-to-day living around its alcohol identity as a central organising principle.

A life-history model of the alcoholic family therefore seems to hold considerable promise. Its ultimate clinical value probably lies in its ability to provide interesting insights into how the presence of chronic alcoholism alters the family's customary life cycle. The developmental picture of the alcoholic family that emerges from the life-history model suggests that, rather than having a life cycle composed of a series of progressive stages, such families tend instead to return repeatedly to stages already experienced. At a microscopic level, the cycling between sober and intoxicated interactional states produces the inflexible stability associated with the Stable-Wet phase. At a macroscopic level, the cycling between Stable-Wet and Stable-Dry family life phases during the mid-life period produces a plateauing effect that profoundly alters the customary slope of family development.

For these families, it is probably accurate to suggest that they have exchanged long-term growth for short-term stability, and it is this emphasis on homeostasis at the expense of growth and change that makes life in the alcoholic family so rigid, inflexible, and ultimately restrictive for its members.

8 THE IMPACT ON CHILDREN

Clare Wilson

The children of alcoholics have been variously described as the 'forgotten children', a 'hidden tragedy', the 'unseen casualties' and a 'neglected problem', by researchers and reviewers. It is not so much that there has been a lack of research, for quite a number of papers about these children has appeared in the last decade. However, this research has failed to develop a coherent picture of the situation of children in families with alcohol problems which could stimulate and inform an active, practical response and workers have been slow in recognising the needs of this group.

One reason for this seems to be the lack of a truly family-oriented, interactional approach to alcohol problems. Despite developments in the application of family theory to alcoholism and growing interest in the use of family therapy in the treatment of problem drinkers, it is still the case that workers in research and treatment, particularly in the UK, tend to operate predominantly from an individual-oriented definition of problem-drinking: the major focus has been on the drinker and drinking behaviour and, where the family is considered, the family members are viewed as isolated individuals with the non-drinkers usually perceived as passive 'victims' of the drinker.. Thus models of treatment tend to concentrate on the drinker and to overlook the rest of the family, particularly the children, whilst research has studied drinkers, spouses and children as separate groups and has not developed an empirical or theoretical perspective on the whole family unit and the way in which excessive drinking relates to family process and the relationships of the family with the community. As one review of research has noted: 'The bulk of the literature represents attempts to delineate specific childhood problems that result from having an alcoholic as a parent; every now and then a new finding is reported and added to an already long list of such problems' (el-Guebaly and Offord, 1977, p. 57). What is missing is information about how exactly having an alcoholic parent can lead to childhood problems, that is, the processes in the family and community which mediate the impact of problem-drinking on children.

In addition the tendency for researchers to think of alcoholism as a 'unique' condition has meant that there has been little attempt to relate work on alcohol and the family to research on families experiencing other kinds of crisis and little comparison of the experiences of children of alcoholics with those of children from other types of disrupted families. Without this information it is difficult to evaluate the list of childhood problems, to predict which children, under what family circumstances, may be at risk and to assess effectively the extent and nature of children's needs for help.

This chapter is designed to draw together and examine some of the main research on children in families with alcohol problems and to suggest implications of the findings for work with these children. It uses the framework of systems theory (see Chapter 7) which seems to offer a useful perspective from which to integrate the available information into some kind of coherent picture. Systems theory asserts that to understand the behaviour of an individual it is necessary to consider the significant group or system of which that individual is a part, the relationships within the group and the individual's contribution to maintaining the system. Thus a number of aspects of family process and factors which influence or modify the nature of family behaviour are examined before considering the catalogue of problems of children in alcoholic families. The theoretical stance of the chapter also entails the assumptions that the impact of parental drinking on children is mediated via family dysfunction, including dysfunctional relationships between the family and the community and that family dysfunction may itself be both a cause and effect of problem drinking.

Marital Relationships

The quality of relationships within the family is obviously a crucial determinant of any child's experience and it is probable that much of the impact of parental drinking problems on children is felt via the reciprocal influences of drinking and family relationships.

Marital conflict, separation and divorce are consistently found to be more common in marriages of alcoholics than in those of comparison groups (Ablon, 1976) and parental conflict is a prominent theme in the literature on children of alcoholics. Cork (1969) interviewed 115 children, one or both of whose parents were in treatment for drinking. The majority of these children described conflict between their parents; 98 said 'parental fighting and quarrelling' was their main focus of concern, whilst only six children reported drunkenness and one drinking as their main concern. An American study interviewed 50 children of alcoholic parents and found that 50 per cent had experienced parental fighting or one parent being victimised (Booz-Allen and Hamilton, 1974). The authors noted that parental arguing, bickering or cursing were constant factors in many of the children's lives. Another study using intensive interviews with members of families with one parent receiving hospital treatment for alcohol problems reported marital conflict in nine of the eleven families (Wilson and Orford, 1978). Parental rows were sometimes about drinking, but often focused on other issues, such as money, gambling, sexual relationships or one partner's fussy or demanding behaviour and it seemed that drinking was not the only, or even the main, source of friction.

These studies showed that children were often present during parental quarrels and would intervene as peacemakers, or become involved on the side of one parent or in tidying up and attending to injuries, although some would adopt a withdrawal strategy, going to their own rooms or leaving the house when arguments began. Some children experienced difficulty in concentrating at school because they were upset over parental rows. Many were kept awake by arguments and were too tired to work or even sometimes to go to school. A few children would stay home from school to try and prevent parental fights or to protect a parent. It is possible that school problems, such as truancy or under-achievement, which have frequently been reported as characteristic of children of alcoholics (e.g. Chafetz *et al.*, 1971; Haberman, 1966; Kammeier, 1971) may be related more to marital conflict than to drinking *per se*.

Marital Violence and Child Abuse

Whilst marital and family conflict are frequently mentioned in the literature on alcohol and the family, it is rare that precise definitions of 'conflict' or clear descriptions of violence are to be found. We have little information on the prevalence of marital violence among problem drinkers, nor on the prevalence of alcohol abuse among persons who batter their partners, although incidence rates of about 45 per cent have been reported for each of these groups (Gayford, 1975; Orford *et al.*, 1975). If this is the case, a sizable number of children are exposed to the combination of parental alcohol abuse and violence, a combination which might be expected to have a particularly severe impact.

Keane and Roche (1974) investigated this question with 169 children of men admitted to an alcoholism unit and a control group of

153 children matched for age (10 years) and size of family. They divided the alcoholic families according to whether or not the father was violent, using a clear operational definition of violence. Boys, but not girls, with alcoholic fathers showed more symptoms of developmental disorder than controls. However, both boys and girls whose alcoholic fathers were also violent showed significantly more symptoms of developmental disorder than those with non-violent alcoholic fathers, or controls.

These results indicate that parental violence may contribute significantly to the risk of problems among children of alcoholics. Indeed, Booz-Allen and Hamilton's report suggests that 'physical violence within the family creates serious problems for children which persist into adulthood.'

There has been very little research on child abuse in alcoholic families and there is little consistency in reported rates of parental alcohol problems among child-abusing families: one review article cites rates ranging from 2 per cent to 62 per cent for dysfunctional alcohol use among abusing parents (Mayer and Black, 1977). These reviewers point out that a number of situational, child characteristic and personality factors which have been associated with child abuse and neglect are also found among alcoholic families, but it seems to be an open question whether alcohol problems are causally related to child abuse or whether both alcoholism and child abuse arise from common factors present in these families. An important question is whether 'alcoholism' or intoxication is the crucial factor. Mayer and Black's research suggests that many alcoholics avoid their children and leave discipline to their partners when they are drinking, to minimise the risk of hurting the children. These workers suggest that persons who are not in treatment and may not have acknowledged their drinking problems may be more likely to harm children when drunk. Other workers have suggested that neglect, rather than abuse, of children may more frequently result from parental alcoholism, especially where the parent is depressed and withdrawn when drinking (Fitch *et al.*, 1975; Booz-Allen and Hamilton, 1974).

Parent-child Relationships

The quality of relationships between children and their alcoholic parents received much emphasis in research around the 1950s, based on the Freudian theory that personality is determined by early experiences in the family. This research, consisting mainly of clinical observation of small numbers of children, tended to give the impression that particular patterns of parent-child relationships are characteristic of all alcoholic families and predictive of certain personality traits. A number of workers have observed that inconsistent and unpredictable behaviour by the alcoholic and, in some cases, the non-alcoholic parent, presents children with 'deficient' role models and that children may be unable to develop a firm self-concept or a stable sex-role identification. Whilst it is the case that many families conform more or less to this pattern of relationships, later research has shown that a variety of patterns of parent-child relationships exists in families with alcohol problems and that a range of factors may determine the pattern in a particular family.

In a detailed, empirical study of parent-child relationships 54 adolescent children of alcoholics were interviewed and tested with measures of social distance, social competence and family harmony (McLachlan *et al.*, 1973). They were compared with an equal number of normal controls, matched for age, sex, education, and father's occupation. Teenagers with actively-drinking fathers rated themselves as more socially distant from fathers than controls or children with recovered alcoholic fathers. Children of unrecovered alcoholic fathers also saw themselves as closer to peers than to their fathers and the authors suggest that close relationships with friends may act as compensation for the poor relationship with the father. There was no difference in assessments of social distance from mothers among children with unrecovered mothers, recovered mothers or controls. A similar pattern was found in the sphere of social competence: unrecovered fathers received very low ratings whilst the groups did not differ in their scores of the social competence of mothers. In general, family harmony was rated lower by children of alcoholics than controls. Families where the father was actively drinking were rated as particularly aloof and insecure, but where the father had recovered the ratings were more similar to those of controls. Families with alcoholic mothers received lower scores for family harmony than controls, whether or not the women had recovered.

McLachlan cautions that this sample is too small to permit great confidence in these results, but the findings suggest that there may be more disruption in father-child than mother-child relationships in families with an actively-drinking parent and that family cohesion may be lower where the father is the drinker. However, whilst the disruption may be more severe, recovery of the father may result in more improvement in family relationships than recovery of the mother.

McLachlan's study was concerned only with relationships between children and the drinking parent, but many workers have stressed the importance of relationships with the non-drinking parent in determining the child's adjustment to the family situation. Cork (1969, p. 49) found that poor relationships with both parents were common among the children she interviewed:

> A few felt close to one parent or the other at times when there was a respite from fighting and drinking, but most of the children said they felt generally rejected by both parents. They seem to feel the rejection of their non-alcoholic mother more keenly than that of their alcoholic father. It was as though they saw him as someone with a handicap and so believed that he could not help treating them as he did. They tended to make excuses for him that they did not make the for non-alcoholic parent.

Booz-Allen and Hamilton found that children's feelings about their parents ranged across a spectrum from love, admiration and respect to fear, anger and hate and Wilson and Orford report similar findings. Some children showed fairly consistent positive or negative attitudes to their parents, whilst others were wildly ambivalent about one or both. Some rejected, or felt rejected by, one or both parents, but others seemed to have quite close, supportive relationships with the non-drinking parent. In some families, especially where the drinker was aggressive or abusive when drunk, there appeared to be a 'coalition' between the non-alcoholic parent and some or all of the children, which was strongest during drinking spells. This was more common where the father was alcoholic, but was also found in one case where the mother was very aggressive when she was drinking. It would seem that the severity of the drinking problem and the degree to which the non-alcoholic partner manages to cope with it and with the associated family difficulties will influence the capacity to sustain close, supportive relationships with the children and to help them cope with their situation.

Family Structure

The nature of family relationships is one aspect of family life which will be profoundly influenced by factors of family structure such as the number, age and sex of children and the absence of one parent, yet surprisingly little attention has been given to them. Most research has used samples where children are living with both parents. But even when the sample has included children with one parent, or whose parents are separated, little attempt has been made to compare the experiences of these children with those from two--parent families — often because the sample has been too small to allow valid comparison. Cork interviewed a few children who were living with their separated non-alcoholic mother and found that some felt things were slightly better and were closer to their mother following the separation, but others expressed conflict about the separation and missed their father.

The general dearth of research on women alcoholics and their families means there is no information about women with drinking problems bringing up children on their own. There is a tendency for husbands to leave their alcoholic wives more often, and at an earlier stage in the development of drinking problems, than wives leave their alcoholic husbands, but there is no information about what happens to children in these cases.

Cork's work is about the only research which examines sibling relationships and the situation of the only child in an alcoholic family. She found that about one-third of the older children 'felt an unusual degree of responsibility towards the younger ones — not only for their physical care, but also for their emotional development. Many tried, without much success, to prepare the younger children for the problems they themselves were facing'. However, whilst some of the younger children had relatively close relationships with older siblings, a number resented the parental role assumed by the older ones. Equally, older children seemed very sensitive to parental favouring of younger children and for a number, 'the apparent need to dominate their juniors was probably the result of deep feelings of aggression or frustration'. Overall, Cork notes 'an abnormal amount of dissension among brothers and sisters . . . they seemed pathetically limited in their ability to give each other warmth and understanding.'

Whilst relationships with brothers and sisters can be unsatisfactory, the situation of the only child may be particularly difficult: Cork found that they expressed strong feelings of loneliness, were sometimes spoiled when their parents were sober and ignored when they were drinking and often became involved in rows between parents. The absence of siblings deprived these children of any source of support or any outlet for their feelings of frustration and resentment.

Drinking Pattern

Whilst all the influences so far discussed are vital mediators of the impact of parental drinking on children, the duration, pattern and severity of problem-drinking, and the way in which the parent behaves when s/he is drinking or drunk must be crucial influences on the experience of children. This may seem obvious, but these factors have been given virtually no explicit consideration by researchers, possibly because of the tendency for research to concentrate on individual family members rather than the family system as a whole.

In the families studied by Wilson and Orford, there was a tendency for men to drink outside the home, usually in pubs, and to return home in an aggressive or incapable state. Women (and one unemployed man who spent his days at home) more often showed a pattern of steady tippling at home, only rarely becoming intoxicated to the point of losing control or being unable to do their work, whether this was housework or work outside the home. Children whose parents drank outside the home were often fearful or apprehensive about aggressive or offensive behaviour on the parents' return. Where parents were less often intoxicated or were more withdrawn when drinking, the children were less afraid and showed more concern for their parent's well-being than they did over aggression, conflict or family disruption.

There are differences in the typical patterns of drinking of men and women alcoholics and these may be important in trying to examine the differential impact of alcoholic mothers and fathers on their children. Unfortunately, until we have more information about how drinking pattern and comportment influence family process and more research on women alcoholics and their families we can do little more than speculate on these relationships. However, it is worth noting that popular belief holds that it worse to have an alcoholic mother than an alcoholic father; this belief seems to be grounded in the fear that whilst a woman's ability to do her household chores may not be impaired by drinking, her ability to provide close emotional relationships with her children may well be adversely affected. It is clear, however, from the work of McLachlan and Cork that children may be closer to an alcoholic mother than an alcoholic father and that wives of male alcoholics may not necessarily show any especially close emotional relationships with their children.

Family Roles and Task Performance

An important tenet of systems theory is that the family evolves a structure of roles through which its functions are achieved. These are social roles (e.g. housekeeper, breadwinner, parent, child) and emotional roles (e.g. comforter, calm decision-maker, trouble-maker) which are necessary for the working of the family system and for the maintenance of emotional homeostasis. These roles are considered to be the property of the system, not of the individuals who play them. Thus, if one member of the system is unable, or unwilling, to play his or her allotted roles, another member must take over if the system is to continue functioning normally. The sex of the drinking parent, the pattern of drinking and the number and ages of children may all affect the nature of role and task allocation in the family and thus the nature of the role responsibilities which children are required to assume. There is little empirical research which directly examines the effects on children of the parental role changes which take place in most alcoholic families and again the lack of research on the families of women alcoholics makes impossible any firm statements about the experiences of their children in this respect.

Cork reported that many children took a large measure of responsibility for household tasks and that older children in particular may assume a large share of housekeeping and child care. Cork felt that many children she interviewed were overburdened by these responsibilities, but Wilson and Orford emphasised the need for comparative data as they felt that for many children the tasks required of them represented normal, age-related activities and that the acquisition of skills and an age-appropriate measure of responsibility could in fact be beneficial. There are obviously cases where children are prevented from going out or from having time and space for their own interests because of their responsibilities for household chores or for looking after younger children. There are also children who have assumed some of the emotional roles of one or both parents, for example in child care or as a source of support for the non-alcoholic parent, for which they are not sufficiently mature. It is perhaps demands of this sort which can be most damaging to children.

The degree to which the alcoholic parent is incapable of performing his/her family roles, the willingness and ability of the non-alcoholic parent to take over these roles and the extent to which s/he can manage the extra tasks will obviously determine how much children have to take on. The heaviest burden is likely to fall on older children, particularly girls, and on children whose parents are both alcoholics.

In some cases children resent their parent's inadequate role-playing, not so much because they have to fill the gap, but because they need advice or discipline and have no alternative source of guidance. Occasionally, an extended family member or close family friend may act as a parental substitute, providing guidance for the children and often a considerable amount of support for the children and for the non-alcoholic parent.

Social Relationships

The social stigma of alcoholism frequently results in isolation for these families. They may have direct experience of ostracism by relatives, friends or neighbours, or they may themselves withdraw from social contacts because of shame and fear of rejection. Both partners attempt to conceal the drinking problem from outsiders and frequently try to hide it from the children. However, even very young children are usually acutely aware that something out of the ordinary is happening in the family. Children often express much of the same bewilderment and confusion we have come to associate with attempts by the spouse of the alcoholic to define and label the problem: the conspiracy of silence by parents who feel children should not know about the drinking often seems to make this a long and stressful experience. Rejection of the non-alcoholic parent may be rooted in this confusion; children sometimes say they would have been more understanding toward their parent had they known earlier the true nature of the problem.

Children become aware of social perceptions of alcoholism as a shameful, degrading condition at quite a young age and the discovery of the parental drinking problem may be a traumatic experience. Parental injunctions against mentioning the drinking problem are usually unneccessary, as children generally have a deep sense of shame and embarrassment about it and a strong fear of ridicule or rejection. These feelings are usually just as strong when the drinking has not been concealed and may lead to some of the most common, and perhaps more serious, effects of living with an alcoholic parent.

Most children will not bring friends home, fearing embarrassment over parental drinking and fighting and the possibility of rejection by their friends. Some will not accept invitations to friends' homes, feeling they cannot reciprocate. Children may avoid close relationships because they are afraid of having to disclose information about the family situation and feel they cannot trust others. A few children in the Wilson and Orford study had 'special friends' whom they felt able to trust and to bring home. Often these friends themselves had alcoholic or violent parents.

The reluctance of the child to disclose the family problem often extends to their relationships with teachers and other adults, sometimes from embarrassment or fear of disapproval and sometimes out of a sense of loyalty to parents. Children are thus not only frequently unable to make or keep close relationships with peers, but are also often deprived of any person in whom to confide or to whom they can express their feelings of anger, fear, resentment or unhappiness about the family. Without the normal opportunities for friendship, children may have long-lasting problems with close or intimate relationships. With no outlet for their emotions they may act out their feelings and risk getting into trouble, or alternatively they may become overly self-reliant or withdrawn.

Effects on Children

The discussion so far has centred on some of the experiences which may be encountered by problem drinkers' children, factors which may modify these experiences and some of the possible consequences. What emerges is the variability in the picture presented depending on the exact nature of the processes at work in these families and the possible interaction between them. For this reason, a detailed review of the large number of reports concerned with the negative consequences of parental drinking problems is beyond the scope of this chapter and we shall just briefly outline the main themes in this literature. More detailed reviews can be found in articles by el-Guebaly and Offord (1977), Jacob, *et al.*, (1978) and Ablon (1976). Original sources are referred to in these and in many of the papers cited in this chapter.

Many of the reported problems concern antisocial behaviour and conduct problems, rather than anxiety, depression or neurotic behaviour. This may reflect the nature of the groups studied as much as the 'reality' of the effects experienced. A group of children from a remand home, court or child guidance clinic may be quite different from one selected from a school or from children or parents in treatment for drinking. Children who come to attention for their problems may represent a minority of children of alcoholics.

Delinquency, truancy, aggressive behaviour, hyperactivity and temper tantrums are among the problems reported by the few care-fully controlled studies as being more common among children of alco-holics. Problems in school, such as learning difficulties, conduct problems and poor performance are also reported, but lack of compari-son groups makes it difficult to say whether these are more common among children of alcoholics than among children from other homes where there is marital conflict and family disruption.

Emotional problems, psychological disturbance and psychosomatic complaints are reported by many workers, but the variety of the symptoms observed and the contradictions between the findings would suggest that this is an area where close attention to the modifying influ-ences discussed above is essential in assessing research findings. Equally, there is an urgent need for comparative research on children in families experiencing other forms of crisis; similar patterns of family dysfunc-tions may operate in famiies disrupted by events such as unemploy-ment, mental and physical illness or bereavement and we need to know whether children experience the same kinds of problems as reported for children of alcoholics.

Whilst little can be said about long-term effects on adult adjustment, it does seem clear that sons of alcoholic fathers stand a relatively high chance of developing alcohol problems in later life, particularly if they show antisocial behaviour and have begun to drink heavily. A recent review (Cotton, 1979) calculated that the risk of children of problem drinkers developing alcohol problems was about 33 per cent. The risk for daughters of alcoholics and for children of alcoholic mothers seems to be rather lower than for sons and for children with alcoholic fathers. However, there is a tendency for high rates of affective disorders among female relatives of alcoholics and studies of adult alcoholics indicate higher rates of parental (particularly paternal) alcoholism in the back-grounds of women than is the case for men.

Cork found that a number of the children she interviewed were drinking, some regularly, and a few experiencing problems. However, about one-third said they would never drink, on health or moral grounds or 'because it hurts other people'. Only a few of these children were against drinking by adults in general, or against any drinking by their parents. More disapproved of their mother's than their father's drinking, which Cork felt reflected the prevailing double standard; moral or attitudinal reasons were advanced against mothers' drinking whilst practical reasons were given against drinking by fathers.

Relatively recently, considerable attention has been drawn to the possibility that excessive drinking by pregnant women can cause damage to the baby. Research, mainly from the United States, has shown that a small percentage of infants born to women with severe, long-standing alcoholism exhibit a pattern of defects which has been termed the foetal alcohol syndrome (discussed also in Chapter 4). These babies are usually short and light at birth, demonstrate facial abnormalities and may have a degree of mental handicap. At present there is little conclusive evidence that alcohol is the principal cause of this syndrome and no definite information as to the level of consumption which may be potentially damaging. Because of the direct connection between the maternal and foetal blood supplies it is unwise for pregnant women to take any drug in large amounts, and alcohol is no exception. Women should be advised to drink only in moderation during pregnancy and those who drink excessively and find it difficult to stop should be offered help and the option of terminating the pregnancy if there are grounds for concern.

Implications for Helping Children of Alcoholics

It must be said at the outset that, despite the impression which may be gained from scanning the literature, not all children of alcoholics suffer ill-effects. Where drinking is not of long standing, is not accompanied by marital conflict or aggressive behaviour, where there are good, supportive relationships within the family and with relatives and friends and the family has a relatively secure financial position, it is unlikely that children will be badly affected. Even if some of the 'protective' factors are absent, children may still manage to cope.

Wilson and Orford asked children whether they felt they needed help and, if so, of what kind. A number said they did not need outside help and that their needs were met by relationships with family or friends. However, others wanted information about alcohol and drinking problems and advice on how to behave towards the drinker. Many felt left out of the hospital treatment given to their parent, unsure about what it entailed and would have liked to talk with treatment staff. Some also wanted the chance to air their own feelings and to discuss family problems with a sympathetic person who was knowledgeable about alcoholism and its effects on family life. In general, children felt neither talking with friends and neighbours nor with a peer group would be useful in this respect. The few who had heard of Al-Ateen did not feel it would help them and none had attended a group meeting.

It would appear that the sort of help outlined by these children could be relatively easily provided by specialist alcoholism services on a routine basis for the children of their clients. However, it is rare that such agencies pay much attention to children. It may be that workers are hesitant to become involved with children because they feel either that they do not know what their problems are and how best to help them, or that they lack necessary skills. It is possible that the provision of advice, information, a chance to talk and an offer of support could be sufficient for many children and of enormous benefit to them.

For children whose parents are not receiving treatment for their drinking, the situation may be very different. Some children develop problems which worry parents and may be referred for specialist help. Others come forcibly to attention through truancy or delinquency. However, many children with more or less severe difficulties never come to the attention of any agency which could offer help. In part, this may be due to the stigma attached to alcoholism: parents who deny the drinking problem may be unable, or unwilling, to recognise their children's problems or to seek outside help. A Yugoslavian study, (Gacic, 1978) for example, found that a majority of 8-11 year old children of parents referred for alcohol treatment showed some degree of disturbance, although no help had been sought for them. Children themselves are usually loath to disclose the family problems and, in addition, their status as children makes it difficult, if not impossible, for them to seek help for themselves.

However, this situation is also related to agency policies and practice. Booz-Allen and Hamilton's report described community agencies as generally inaccessible, lacking in understanding of the children's problems and feelings and unhelpful to children involved with them; in short, as potential rather than actual resources. This was an American study, but the position in other countries is probably not too different.

Inaccessibility results, in part, from children's inability or unwillingness to come forward for the reasons just mentioned, but also from the lack of an active approach by services to the recognition of and response to the needs of these children. We have already noted the lack of response to children by specialist alcohol services and the position is similar among the majority of non-specialist agencies contacted by families for help with drinking problems. Most frequently the drinking problem is not the presenting problem in referrals to community agencies and may not be recognised for some time, if at all. Many workers are reluctant to ask about drinking, often because they feel the lack of necessary knowledge, skills, experience and support to work with problem drinkers (Shaw *et al.*, 1978). Thus the lack of an active approach to children of alcoholics is part of a more general lack of an active response to the recognition of drinking problems, as well as a phenomenon in its own right.

Booz-Allen and Hamilton's second point, that agencies did not understand the children's situation, was illustrated by the mismatch between the perceptions of workers and the children's own views: children said that family conflict was their main problem, whilst agencies did not mention conflict, but felt that non-fulfilment of parental responsibilities was the main problem. Similarly, agencies felt that confusion and guilt would be the children's predominant feelings, whilst children most frequently reported feeling embarrassment and resentment. This situation is perhaps often the product of a lack of accessible information about children of problem drinkers but also seems to reflect the predominance of an individual-oriented, rather than a family-oriented approach, in both research and practice.

From the discussion in this chapter, the main message seems to be that parental drinking *per se* does not result in negative consequences for children, but that childhood problems (with the exception of the foetal alcohol syndrome) stem from the associated family dysfunction and disturbed relationships with the community. Thus, in order to understand the situation of these children it is essential to begin by constructing as full a picture as possible of the family's circumstances, relationships and position in the wider community and to look at the child as a part of this dynamic system.

Over thirty years ago, a social worker in a child guidance clinic wrote that treatment for children of alcoholics was unlikely to be successful unless there was improvement in the drinking and in marital and parent-child relationships. Whilst she was working with children with quite severe problems, it is likely that improvement in these areas is a prerequisite for long standing improvement in the situation of any child with problem-drinking parents.

Where possible, treatment of the whole family would seem to be the method of choice. An experimental project in America using family therapy for behaviour problems among children of problem drinkers found that not only was this method helpful to the children, but it also resulted in earlier recognition of and treatment for parental drinking (Hindman, 1975). From another direction, the Yugoslavian study mentioned above found that the use of conjoint family therapy as part of a multi-method programme (grounded in a systems perspective) for problem drinkers and their families resulted in greater improvement in family relationships, psychological and social adjustment of family members and in drinking, than a traditional, individual-oriented programme.

Family therapy may not be feasible for many agencies because of lack of experienced workers or resources for training. In this situation, referral of parents to specialist alcohol units and/or for marital counselling may be an appropriate strategy. What must be avoided, however, is the situation where a number of different services are involved with a given family with little or no co-ordination between the workers concerned. This can only result in fragmentation of the family with a loss of any sense of the family as a whole and consequent frustration of the workers' attempts to help.

Treatment of the whole family may also be impossible because one or more members refuse to participate. In some cases it may be possible to work with part of the family constructively, for instance with the non-alcoholic parent and children. This can sometimes result in the drinker seeking treatment and the ultimate resolution of many of the family problems. In some cases, though, separation of the family may be a more constructive solution for all concerned and counselling may be more usefully aimed at enabling the family to make the break and adjust to their new situation, in practical and emotional terms.

Whilst such drastic measures may be necessary in some cases, these may well represent a small minority of children from severely disrupted family backgrounds. It is likely that a large number of children with alcoholic parents can be assisted with quite simple, but sensitive, counselling in conjunction with help for the family problems, including drinking. Nevertheless, until a more active policy towards involving these children is adopted, we can only speculate about the real extent of their needs for treatment and the methods which will prove most useful.

9 FAMILY LAW AND ALCOHOL PROBLEMS

Heather Johns

We are all aware that many crimes are committed when the offender is drunk. In the home, too, crimes associated with alcohol are daily perpetrated, although many of them will never be recorded in police statistics. Wife beating and child abuse are the obvious horrifying examples, but there are others that although not officially categorised as crimes, amount to serious violations of human dignity and self-respect. Living with a person who has a drink problem may mean living with problems that fall within the twilight zone of the hidden misery statistics.

There is very little substantive law that deals directly with problems of drunkenness within the family. Indeed, the law in general has little to say about alcohol problems at all. Rather the recognition of alcohol problems is manifested indirectly by the way in which the law responds to other family problems, which may or may not be alcohol linked or based. It should also be stressed that the law provides no definition of what constitutes an alcohol problem. It will be seen, however, that the legislation which responds to such problems generally requires that there is a persistent and serious level of drinking, which affects the behaviour of the drinker in an anti-social manner. The object of this chapter is therefore to look at those laws which do in fact go some way towards alleviating the problem of drunkenness, albeit that they are designed to remedy perhaps more clearly defined forms of family strife, such as matrimonial violence and child custody disputes. We must then evaluate the efficacy of those laws in their attempts to relieve the perhaps hidden and underlying problems, such as drunkenness. Before discussing the legal remedies currently available I shall outline the sorts of problems that the law is asked to redress.

Numerous studies have been conducted which attempt to show a correlation between alcohol and familial violence, notably Gayford's survey of 100 battered wives at Chiswick Women's Refuge where he recorded that 'the survey shows pointers of correlation between alcoholism and wife beating . . . with 44.1 per cent of women claiming that violence only occurred when their man was under the influence of alcohol.' In his evidence to the Select Committee on Violence in the Family (1975) Gayford further remarked that 'alcohol is a very big problem so far as the men are concerned . . . 50 per cent of the men regularly get drunk, in 75 per cent of the men drunkenness is a very frequent occurrence in their lives'. In 1976 Orford *et al.* (1976b) reported the findings of their hardship questionnaires to wives of alcoholics and found that '72 per cent had been threatened, 45 per cent beaten, 49 per cent had witnessed the man breaking up furniture, windows and china.'

Incest is yet another example of the insidious type of problem that so often remains hidden within the family. Little research has been conducted in this area. However, in 1971 Hall Williams made a study of 68 offenders convicted of incest and considered for parole between 1970 and 1971, and found that 18 per cent had a drink problem. A similar study by Maisch in 1973 revealed that 'a high proportion' were alcoholics.

Solicitors are likely to deal with a number of cases involving child abuse and neglect. In a significant number there is evidence that problems associated with drinking of varying severity plays an important part. Nevertheless we do not know precisely what leads a parent to abuse his or her child. Whatever psychological or social problems may exist, these may well be exacerbated by a drink problem (Belsky, 1978) or indeed may lead to the creation of a drink problem. No one can be sure whether excess drinking is the cause of abusive behaviour or a result of the frustration which produced it.

Finally, there are of course other insidious problems associated with drunkenness. Obviously a family may be faced with an acute lack of money if one member needs to finance his alcohol addiction.

Clearly familial disputes are as multifarious as are their causes. Whether alcohol problems are precipitous or symptomatic of family strife is a moot point. The courts, however, are daily asked to resolve such family problems. It is therefore essential to examine how they do this, the equipment that is available to them to do so and indeed how sensitive they are in detecting and dealing with underlying problems, such as drunkenness.

In England the legislation that specifically attempts to regulate alcohol problems within the family is limited. What little there is has emerged in an arbitrary fashion and stems largely from the work of the temperance workers at the turn of this century in drawing Parliament's attention to the appalling problems of drunkenness prevailing at that time. In 1874 a government inquiry (Reports to the Secretary of State, 1875) into the law on brutal assaults revealed a consensus among the Police and judicial authorities about the serious level of violent crime ascribed mainly to drink. Thirty-five years later in its evidence to the Royal Commission on Divorce and Matrimonial Causes (1912) the NSPCC similarly attributed a high proportion of conjugal and parental violence to drunkenness. The Liverpool Society reported this was responsible for nine-tenths of child cruelty. Undoubtedly the emphasis on drink partly reflected the influence of the temperance workers in exposing the problem, but partly also the more general public concern from the 1870s with high alcohol consumption and consequent street violence.

As a result of this concern ad hoc legislation emerged relating mainly to the protection of wives and children: (1) Licensing Act 1902 S.2 whereby it became an offence to be drunk in a public place while in charge of a child under seven, and S.5 of the 1902 Act whereby habitual drunkenness became for the first time a ground for separation, maintenance and custody; (2) S.1 (b) Children and Young Persons Act 1933 whereby a person having care or custody of children may be criminally liable for causing the death of a child under three years by overlaying it in bed whilst drunk. (It was thought to be a fairly common occurrence for parents accidentally to suffocate their children by falling asleep on top of them when drunk.)

Although most of these laws still remain on the statute book, they have largely fallen into disuse, as a result of the changes that have taken place in the structure of the family and by the changes in attitude towards what constitutes acceptable behaviour within the family.

Having thus outlined briefly the major areas of family problems as they present themselves to the practitioner today, I propose for the remainder of this chapter to describe the broad remedies available for each loosely-defined area with particular reference to alcohol problems.

Obviously the ultimate relief for all forms of disputes between spouses is divorce. Habitual drunkenness however has never been accorded the status of a ground for divorce *per se*. Nevertheless, habitual drunkenness has for many years been regarded as behaviour sufficiently serious to warrant divorce. Before the Matrimonial Causes Act 1973 the former matrimonial offence of cruelty was established on a finding of habitual drunkenness. Davis J. stated the principle in the case of *Baker v Baker* (1955) 1 Weekly Law Reports, p. 1011, 'persistent drunkenness after warning that such a course of conduct is inflicting pain on the other spouse, certainly if it is known to be injuring the other spouse's health may well of itself amount to cruelty'.

The Act of 1973 provided that the sole ground for divorce and judicial separation is that the marriage has irretrievably broken down. This is proved by establishing one of five facts:

(1) The respondent's adultery.

(2) The respondent's unreasonable behaviour.

(3) Two years desertion.

(4) Two years separation plus consent.

(5) Five years separation.

The relevant fact so far as problems of drunkenness are concerned is obviously that of unreasonable behaviour. S.1. (2) (b) of the 1973 Act states that the test must be whether 'the respondent behaved in such a way that the petitioner cannot reasonably be expected to live with the respondent'.

The behaviour complained of must be serious, grave and weighty, virtually amounting to the former matrimonial offence of cruelty. The test to apply is an objective one: can the petitioner 'reasonably be expected' to live with the respondent? It is not 'has the respondent behaved reasonably'. The court must make the decision. It does so on a value judgement about the respondent's behaviour and the effect of that behaviour on the petititioner. The case law has established the principle that the respondent's behaviour must be looked at in the light of the petitioner's behaviour and thus it has been held that 'a violent petitioner may reasonably be expected to live with a violent respondent (and) a petitioner who is addicted to drink can reasonably be expected to live with a respondent similarly addicted . . . ' (*Ash v Ash* (1972) FAM 135). It is not possible to ascertain what proportion of unreasonable behaviour petititions are based wholly or in part on drunken behaviour. However, it is interesting to note that in 1976 behaviour petititions formed the second largest grounds for divorce after adultery. Furthermore, out of a total of 38,364 behaviour petitions, 34,884 were brought by wives, this discrepancy being much greater than for any of the other grounds for divorce.

In contrast to the British system of 'marital offence' divorces, the majority of states in North America have in recent years established a system of 'no fault' divorces and have abolished the concept of the guilty spouse. However, before this radical reform all the divorce codes included habitual drunkenness as a grounds for divorce. The standard test applied by the majority of states in defining habitual drunkenness was broadly similar to that provided by S.106 California Divorce Code as 'that degree of intemperance from the use of intoxicating drinks which disqualifies the person a great portion of the time from properly attending to business or which would reasonably inflict a course of great mental anguish upon the innocent party'.

Since 1938 habitual drunkenness has been a ground for divorce in Scotland. Indeed the Licensing (Scotland) Act of 1903 had established that habitual drunkenness was the equivalent of cruelty for the purpose of obtaining a decree of judicial separation. The Divorce Act of 1938 enacted that any cruelty that would justify a judicial separation should be a ground for divorce and therefore since habitual drunkenness had been placed in the same category as cruelty it has in fact been an additional ground for divorce in Scotland since 1938. The Royal Commission on Marriage and Divorce (1951-1955) in England reported in 1956 that it did not consider that any advantage would be gained if habitual drunkenness were deemed to be cruelty in England. 'We think that such hardship can be suficiently relieved under the law relating to cruelty and desertion as grounds of divorce.'

A marriage may also be annulled if certain defects pertained at the time of the formation of the marriage contract. S.12 (c) of the Matrimonial Causes Act 1973 provides that a marriage should be voidable if either party did not validly consent to it whether in consequence of duress, mistake, unsoundness of mind or otherwise. Marriage is a contract and consequently absence of consent will invalidate the ceremony. Thus a marriage may be voidable if one of the parties was so under the influence of drink that he or she was incapable of understanding the nature of the contract into which they were entering. The significance of this legislation must be doubted however when one considers that in 1976 the total number of nullity decrees based on S.12 (c) Matrimonial Causes Act 1973 was three (all brought by women).

Here again we find the United States Divorce Codes have long recognised severe drunkenness at the time of the marriage ceremony as a specific ground for annulment. For example, S.82 of the California Divorce Code provides that 'one participating in the marriage ceremony while under the influence of intoxicating beverage to such an extent as to be of unsound mind and without knowledge of what is happening is entitled to an annulment of the marriage'.

Clearly provisions exist whereby a marriage that has foundered because of severe alcohol problems may be terminated. But how successful is the law in dealing with problems where the remedy sought is not final separation but help and guidance in solving those problems while preserving the family unit?

Where a marriage has not yet been terminated by divorce the Magistrates' Court has power to make orders for the maintenance of the parties to a marriage and for custody and maintenance of and access to children of the family. The Domestic Proceedings and Magistrates'

Court Act 1978 (implemented on 1 February 1981) enables the court to make such orders if the applicant can establish that the respondent (1) has failed to provide reasonable maintenance for the applicant or for any child of the family or (2) has behaved in such a way that the applicant cannot reasonably be expected to live with the respondent or (3) is in desertion. Orders may also be made where a voluntary separation of at least three months has taken place and one party has during this period made payments of maintenance to the other.

The Act is a major innovation in family law and will implement a number of reforms that have long been overdue. In 1971 the Law Commission set up a working party to consider the matrimonial jurisdiction of Magistrates' Courts. The Commission's report published in 1976 (Law Commission, 1976) made detailed proposals for reform of the substantive law, to bring it broadly into line with the law administered by the divorce court. These proposals have been implemented in the Act presently under discussion.

Use of the Magistrates' Court has declined steadily over the last few decades. At the beginning of this century over 90 per cent of all matrimonial suits were heard by magistrates, whereas in 1975 the number of divorce petititions filed totalled 138,048 but the total of magistrates' matrimonial orders was only 12,027. The reasons for the decline in popularity of the Magistrates Courts are obviously beyond the scope of this chapter. It is, however, relevant to note that certainly since the reform of the divorce law in 1973, the magistrates' jurisdiction over matrimonial matters was felt by many to be based on the wholly archaic public morality of the latter part of the nineteenth century. Under the former law administered by the Matrimonial Proceedings (Magistrates' Courts) Act 1960 orders for maintenance and custody could only be obtained by proving that the defendant was guilty of one of the offences laid down in the Act. The offences included compelling a wife to submit to prostitution, being a habitual drunkard or drug addict, adultery or cruelty. The expression 'habitual drunkard' was so defined as to ensure that only in really serious cases could a complaint be made. The defendant had to be 'a person (not being a mentally disordered person within the meaning of the Mental Health Act 1959) who by reason of habitual drinking of intoxicating liquor (a) was at times dangerous to himself or to others or incapable of managing himself or his affairs or (b) so conducted himself that it would not be reasonable to expect a spouse of ordinary sensibilities to continue to cohabitate with him.

Judicial statistics for the numbers of applications made on the individual grounds of complaints are regrettably not recorded. However, in 1966 the Bedford College survey produced a breakdown of complainants applying for orders and the grounds cited:

> Desertion 593; wilful neglect to maintain 397; persistent cruelty 183; adultery 94; others (including drunkenness) 4. Total number of complaints: 1271.

The complaint of habitual drunkenness was clearly little used and obviously will now fall under the umbrella of the 'behaviour' complaint, as in divorce law. The under-utilisation of habitual drunkenness may be largely explained by the fact that only under this complaint could a *complainant* be ordered to provide maintenance for the *defendant*. Thus in order to avoid this the practitioner would advise the complainant, where appropriate, that the defendant's drunken behaviour amounted to either constructive desertion or persistent cruelty and thus a complaint would be made on either of these grounds rather than drunkenness. The idea of the habitual drunkard meriting support was at odds with the rest of the legislation which was almost exclusively designed as a method of support for wives and children and reflects an interesting aspect of indulgence on the part of the legislators which is virtually lacking elsewhere. Under the 1960 Act a husband could only obtain maintenance where, in addition to proving an offence, his earning capacity was impaired by some physical or mental disability. It is perhaps reasonable, therefore, to assume that habitual drunkenness was similarly recognised as a disability. One of the original tenets of the concept of maintenance was to prevent a deserted wife becoming a burden on the state. It is a logical extension of this to require the support of those husbands who suffer from some incapacity and who would otherwise be dependent upon the poor law authorities.

The new legislation provides no facility for maintenance payments in such circumstances, the payment of maintenance being based entirely on the financial circumstances and responsibility for any children of each of the parties. The emphasis in the legislation is clearly to eliminate as far as possible the apportionment of blame when family breakdown has occured. The Law Commission rightly felt that the hostility inevitably introduced by the concept of the guilty party severely handicapped any efforts to decide questions such as custody and access on any sort of rational basis. Indeed the new Act accepts the principle of complete equality between husband and wife and either party to the marriage may apply for any of the orders.

Disputes regarding the custody of children may be dealt with by the courts either while the marriage is subsisting, after divorce or as between unmarried parents. The law relating to custody disputes in general, whether between parents or parents and local authority, places great emphasis on the moral conduct of the parents. No specific reference is made to drunkenness in the relevant legislation but such a problem would undoubtedly count heavily against the offending parent. S.1 of the Guardianship of Minors Act 1971 (disputes between parents) expresses the principle that so far as matters such as the custody, care and control of, and access to a child are concerned the paramount consideration is the welfare of the child. In determining this the court has regard *inter alia* to the conduct of each parent. Although the courts are very reluctant to upset the status quo and remove a child from the care of the parent with whom he/she is settled, allegations of drunkenness leading to the possible neglect of the child would undoubtedly greatly influence the court's decision.

Certainly the grounds laid down for care orders in English legislation by the local authorities in the Children's Acts 1948 and 1975 and in the Children's and Young Persons Act 1969 are concerned with the moral behaviour and capabilities of the parents but again without specifically alluding to problems of drunkenness. A drink problem that leads to the physical or emotional neglect of a child and which is likely to impair the child's natural development would justify the making of a court order in the majority of cases.

Violence in the family poses serious logistic problems not only in securing effective remedies but also in detecting the extent of the problem. In discussing domestic violence we should include not only wife beating and child abuse but also child neglect. Although child neglect will not always involve incidents of violence, the results of some forms of neglect are tantamount to serious violations of the person.

Domestic violence like any other form of violence is subject to the control of the criminal and civil law. It is indeed fairly common for incidents of child abuse and neglect to be dealt with by proceedings under both jurisdictions; that is, by the removal of the child by a civil care order and the punishment of the offending parent in the criminal court. Incidents of wife beating are, however, far less likely to be the subject of criminal proceedings, the Police being noticeably more reluctant to interfere in a dispute between husband and wife than where a child is the victim. Consequently the majority of such actions are dealt with by the civil law. Obviously we require the immediate protection of children who are unable to defend themselves. However it is evident that in many cases the beaten wife is equally trapped in the home environment.

Police reticence to get involved in 'domestics' stems from a number of factors. The situation is often very volatile and there is a serious risk of physical injury to a police officer who attempts to restrain a husband at the crisis point. In the USA it has been said that 40 per cent of injuries to the Police occur while they are intervening in family disputes (Bard, 1974). However, once called to the scene the Police will often refrain from pressing criminal charges in favour of advising the woman to institute her own civil proceedings. Primarily, the Police reason that in many instances, once the initial crisis period has passed, the woman is often very reluctant to continue with the criminal prosecution of her partner.

The remedies for matrimonial violence under the civil law are: in the High Court an injunction coupled with divorce proceedings; in the County Court an injunction under the Domestic Violence and Matrimonial Proceedings Act 1976 (available to both married and unmarried couples living together); and, since 1979, an injunction in the Magistrates' Court. In each court the relief available is broadly similar: a non-molestation order and, where appropriate, an ouster order excluding the guilty spouse from the matrimonial home. The penalty for breach of the court order is imprisonment. No attempt is made by the court to analyse the individual and specific problems of the parties, be they psychiatric, alcohol-linked or otherwise. Indeed apart from the Magistrates' Court's power to order maintenance payments, our courts in the United Kingdom are ill equipped to do anything other than terminate the relationship.

In dealing with battered wives the solicitor is forced to acknowledge that many women are not seeking merely to be rid of their partner but seek more positive support and guidance in coping with a particular matrimonial problem. Many women either drop proceedings against their husbands before the court stage is reached or return to their husbands within days of an injunction being granted in their favour. The court is able to pay only scant regard to the complex bonds of interdependence that can so effectively bind a couple together. At present many women feel unable to cope without their partner however antisocial his behaviour may be. In such cases the law is often used as a desperate attempt to bring the man to some realisation of his behaviour. The law very rarely achieves this. Men who batter women need positive help. Some authors have suggested that many of them are mentally unstable (Belsky, 1978) and exceptionally dependent on their women and children. They may have nowhere else to live except the homes of the women they assault. Sending a man to prison may temporarily protect the women but it can do nothing to solve his own difficulties or help in changing his behaviour pattern. It is quite common for a man who had just been released from prison to go straight home and beat up the woman again (Coote and Gill, 1977).

In Britain no attempt is made to counsel parties with a view to either reconciliation or to accepting that a relationship is over. Unless a man is legally represented he may not even be aware of the effect and meaning of any injunction or order of the Magistrates' Court which has been made against him. English courts remain in a state of confusion as to their powers to interfere in inter-spousal relationships. In dealing with children they have recognised the use of placing a child under the supervision of a social worker while the child continues to live at home. The idea of any such monitoring of the affairs of a husband and wife is completely taboo. However, the misery of many couples trapped in a marriage cannot continue to be ignored.

In contrast in the United States and particularly in New York an attempt has been made to take a much broader view of domestic relations as a whole. The New York Family Court Act S.811 expresses the philosophy which led to the setting up of the Family Court system in New York:

> In the past wives and other members of the family who suffered from disorderly conduct or assaults by other members of the family or household were compelled to bring a criminal charge to invoke the jurisdiction of the court. Their purpose with few exceptions was not to secure a criminal conviction and punishment but practical help . . . this article . . . authorises the Family Court to enter orders of protection and support and contemplates conciliation proceedings.

The New York Family Court has jurisdiction over all family matters which must be brought before it. Proceedings for family offences can be brought by the victim, authorised agencies, the Police or other persons with the court's permission. The Probation Service attached to the court has power to attempt preliminary informal adjustment of suitable cases, e.g. by counselling or referral to the court's mental health service or to the voluntary marital counselling agencies again on the court premises. The Probation Service cannot compel this nor prevent a petition being filed if the party so wishes. The court has power to dismiss the petition, suspend a judgement for six months, order one year's probation or make a civil protection order. The court most commonly imposes a civil protection order to which it may attach reasonable conditions of behaviour to be observed by the petitioner or respondent or both for a minimum of one year. For example it may: order the respondent not to molest the petitioner; exclude the offending spouse; order either party to give proper attention to the care of the home or to refrain from acts of commission or omission that tend to make the home not a proper place for a child or to co-operate in seeking and accepting medical and/or psychiatric diagnosis and treatment including family case work or child guidance. The penalty for breach of such an order is a maximum of six months' imprisonment. This may be suspended with conditions as to appropriate treatment.

In Washington DC an intra-family offence is defined as an act which could be punished as a criminal offence, is committed by one spouse against the other, by a parent against a child or by any person against another with whom he shares a mutual residence and is in close relationship (Divorce Code S.16 sub. s. 10101). The Family Court here has power to order either spouse to participate where appropriate in such a programme of alcoholic rehabilitation as may be established by the Department of Social Services.

Similar provisions exist under the German Civil Code whereby a person who through alcoholism 'is not able to minister his own affairs or exposes his family to distress . . . may be subjected to tutelage'.

There are no overall figures available which would enable comparisons to be made of the success rates of Britain and the USA in resolving family disputes. Certainly any course of counselling must rely on the willingness of both parties to participate. In Britain there is a traditional reluctance to compel treatment of any kind. Over a period of nearly 100 years piecemeal attempts have been made to compel the treatment of alcoholics under the provisions of the criminal law. In 1897 the Habitual Drunkards Act provided for the establishment of inebriate reformatories or retreats for those persons convicted of offences of drunkenness. In 1972 the Criminal Justice Act enabled a police officer to take a person arrested on a charge of drunkenness to a medical treatment centre for alcoholics. There are only two such detoxification centres in Great Britain, neither of them in the Metropolitan area. These are treatment centres to which the Police may take offenders although there are no powers to detain them, and of course they cater for single people.

It is a widely-held belief that treatment or counselling will only succeed if conducted on a voluntary basis. There are of course compulsory powers to admit patients to hospital for psychiatric treatment. Alcoholism however is not of itself a mental disorder and detention under the Mental Health Act 1959 on the ground of alcoholism alone is therefore not possible.

In an article in the **British Medical Journal** in 1966, Scott observed that 'there is an obvious problem in the stage army of alcoholics circulating in self destructive manner round the courts and prisons and there is an understandable urge to force a solution through legislation, yet compulsion is a double edged weapon and expensive of human effort and resources, it should be a final resort when voluntary measures have been tried and failed'. Nevertheless, in advanced stages of alcohol addiction when a patient could be said to have lost nearly all his free will in the disease process, compulsory power of treatment would at least amount to an effective means of containing a perhaps violent and abusive spouse, in an environment more conducive to rehabilitation than prison.

At earlier stages in the development of a drink problem, compulsion to participate in informal discussions of familial relationships, whether or not the courts then have power to compel a designated course of treatment, would provide a setting more conducive to the revelation of the perhaps more hidden anxieties within the relationship than the present court structure allows.

Whether a course of treatment, which is imposed rather than voluntary, can ever be successful is beyond the scope of this chapter. However, given our present abysmal failure to deal effectively with family strife, the concept of compulsory treatment should at least be accorded the status of a viable alternative. The inherent infringement of personal liberty can surely be no more demeaning than a term of imprisonment.

There has been much debate over the past few years about the setting up of a family court system in Britain. It appears that no government feels able to make firm proposals for the inauguration of such a scheme. In extending power to make exclusion orders to the Magistrates' Court the Law Commission (1976) envisaged the Probation Service being involved with the preliminary counselling of the parties. However, matrimonial case work undertaken by the Probation Service is regarded as an extra-statutory duty.

In Britain we clearly do not yet know how we wish to regard family problems. We do not know the causes and we do not know the remedies. Surely where such uncertainty prevails we must at least allow flexibility. In many cases an approach to the courts indicates a plea for professional help in a sincere effort to salvage a marriage. The courts are an expensive machinery to set in motion. They must therefore be restructured to provide families with what they want. The Select Committee on Violence in Marriage envisaged the setting up of family crisis centres to provide counselling and advice from experts in the relevant fields at the pre-court stage. To date nothing has come of these proposals. The court as it exists today still has no power to utilise the problem-solving agencies and techniques that do exist.

There must obviously always exist the means to terminate a relationship with the minimum amount of acrimony. However, we must always be aware that in domestic disputes underlying causes are often subject to continual eruption because of the close contact of the parties. Indeed, it is this very intimacy that so often inhibits the ability to recognise the existence of such problems let alone the possible solutions to them. We need a family court both to assist in the delicate unravelling of these complex bonds and to ensure that once family problems are revealed underlying problems such as drunkenness can be given the expert advice and assistance that is required whether or not the relationship continues. But obviously before we put all our eggs into the family court basket we must ensure that the standard of our support agencies is sufficient to meet the task.

10 ORGANISATION OF SERVICES TO FAMILIES OF ALCOHOLICS

E. Bruce Ritson

It is well-known that alcohol-related problems can have a corrosive and distorting influence on family life. This raises one simple question which forms the basis of the present chapter. If we are confronting something which is so clearly a family problem, why is the family so rarely involved in conventional therapies?

The case for family involvement is further strengthened by the evidence that those alcoholics who enter treatment with an intact and supportive marriage have a much better chance of overcoming their drinking problems than those who lack such support and have divisive embattled marriages (Orford and Edwards, 1977). The family is in fact one of the most important resources available to the therapist, but very real difficulties often exist in making effective use of its resources and these are examined below. Some of the barriers arise from the way in which services are organised; others reside more in the attitudes of agencies and families themselves.

Barriers to Seeking Help

The decision to seek help from an outside agent usually follows some personal or family crisis. The 'last straw' may have been a breakdown in health, or in a relationship, or some social catastrophe such as loss of job or an arrest. A crisis is a turning-point from which the person may emerge with a new sense of competence and an enlarged repertoire of coping skills, or conversely it may presage further disintegration and regression. This would imply that a crisis is an opportunity for change so that the task of the agency is to ensure that the client and the family take full advantage of this opportunity (Caplan, 1964).

Most families are reluctant to admit that one member has a drinking problem. Commonly the family share in various ways a feeling that all is not well, that the coping strategies which have sustained them over the years are no longer effective. To understand the difficulties in organising services for the families of problem drinkers it is useful to start by examining the differing perceptions which may co-exist within a family, because these determine the construction family members place on the changes they observe and the kind of help they are likely to seek.

The following case illustrates the way in which three significant family members held different priorities and perceptions when confronted by a similar sequence of events.

Mr A (aged 42) has been working longer hours than usual, trying to cope with a recent merger which complicated his company's accounting methods. He has a new boss whom he feels has no appreciation of the task he has been set and takes out his frustration on Mr A by finding trivial mistakes in his accounts. Recently Mr A has increased his alcohol intake to help him cope with the situation at work and is keeping half a bottle of whisky in his desk to sustain him whilst working overtime. This has caused him some embarrassment when one evening he falls asleep at his desk and his secretary drives him home in her car. This leads to a row at home and adds further to his worries. Eventually the strain of work affects his health, his sleep is poor, he has no appetite and is sick most mornings. His general practitioner has given him a 'sick note' and he is currently off work due to his gastritis. He feels relieved to be away from the responsibility of work. Despite the doctor's advice and his wife's nagging he finds the most relaxing way to enjoy his convalescence is to spend most of the day drinking in the golf club and to have an occasional round of golf between drinking sessions. He says that if his wife didn't nag about drinking so much he would spend time at home in the garden but he feels he has to get away from the atmosphere at home.

Mrs A (aged 40) views events differently. She has noticed her husband becoming less involved with the family over some years. He has been working hard, or at least longer hours, and seems more easily upset by trivial incidents which previously he coped with easily. She wonders if he could be having an affair – he certainly seems less interested in her sexually than he has been in the past, so the night his secretary drove him home only highlights her suspicions. She has been worrying a lot about his drinking. He was spending money they could ill afford on drink and he often has a terrible hangover in the morning. Little wonder he couldn't cope with his work, although the new manager seemed very understanding and tolerant. She worries that the office will notice he is not coping and drinking far too much. When she suggests he cut down his drinking he flies into a temper and sulks at the golf club. She is particularly perturbed that even when the doctor has given him a chance to pull himself together there has been no real change in his drinking habits and he is still avoiding the family. She has spoken of her worries to her friends, and to the minister. They advise her to see her doctor who has given her a tranquilliser and the address of the Marriage Guidance Council. The fifteen-year-old daughter finds her father so objectionable when drunk that she refuses to join in the family meals. For years she has been unable to have friends into the house for fear of the state her father would be in. She is a curiously friendless, awkward child who has not really fulfilled the promise of her earlier years at school and her teachers view her as something of a problem.

This vignette depicts a commonplace situation which illustrates the range of presenting problems which have masked for some years the underlying issue of the father's growing dependence on alcohol.

We have seen in an earlier chapter (Chapter 7) that the interrelationships within the family are geared to sustain a certain homeostasis. The decision that this balance has been so severely threatened that outside help must be sought is not easily taken. Indeed, the family often tries to cope without seeking outside aid from the outset and may continue in this way for many years. This seems to be particularly true in certain cultures when the kinship bonds of the family are highly regarded and where every effort will be made to conceal deviant members. We do not know how often the families' own coping strategies prove effective, though there is evidence to suggest that apparently unaided remission of even established dependence is not uncommon (Cahalan, 1970). It would be interesting to make a close study of those families which have shown the internal capacity to achieve this reversal.

Individuals who are dependent on alcohol make greater than average use of health and social services. One recent study showed that problem drinkers identified in a community survey visited their general practitioner three times more often than others in the sample (Cartwright *et al.*, 1975). General practitioners themselves often comment on the regularity with which wives of alcoholics come to them requesting tranquillisers or anti-depressants when further enquiry reveals that their spouse's drinking is the underlying problem. Moreover, research has indicated that social and family problems are much the commonest presenting characteristics of alcohol dependence in general practice (Wilkins, 1974). Women often complain of their husband's drunken behaviour but implore the general practitioner to say nothing about it because their husband would regard it as a personal betrayal.

It should therefore be clear that there are a number of barriers which make it difficult to talk frankly about a drinking problem either within the family or with the agency from which help is sought. In practice, a number of recurrent obstacles may be observed.

Barriers to the Recognition of Alcohol Abuse within the Family

Denial

This common defence sustains us all at times and excessive emphasis has perhaps been placed on it as a frequent resistance in the problem drinker. Many patients and their families do not necessarily deny that drinking is a problem, although there is often disagreement over its seriousness and the measures which need to be taken to improve the situation. In common with most other ailments the sufferer experiences, the family encourages various strategies of self-cure, such as avoiding spirits or 'going on the wagon' intermittently. The family may reward periods of abstinence, and encourage the development of new interests. Help-seeking comes only after these essays in self-treatment have been exhausted.

Projection

The family is commonly more comfortable attributing blame for an alcohol-related crisis to some external situation or person who then becomes the scapegoat for the family's difficulties. This token problem is then offered to the agency for resolution. For example, a wife may consult the social worker about inadequate housing or her dislike of living in a neighbourhood where there are so many drunks and pubs. The problem presented may indeed be a very real issue requiring resolution; however it may also serve as a means of masking the family's concern about the husband's dependence on alcohol and his drunkenness, in the hope that a change of neighbourhood would also resolve the drinking problem. In consequence the agency feels comfortable in dealing with a housing problem and refers the case on to the appropriate 'housing department'.

The family has thus yet again avoided the issue that is disturbing its homeostasis. Projection, in common with other defences, is a way of dealing with intolerable anxiety. The family may at first only feel able to discuss the token problem which is presented and only when they feel secure with the agency and able to trust its staff can they mention alcohol abuse.

The Scapegoat

The scapegoat is endowed with feelings and impulses which other members of the family cannot accept. The drinker is often given this role so that involvement in family therapy means acknowledging an unpalatable facet of family life. For instance: a middle-aged woman, Kate, with a serious drinking problem rebelled against her mother's hostility towards men and sexual relations by becoming quite promiscuous. She had several children and found to her surprise that her mother immediately took great interest in them and effectively became responsible for their care together with the 'good' sister who never married. Kate, for her part, was excluded from the family because of her drunkenness and loose life. Little wonder that her sister and mother would have nothing to do with her but remained happy to protect the children from her evil influence.

Guilt

The spouse of a problem drinker commonly feels that he or she is in some way to blame for the drinking. This belief was often reinforced by the earlier literature on alcoholism which suggested, without much foundation, that commonly the wife engendered or at least encouraged the spouse's drinking (see Chapter 6 for full discussion). The guilt may also be founded in the unacceptable feelings of hostility which commonly reside in the alcohol-impaired marriage. It is not uncommon for a spouse to have wished that his or her partner had died during a drunken bout or that the problem drinker would leave the family for good. The spouse subsequently feels guilty about these thoughts and may even come to believe that such inner 'badness' has contributed to the drinking problem. Many spouses come to view alcohol as a rival and wonder how they have proved so unattractive that drink should seem preferable. In such circumstances guilt and low self-esteem may deter spouses from seeking advice because they *know* that the fault lies in themselves.

Disloyalty

As already indicated, a spouse often feels extremely disloyal talking about the problem drinker without his knowledge or consent. This feeling is stronger in some cultures than others and in some more paternalistic societies there is a virtual taboo on a wife talking about her husband outside the home in this way. There is also sometimes a further anxiety that a man may physically assault his wife for speaking about him to outsiders.

Shame

A considerable stigma is still attached to the word 'alcoholic' and this is little improved by some of its contemporary synonyms, such as problem or excessive drinker. Excessive drinking is far from being a socially acceptable complaint and is often used as a term of abuse. The problem was highlighted for the author in a recent conversation: 'Her man's nothing but an alcoholic and he's from such a respectable family, too. I can't understand what she sees in him.'

These familiar views abound and naturally make any family member think twice before attracting such a label to their own family. The stigma is particularly acute for female problem drinkers. Many recent studies have shown that society remains extremely critical of women who drink heavily and judges them more harshly than their male counterparts (Camberwell Council on Alcoholism, 1980). Women and the family incorporate these values and the heightened sense of shame prevents them from seeking help. One patient vividly illustrated this by saying she would only come to the clinic after dark when no one would see her.

Ignorance

Sheer lack of knowledge may be a barrier for many. Symptoms of alcohol dependence may be recognised but not associated directly with alcohol. For example, the mother of a young alcohol addict would regularly buy cans of beer for him to take in the morning so that he would feel more 'settled'. Neither had truly ascribed his morning shakiness to alcohol, preferring to believe that it was simply due to 'bad nerves'. The acute abdominal pain which accompanies alcohol-induced gastritis may be ascribed to a 'weak stomach' or a supposed ulcer rather than the direct effect of excessive drinking. A strong smell of alcohol on the breath while at work in the morning is common evidence of an alcohol problem and yet it is often overlooked and the employee's deteriorating work performance attributed to other factors.

Despite these barriers to seeking help, we know that a disproportionately large number of problem drinkers attend their general practitioners, visit social workers, get arrested, consult lawyers and seek various forms of counselling and advice. Unfortunately, they rarely reveal the core cause of their problems. The same is true of spouses and of children. We should now explore the factors which prevent skilled professionals from recognising alcohol problems when they are clearly causing havoc within the family.

Barriers to Problem Recognition within Agency Staff

A general practitioner colleague of mine recently documented the history of those patients within his practice in which an alcohol problem was ultimately detected. The following is a fabrication, but none the less typical of his casebook and it illustrates the frequent opportunities for recognition and points to some of the difficulties inherent in making an effective intervention.

Aged 30 – Married

First attended practice aged 19 having injured ankle falling in the street – X-ray arranged, no further action.

Same year, sustained laceration in fight with 'friend' at dance – GP adds: 'I suspect she and her friend had been drinking too much.' Laceration sutured, no further appointment.

Age 21. Complaining of abdominal pain – looks pale and tired. Recurrent gastritis, pain and nausea, losing weight. Consulted physician – Barium Meal arranged, nothing found. (She is now married.)

Age 22. Broke her arm falling downstairs, smelling strongly of alcohol when I was called – referred to casualty department, plaster cast applied.

Age 22. Called to see her baby who was suffering from gastroenteritis – house looks in dreadful state. Patient and her husband both drinking gin when I called.

Age 23. Health visitor worried that child is being neglected. Mother angry about this and seems to resent visits. Social worker reports similar experience. Suggest that case conference arranged as child at risk of abuse or neglect. Conference arranged – agreed that the child was at risk, regular visits from health visitor and social worker planned.

Age 25. Attended for vaccination – home situation seems to have improved.

Age 28. Sore throat – smokes 40 per day. Advised to stop. No mention of drink.

Age 28. Acute abdominal pain – Pancreatitis diagnosed and admitted to hospital — discharged improved, advised not to drink by physician.

Age 29. Says she is depressed, can't cope with the children (now has two), husband not interested in her. Breath smells of alcohol at morning surgery. Enquire about drinking. Says she takes Bacardi 'for her nerves'. Agrees to give it up.

Age 30. Overdose Paracetamol with alcohol following row with husband. He has left, saying he can't stand her drinking any longer. Admitted Intensive Care Poisons Unit.

This common sequence of events illustrates the way in which social workers, doctors and others intervene at times of crisis but rarely extend this to enquire into the workings of the family or the place alcohol may occupy in causing the problems. Some of these barriers to recognition and family involvement reside in the structure of the services and others within their staff. It is also evident that most of our knowledge about the early recognition of alcohol problems relates to signs and symptoms associated with the drinker. A family perspective to recognition barely exists and a great deal more work needs to be done to clarify the patterns of family disruption which could alert the agency to the existence of a drinking problem.

Some workers find it extremely difficult to ask about their clients' drinking habits. It is perceived as almost a taboo subject since drinking is largely regarded as a personal matter. This reticence and hesitancy about making a straightforward enquiry into families' drinking habits provides fertile ground for collusive denial. The helping agent's own drinking habits and views about drinking may also hamper truly objective enquiry. We know for instance that doctors have themselves three times the average risk of alcohol problems (Murray, 1977) and it is not too unrealistic to postulate that those drinking less than their medical adviser will be unlikely to be defined as having alcohol-related disabilities.

Judgementalism

Some agencies and individuals have established a reputation, not always deserved, of adopting a moralising and hypercritical response toward those who drink too much. Such anti-drink views may cause the client to avoid raising the topic of a family drinking problem, preferring to stick to safer ground.

Labelling

Many agencies catering specifically for problem drinkers and their families use the word alcoholic in the title — for example 'Council on Alcoholism' or 'Alcoholics Anonymous'. While this serves to make their function explicit and prevents defensive evasions, for some the label itself proves an insuperable hurdle to attendance. A recent unpublished enquiry by the author showed that as many as half of the clients referred to the Edinburgh Alcoholism Treatment Unit failed to attend and that this failure was unrelated to time spent waiting for an appointment. Families who may have summoned courage to confide in a trusted family doctor or minister often cannot bring themselves to accept referral to another less familiar agency, particularly if it carries an unacceptable label. If a professional worker himself believes there is stigma in identifying an alcohol problem he will be reluctant to do so and will settle for a more 'comfortable' description of the problem such as 'nerves' or 'domestic stress'.

Lack of Knowledge

Lack of specific knowledge about the symptoms of alcohol dependence and uncertainty about the patterns and quantities of alcohol intake which are likely to be harmful are important blocks to identification. Evidence (Shaw *et al.*, 1978) shows that many professionals are quite ill-informed about alcohol abuse and often their own training has been surprisingly deficient in information about this common problem. It is worth noting however, that while Shaw *et al.* found that receiving information about alcohol was an essential prerequisite of improved therapeutic confidence, it was not sufficient in itself to dispel the attitudes of helplessness or hostility some agents felt towards problem drinkers. It thus demonstrated that improving knowledge does not, by itself, create a capacity to help.

Attitude

A pessimistic and fatalistic view of alcohol problems is also a significant impediment to effective helping. There is a widespread feeling amongst practitioners that there is little point in pursuing the role which alcohol plays in families' problems because nothing can be done about it. Those who work with alcoholics are all too familiar with the consoling friend who says 'I don't know how you manage to work with alcoholics, you must get very depressed, they never change, do they?' It is strange that this view remains widespread despite the abundance of follow-up studies which show that most alcoholics do improve (Costello, 1973).

     As a consequence of such factors, many workers in statutory and voluntary agencies may feel sorry for and sympathetic toward the family of the alcoholic, but nevertheless adopt a profound therapeutic nihilism when faced with the challenge of confronting the harmful drinking itself. Recent research (Shaw *et al.*, 1978) has shown that with appropriate staff support it may be possible to inject a more realistic and optimistic attitude into those community-based personnel whc currently exhibit such despondency towards problem drinkers.

Barriers to Working with the Family

Even when alcohol misuse has been recognised as a family problem, barriers to working with the family still remain. Social worker, minister, 'family' doctor and counsellor will all have learned about the importance of family dynamics in their training but their practical experience is almost invariably rooted in a dyadic relationship, confined to the client and the therapist. They often feel ill-equipped to work with a family, particularly one in conflict. Therapists' experience of family rows will probably come from their own personal life and such scenes will often be viewed as something to be avoided. Most therapists feel more 'in control' with a single client than if they are buffeted by the uncertain storms of family life.

Opportunities for training in family therapy, now well developed in the USA, are minimal in Britain and other European countries. The development of formal training will be discussed later but the immediate issue is whether the worker untrained in family therapy should keep away from working with families. I think not. In many cases the spouse and other family members will be so bound up in the drinker's problems that to exclude them makes no therapeutic sense. At its simplest, working with the family can start by interviewing significant family members sequentially and subsequently bringing them together. This helps the therapist develop from more familiar territory and gives him an understanding of the focal family conflicts before bringing family members together to examine them. The therapist who is reluctant to embark on working with the family will probably find that much of this reticence has its origins in his or her own sense of anxiety or inadequacy at working in an unfamiliar field. But confidence can be considerably increased by providing the worker with access to staff support and consultation. It is very important that the family is approached tactfully, avoiding any implication that the family is to blame for the drinking of one of its members. Instead it needs to be acknowledged that the whole family must be very distressed by their problems and that a joint examination of this distress will ensure that it is fully understood.

Structural Barriers to Working with Families

Family therapy with alcoholics has a somewhat different provenance from most family therapies. The majority of contemporary British schools of family therapy have their origin in work with children or adolescents, while our interest in the family has grown from an interest in the marriages of alcoholics. In common with other specialities there has always been a tendency to plough our own furrow without recognising the growth of knowledge in contiguous fields. A brief résumé of the development of services for alcoholics in Britain will help the reader understand our current position.

These services have developed in a piecemeal way, usually reflecting the enthusiasm of a small number of individuals who have championed the cause of the alcoholic and less often that of his or her family. In the self-help sector Alcoholics Anonymous has been a very significant influence. It drew public and medical attention to the disease of alcoholism and stressed the importance of abstinence as a cure. Although both these tenets have been seriously questioned in recent years those beliefs have left their imprint on the pattern of services for alcoholics throughout this country. Beginning in 1962, the Department of Health and Social Security has produced a series of papers emphasising the prevalence of alcoholism and the need to develop specialised services for their treatment. At first emphasis was placed on specialised in-patient units where patients were treated for periods of up to three months. Spouses of patients were often involved in the treatment programme. A number of evaluation studies (Edwards and Guthrie, 1967; Ritson, 1968) raised serious doubts about the superiority of in-patient treatment over out-patient therapy. In recent years there has therefore been a tendency for specialised services to invest more energy in out-patient treatment and follow up. Often the spouse is also involved in therapy in the belief that excessive drinking is often symptomatic of marital stress and that recovery would be facilitated by finding new ways of handling marital conflicts. Specialised units commonly interviewed the spouses but very rarely involved other family members. In the early years these interviews were mainly to help obtain background information to augment the clinic's understanding of the patient. A little later some clinics began to use joint interviews with couples as a means of clarifying the relationship between the spouses and to make use of this interaction to facilitate mutual understanding. In some cases groups of couples participated together in examining problems in common and fostering a supportive atmosphere in which difficulties could be explored (Ritson and Hassall, 1970). We found that the spouse (usually female) welcomed the support of others in a similar situation. This helped to counteract any feelings she had of being unsupported which arose because she imagined the patient had an alliance with the treatment staff, which she could not enter.

These endeavours remained firmly centred on the problem drinker as patient. They did however enhance therapeutic appreciation of the difficulties which the couple experience in adapting to a new, usually abstinent, life style.

Alcoholics Anonymous also recognised the domestic stress which exists when alcohol is misused and encouraged the development of two parallel organisations for family members, Al-Anon and Alateen, which are concerned respectively with the spouses and teenage children of alcoholics. They hold regular meetings which have many similarities to AA gatherings. They provide considerable mutual support, they do not insist that the problem drinker joins AA, and are quite clear that the relative may gain strength in his or her own right by involvement with the organisation.

Throughout Britain there are an increasing number of Councils on Alcoholism. These are voluntary organisations which provide a counselling advice service not only to sufferers from alcohol problems but also to their relatives. Counsellors often comment that working solely with the non-drinking partner can effect a beneficial change in the total marriage. Such experiences suggest that there are many different routes into working with families where alcohol is a problem — the important element underlying each of these approaches has been the recognition that drinking cannot be taken in isolation from the setting in which it occurs.

At present many Alcoholic Treatment Units and Councils on Alcoholism recognise that specialist services alone cannot cope with such a common phenomenon as harmful drinking. As a result they are already devoting more time to the development and support of the existing network of community agencies which, while not labelled as 'specialist' in dealing with alcohol problems, are the front-line organisations to whom people turn at times of crisis. In fact most alcoholics already receive treatment from non-specialist units. In Scotland, for instance, alcoholism is the primary diagnosis for at least one-quarter of the men admitted to general medical hospitals. These far outnumber referrals to specialist units.

The diverse range of agencies to whom different members of the family turn at times of crisis is illustrated in Table 10.1.

Table 10.1: Crises which Commonly Bring Families to Contact Agencies

Alcohol Related Crisis		Front Line Agency
Marital:	marital unhappiness	general practitioner, marriage counsellor, Samaritan
	assault	Police, Women's Aid
	separation	marriage counsellor, lawyer, minister
	sexual inadequacy	sex counsellor
Family:	unhappiness	primary health care team, social worker
	behavioural problem in childhood	teacher, child guidance, psychologist
	financial difficulties	social worker, Women's Aid
Work:	poor attendance, performance	employer, personnel officer
	loss of work	Social Security, Industrial Medical Officer
	accidents	factory nurse
Legal:	divorce	lawyer
	drunk driving	Police, Court, lawyer
	violence	Police, Court, lawyer, social worker, Citizen's Advice Bureau
Health:	gastritis	family doctor
	liver failure	family doctor, physician
	accidents	hospital, surgeon

The Shaw *et al.* (1978) research report, quoted earlier, suggests that front-line workers of the kind named in the table become much more effective in responding to alcohol problems if they receive adequate specialist consultation and support. In the course of their work, social workers, probation officers and general practitioners working within a particular district of London were offered a brief course on alcohol-related problems which was supplemented by consultation about cases which they had identified in their case load. Although this project was of brief duration it showed that the front-line workers' sense of competence in identifying and dealing with alcohol problems improved rapidly during this time although it was unfortunately impossible to assess how lasting a change had been engendered.

An advisory committee on alcoholism, set up by the Government Department of Health and Social Security (DHSS, 1978), supported the trend towards providing treatment and care at a primary level. The committee stated that the main task of primary level workers in the management of the problem drinker should be:

(1) to recognise problem-drinking and its causes and effects;
(2) to have an adequate knowledge of the help required by the problem drinker and the family;
(3) to give this help as far as it lies within their scope;
(4) to know where and when to seek more expert help;
(5) to provide continuing care and support before, during and after any period of specialist treatment;
(6) to provide adequate follow-up.

Not only does the strategy described increase the likelihood of recognition, it also facilitates early intervention. Every effort should be made to minimise the gap between the crisis that prompts help-seeking behaviour and effective intervention. This means bringing specialist services as near to the client as possible.

Hopefully, this emphasis will facilitate involvement of the total family and should certainly make it easier for them to attend without experiencing the stigma and anxieties described earlier. Whether the primary level staff will feel equipped to help families rather than individuals remains to be discovered.

Another strategy which has been developed is to bring specialist help into easily accessible and familiar centres. Experience of at least one counselling service for alcoholics (Wesson, 1979) suggests that the presence within a health centre of a counsellor trained in alcohol problems greatly facilitated referral of both problem drinkers and their families. In such circumstances, the non-attendance rate dropped appreciably. Wesson found that 81 per cent of those referred attended, and amongst the 27 identified clients and 11 relatives of problem drinkers who did attend, the majority were concerned with alcohol-related disabilities which had been identified at an early stage. Close examination of the characteristics of clients who had not attended showed they all had a long history of problem-drinking with many previous treatment experiences in contrast to the new hitherto unrecognised cases who did attend. Services of this kind should facilitate family involvement at an early stage but again this assumption has not yet been properly tested.

In examining trends in the provision of services and some of the obstacles which may prevent either the problem drinker or a family member from obtaining appropriate recognition and help, it is noticeable that the organisation of existing services is, in almost every situation, case- or patient-centred. At one time, I had the opportunity of attending a specialised eye hospital, where the case notes were simply divided into two columns marked 'right eye', 'left eye'. Not much space there to enquire about the whole person! Whilst this might be dismissed as an extreme case of specialisation, the same process is also to be seen in the much more common priority allocation lists of social work departments which define categories such as child abuse, care of the elderly and homelessness. Obviously such strategies are administratively tidy; they help the agency to discuss the categories of client with which it is concerned. None the less enthusiasm for fitting individuals into categories can generate the kind of tramline thinking which may limit an agency's perception and response to the presenting complaint and facilitate the client's avoidance of the underlying issue by accepting the category offered. The housewife, for instance, gratefully accepts antidepressants or hypnotics without having to reveal that her sleeplessness and depression are engendered by her realisation that her life is now dominated by alcohol and her children are being neglected.

The term 'family doctor' sounds promising if we are concerned with treating the 'whole family', and indeed many general practitioners rightly stress their concern with all members of a family. In practice, this objective is not so easily attained for a number of reasons. For one thing, by no means all family members are registered with the same general practitioner and this is particularly true between spouses. An emphasis on the family may also conflict with the strongly-held professional tenet that the doctor's first concern is his or her patient. Some general practitioner colleagues have doubted the feasibility, and even advisability, of treating the whole family at one time, pointing out that the individual's unique needs and the right to a one-to-one confidential relationship become eroded within the family interview. These valid ethical doubts should serve as a reminder that family or marital therapy is not always the most appropriate initiative and space must be left within the organisation of services for individual counselling needs.

At present there seems little need to fear that the independence and uniqueness of the dyadic helping relationship will be swamped by a deluge of family dynamics. Consider the booking procedure of a clinic, hospital or case-work agency. A receptionist asks the patient's/client's name, finds out whether there are any relatives, and who are the next-of-kin and so on. The case notes are made up for the client/patient. All of these everyday activities underscore the identity of the person with the problem that is the focus of the agency's attention. Changes in attitude and reorganisation of simple reception procedures might help services seem less 'case'-centred.

Family therapy may disrupt other traditional patterns of work. It is difficult for a family to meet during the working day and this may necessitate greater emphasis on evening clinics and improved access-ability of services. For most people it is difficult and expensive to bring a family across town regularly. Work, particularly with poorer families, requires the services to be near at hand. Family therapy need not be thought of as relevant only for the articulate, introspective middle class but can be used very effectively with the most disadvantaged populations, provided accessibility is assured (Minuchin *et al.*, 1967).

Some specialist facilities now stress the need for as many close relatives as possible to attend for the initial interview and some even make the willingness of the family to participate part of the treatment contract. A frequent objection to conditions of this kind is that the family members may feel that they are being turned into patients, a label which they have reserved for only one family member. It is particularly trying for the spouse to feel that s/he is going to be drawn into the work of therapy when s/he has had to work so hard for so long with an alcoholic in the family. The message at first is often simply, 'Look, I can't cope, I need a rest, don't ask me to be involved.' In some cases it may be best to respect such views at first, knowing that the interpersonal dynamics which commonly underlie such as assertion will need to be explored at a later date.

Such phenomena make it difficult for a family, or even couple, to present a problem as residing within the family matrix. In most cases, the family has, of necessity, to offer some individual as the patient or client with the considerable danger that the family members will remain fixed into the roles which exist at the time of contact. These roles may be, for instance, those of patient and therapist, whilst the spouse and the rest of the family remain as witness-rapporteurs or assistant-therapists. The onus rests with the therapist, or counsellor, to translate the presenting symptoms into terms of family dynamics and to redress the potential distortion induced by the referral process. There is none the less a growing interest in reorganising traditional services so that the family can be treated as a unit.

Towards Family Therapy for Alcohol Problems

'Alcoholism therapists have come relatively late into the family field, and family therapists have only recently begun to view alcoholism as an area of interest' (Steinglass, 1976). Recognition of the importance of 'significant others' started with the spouse of the alcoholic. Joint assessment and joint therapy for couples are now routine parts of some clinics' work. Group therapy has long been one of the most popular treatment-modes for alcoholics themselves and during the past decade alcoholism treatment units have offered a discussion group and even therapy groups for the spouses of identified alcoholics. In Edinburgh, a regular group of this kind has been in existence for many years (Smith, 1969). Although the therapeutic advantages of such groups have never been conclusively demonstrated, they appeared to improve the attendance rate of both patient and spouse. Moreover, one study in the USA, which was unfortunately not controlled, showed significant improvement in drinking patterns and enhanced quality of marriage after this experience (Ewing and Fox, 1968).

Another development was to bring couples together in the same treatment group. This is quite widely practised in Britain, although totally unevaluated. Its attractiveness probably lies in the meeting of two well-tried therapeutic styles: that is, the traditional emphasis on group methods with alcoholics, combined with the recognition that marital dynamics are important. Cadogan (1973) provides the only serious attempt at evaluating this approach. Forty married alcoholics were offered this form of treatment on their discharge from an alcoholism treatment unit. The forty couples were then randomly allocated to treatment or waiting lists. The treatment consisted of weekly 90-minute sessions. The follow-up that was provided was very brief but at six months the therapy group showed significant progress compared with the others.

A number of American authors have described their work with the families of alcoholics. For instance, Meeks and Kelly (1970), Steinglass (1976; and Chapter 7 in this volume) and Howard and Howard (1978) describe treatment in which they make a conscious endeavour to involve the problem drinker by way of counselling the 'significant other', this being 'any person who had developed emotional ties to the alcoholic'. Their approach has been influenced by the experience of Al-Anon and they encourage families in which there is a problem drinker to contact them and thereafter draw the remainder of the family into treatment.

They are conscious that the best family therapy is of little value if most people do not know of its existence. They have developed a system of community education (which some would call advertising). They would, for example, use car bumper stickers reading, 'Do you have a family drinking problem? Call . . .' and place similar messages on matchbooks in bars and restaurants and on wrappers used in grocery and liquor stores. This kind of aggressive campaigning has no real counterpart in Europe, although the Scottish and English Health Education programmes have actively encouraged alcoholics to seek help, often using the havoc caused in family life as an important part of the appeal. However, these promotions have assumed that the drinker rather than the family would be inspired to seek help and it might be helpful in the future if the message could be extended to make it clear that any family member who was suffering as a result of someone's drinking could make the first contact.

The USA has a more entrepreneurial system of delivering social and health care with a much greater emphasis on a private fee-paying contract between client and agency. There is ample evidence for this both in the way in which new therapies catch on and achieve the status of a cult long before their value has been tested and also in the way in which health services are much more responsive to market demands. If such a system is somewhat wasteful, with inequalities of service provision, it does facilitate innovation and the rapid creation of new systems for care. The American delivery system of care makes it much easier for the family therapists to offer their services directly to families and the concept of seeking help as a family is more readily accepted. Institutional structures within the British health and social services may be more equitably distributed, but they are much less flexible when it comes to introducing and experimenting with new patterns of service.

British and other European health and social work services are based on the identified client or patient in need. This is true of all the primary level health and social work services which act as a filter to more specialist facilities. Family therapy has grown in Britain during the 1970s from its origin with Skynner at the Institute of Group Analysis, and the family therapy training programme developed by Howells in Ipswich. Since then, Walrond-Skinner (1976) formerly in Cardiff and her colleagues in Cardiff and the Tavistock Institute in London have developed foci of family treatment in England and Wales. These developments are reviewed by Skynner (1976). In recent years Evans and others have fostered the growth of family therapy in Scotland and there is now a training course available at the Scottish Institute of

Human Relations. Since 1975 there has been an Association of Family Therapy which now publishes a quarterly journal. We can therefore look forward to a much higher level of ability and concern for family work in the next ten years which should make itself felt within the existing network of client-centred agencies, where most staff will still be working.

The Future of a Family Approach

In conclusion let us examine how the understanding of family needs which has been developed can be simply applied within a framework of existing services. Britain, in common with many other countries, cannot afford to develop a whole range of new services (even if that was desirable). We can, however, explore ways of grafting on new attitudes towards the family and of introducing modest changes in practice which could turn the family from being bystanders in the therapeutic encounter into resources for effecting change.

The simplest and most readily applicable technique is for primary level agencies to ensure that the spouse, and where possible, other significant family members, are seen at the time of first assessment, interviewed separately and finally together. This is not an exceptionally time-consuming procedure, particularly if the interview focuses on the presenting crisis and the current problems and capacities of the family. The interview will at least ensure that the couple has had a chance of expressing its views of the situation, and of hearing the other partner, or family member's opinion. They can then share a perception both of the issues to be faced and agree on necessary changes. This agreement about family goals reached in the presence of a third party can prove a useful basis for a contract for future change. Some families can work effectively on such a plan even after one interview. Orford and Edwards (1977), for instance, demonstrated that for married male alcoholics one session of detailed assessment and advice for the future given to the couple proved just as effective in influencing subsequent progress as a much more intensive therapeutic approach.

Almost all of the approaches described have been concerned with couples rather than with families. We know that the children of alcoholics are themselves more vulnerable to a number of behaviour problems in childhood and to drinking problems themselves in later life (see Chapter 8).

Schools, child guidance and child psychiatry services should be aware of the problems which alcohol causes within a home and be willing to extend their skills to incorporate the drinking member within therapy. A specialist consultation service might well prove a useful resource to these facilities. This seems preferable to the present tendency to refer the drinking member to a specialist alcoholism unit, thereby fragmenting the treatment process and possibly losing clear understanding of the role alcohol plays in the family.

Walrond-Skinner (1976) points out that family therapy 'involves the treatment of the natural system itself; not the treatment of one or more of its components, not the treatment of one part of the system by another'. The treatment of the system of interactions which constitute a family involves a step away from the identified patient.

Beels and Ferber (1969) have reviewed general styles of conducting family therapy. They identified two principal therapist styles: the first they labelled 'the conductors', the second 'the reactors'. The former tended to be dominant and intrusive with the family; the latter appeared more passive, reflective and analytic. The relationship between alcoholic families and optimal therapist style has not been explored and is obviously an area in which much research is needed. Evaluation of family therapy has been marred by inadequate research design (Wells *et al.*, 1972) and the use of specific family therapy as opposed to an awareness of family dynamics is at present a minority pursuit. It is likely to remain so until training opportunities are improved and the few agencies which are geared toward families have expanded in number and shown a greater interest in problem drinking. At present we should ensure that some members of specialist services for alcoholics develop skills in family therapy so that they can treat selected families and train others.

Rather than ending with any blueprint for future plans I would like simply to list six requests for the present:

(1) Increased awareness that excessive drinking is not a personal matter but involves others.
(2) Willingness to involve the family in the initial assessment of problem drinking.
(3) More inquiries into drinking and its effect on the family.

These simple procedures are available to us all. From this the family and counsellor or doctor can build up a plan of action aimed at changing the family's existing life style in a way which will help family members to communicate their needs and feelings more openly. It is often difficult to progress from this stage to more protracted therapy without having first gained experience and training. We require therefore:

(4) More training opportunities in family therapy.
(5) Easier access by families to existing treatment facilities.

Finally there is a tendency for new developments in therapy to flourish in an uncritical way and consequently to die prematurely because they are vulnerable to critical enquiry. Therefore:

(6) Evaluation of family therapy, both as a personal daily enquiry by the individual therapist and as part of a broader research project, is essential.

11 THE EXCESSIVE DRINKER AND THE FAMILY: APPROACHES TO TREATMENT

Judith Harwin

Alcohol abuse is commonly described as a family illness. There are two interpretations of this view. The first focuses on the contribution the family may make to the genesis and maintenance of drinking problems; the second draws attention to the wide range of social and psychological repercussions which are frequently experienced by the spouse and children. These two views are entirely compatible and indeed both would logically point to the importance of fully involving the family in treatment. Yet this involvement is by no means always the case in practice (Meeks and Kelly, 1970; Gacic, 1980). It is still unusual for families to participate in all phases of the drinker's treatment. Frequently, relatives are regarded as useful adjuncts to the initial assessment, thereafter to be ignored. Sometimes they are actively discouraged from any contact with the therapeutic process, as vividly described by the wife of an alcoholic in an autobiographical account written less than ten years ago (Burton, 1974).

The variability in the provision of family-focused help is surprising since experimentation in this area first began over 25 years ago. Until then help for the excessive drinker was mainly based around the needs of the individual and was provided either through the statutory medical and psychiatric services, or else through the self-help movement, Alcoholics Anonymous (AA). Despite differing in many important respects, both treatment modalities rested on a shared belief in the disease nature of alcohol abuse. As such, it was held that alcohol abuse ran a characteristic, progressive course, the central feature of which was the development of dependency. Treatment was based on the goal of abstinence and therefore depended exclusively on the co-operation of the individual and could proceed without the participation of the family.

Many commentators now acknowledge (Room, 1972; Shaw et al., 1978) that the formulation of alcohol abuse as a disease was in part a political artifact, aimed at providing help for the excessive drinker without the moral censure that was part of the legacy of the nineteenth century temperance movement. But if this succeeded in cloaking alcohol abuse in medical respectability, it also created an organisational structure ill-equipped to deal with the increasingly strong evidence pointing to the social origins and effects of alcohol abuse. The disease model was further challenged by recent research showing that dependency is not an inalienable element of alcoholism, but rather that social and psychological harm may arise without any evidence of concomitant dependency (Shaw *et al*., 1978).

The disease model undoubtedly contributed to the subsidiary status occupied by the family of the excessive drinker and it was only when alcohol abuse was redefined as a medicosocial problem that family needs came to receive greater prominence. Even so, traces of the individually-oriented disease model still existed in the earliest policy memorandum to adopt a medicosocial perspective (Ministry of Health HM (68)37). This memorandum emphasised the role of both medical and social agencies, but stated quite clearly that any contact with the family depended on the consent of the alcoholic, who in this way acted as a gatekeeper. While this advice obeyed the strict medical ethic of loyalty to the patient, many families may thereby have been deprived of access to treatment. It is worth noting that in subsequent circulars (DHSS, Circular 21/73; DHSS, 1975) no reference is made to the necessity of seeking the consent of the patient: indeed these documents began actively to encourage experimentation with social treatments for the family.

Thus two quite separate roots may be identified in the treatment of excessive drinkers and their families — the medical and the social. Sometimes these roots have operated independently of one another and at others have been moulded together, symbolised most clearly in the awkward metaphor 'family illness'. Together they have produced a rich variety of strategies which include group therapy, family casework, family therapy, behavioural and ecological counselling. The purpose of this chapter is to review and evaluate the main forms of family-focused treatment and to trace the theoretical frameworks from which they have evolved. Since patterns of intervention may carry implications for the organisation of services, in the final section consideration will be given to the influence of developments within treatment on recent policy initiatives for the care of excessive drinkers and their families.

Group Therapy

Concurrent, Separate Group Therapy for Excessive Drinkers and their Spouses

Group therapy was one of the earliest strategies to cater for the relatives of the excessive drinker and experimental reports recommending its usage first appeared in the 1950s. The main impetus sprang from clinical observations in which it was noted that the wives of alcoholics in some cases unexpectedly developed psychiatric symptomatology following the recovery of their partner (Macdonald, 1958). This finding led to an investigation into the characteristics of what has come to be called 'the alcoholic marriage' in which particular attention was paid to the personality attributes of the non-alcoholic spouse. It generated a highly elaborate theory known as the 'disturbed personality hypothesis' (DPH) which focused on the characteristics of non-alcoholic spouses.

The DPH proposed that in the alcoholic marriage a process of subconscious assortative mating determined that the choice of partner should be someone who is sick. Such a choice, it was suggested, would satisfy the two aspects of personality that were claimed to be characteristic of the spouses of alcoholics — the combined need for dominance and dependency. This view also suggested that the return of self-reliance to the alcoholic, which would be likely to be associated with recovery, would deprive the spouse of a role. As a result the spouse would then become sick. The theory was largely based on psychoanalytic concepts and has been extensively reviewed in Chapter 6 of this volume.

The DPH discounted the possibility of an alternative explanation put forward by Jackson (1954) suggesting that the spouse's behaviour could have developed as a direct reaction to the pressures that arise from living with an alcoholic, rather than representing an enduring personality trait. This viewpoint became known as the 'stress school' (see Chapter 6) and in accord with its tenets came a shift in the focus of treatment, which placed less emphasis on the personality of the spouse and looked more at the marital situation and social circumstances of the case, drawing on the sociological concepts of norms, rules and roles to explain the spouse's difficulties.

However, the 'stress school' appears to have gained less influence on the aims and methods of separate concurrent group therapy than has the DPH, which led to the formation of psychotherapeutically-oriented groups for spouses in which the group became a medium for the expression of emotions such as anger, hostility and rivalry.

There are many accounts in the literature attesting to the benefits of group therapy (Pixley and Stiefel, 1963; Yalom, 1974; Berman, 1968) but the majority of these are descriptive rather than evaluative and concentrate on interpretations of behaviour based on psychoanalytic constructs of personality. The aim of therapy was to bring about what one therapist described as a 'significant reorganisation of personality structure' (Berman, 1968) though most expressed their aims more modestly, if with no greater precision.

Gliedman *et al.* (1956) provided an early evaluative study representative of the psychoanalytic model of group therapy. The specific aim of the authors was to establish the effects of separate concurrent group therapy on drinking behaviour and associated social and marital functioning. Unfortunately out of 45 couples to whom this approach was made available only 9 agreed to participate and no attempt was made to secure a control group. At the end of treatment two patients were recorded as having become abstinent while a further three said they had reduced their expenditure on alcohol, which the authors claimed 'represented a reliable index of improvement'. Data on the drinking status of the remainder are unaccountably not provided.

Using instruments of questionable suitability, few improvements were found in either psychiatric symptomatology[1] or 'social ineffectiveness'[2] although marital satisfaction[3] was reported to be improved in several cases. However the very small sample size in conjunction with the obvious methodological defects already noted cannot support the authors' claim regarding the benefits of this type of treatment.

Although this study illustrates the difficulties in engaging couples in group therapy, it remained a popular form of treatment and several studies have suggested that if the wife could be involved in therapy, the husband was more likely to improve (Gerard and Saenger, 1966; Ewing and Fox, 1968; Smith, 1969). Perhaps this was the most potent factor in encouraging further experimentaton with different ways of involving the relatives. Conjoint group therapy was one such approach.

Conjoint Group Therapy

This form of treatment, in which a small number of couples meet together with a therapist, developed after separate concurrent groups had become well established. Both methods rested on a belief in the value of the group as a forum for discussing marital and drinking difficulties. However, it was suggested that conjoint group therapy afforded special advantages in both assessment and treatment. First, it enabled therapists to observe marital interaction directly rather than to rely on the separate and possibly conflicting accounts of each partner as occurred in separate concurrent counselling. Secondly, it provided an opportunity to deal with issues that affected both partners jointly. As such the focus of therapy lay more clearly on marital than on individual difficulties.

Burton and Kaplan (Burton, 1962; Burton and Kaplan, 1968a, b; Burton *et al*., 1968) were among the first to attempt a systematic study of the value of conjoint group counselling. In 1959 the Division of Family Study and Marriage Council of Philadelphia changed from a programme of individual to conjoint group counselling for couples with an alcoholic member and subsequently attempted to compare the outcome of these two types of therapy on family pathology and drinking behaviour. But although the study had the potential merit of using large numbers (227 couples) and comparison groups, both of these advantages were lost because difficulties in securing adequate numbers in the comparison groups at follow-up resulted in the omission of crucial comparison data. It was originally hoped to derive two additional comparison groups from (a) clients who refused group treatmet and (b) couples in which only one spouse participated.

Criteria for selection into group treatment were based on evidence of drinking problems and family pathology.While the latter, which covered a wide range of areas (including discord over household management, occupation, children and sexual adjustment) had the merit of quantification on a rating scale, unfortunately there was no equivalent objective measurement of alcohol consumption, since it was claimed that equal amounts of alcohol do not necessarily affect people uniformly. But as the research subjects had first sought help for marital rather than drinking problems, precise measurement of their consumption would seem especially important to establish whether or not alcohol misuse was a major difficulty. The additional criteria of either a medical diagnosis of alcoholism or a history of having sought help previously for drinking difficulties do not seem reliable substitutes for quantifiable data. Furthermore an unstated number of clients were completely abstinent at intake and were receiving help from Alcoholics Anonymous, though no further reference is made to these points.

Group counselling, which varied considerably in intensity from 1 to 44 sessions, took as its primary focus the alleviation of marital conflict and dealt with drinking problems only as a subsidiary area in accordance with the authors' interesting hypothesis that the relief of marital stress could in itself modify excessive drinking.

The results, based on a sample of 73 per cent who were followed up over a period which varied markedly from only 9 to a maximum of 77 months, were claimed by the authors to provide support for the benefits of group counselling. Some 55.6 per cent reported a decrease or cessation of excessive drinking and 75 per cent were assessed as having fewer marital problems. Moreover, a statistical correlation was found between reports of a decrease in consumption and a decrease in marital conflict, although it is not made clear to which specific areas of marital functioning this was applicable.

Confidence in these results, however, is undermined by a series of methodological weaknesses. Variations in extent and type of treatment (some couples received individual counselling while awaiting placement in groups) and in length of follow-up have already been noted. So too has attention been drawn to the subjective, imprecise nature of much of the data, which were not in all cases collected by independent observers; and, in the case of drinking outcome, the data unaccountably excluded the evaluation of the non-alcoholic partner despite the fact that the basic research unit at intake had been defined as the couple. Finally the absence of a control group precludes any possibility of establishing whether the results can be attributed to the administration of group therapy.

Similar criticisms can be levelled against another study (Corder *et al*., 1972) which purported to demonstrate the superiority of treatment based on conjoint group therapy, although this study had the merit of including a control group matched in respect of age, income and educational level, but without the additional participation of wives in therapy. Reference is made to this study because of its innovative feature of inviting wives in the experimental group (numbering 20) to join their husbands as patients for the final week of a month-long programme of treatment. When the two groups were compared at six month follow-up statistically fewer of those receiving conjoint group therapy were drinking, unemployed, divorced or separated. However a failure to define the criteria by which drinking behaviour was assessed and variations in follow-up procedure reduce confidence in these findings.

The reports described so far have focused either on the personality attributes of the spouse or on the extent of marital conflict, but have paid very little attention to the overall social context. A study by Pattison *et al*. (1965) stands out in this regard because it attempted to examine the complex interplay of sociocultural factors, personality and marriage. Classes were held for the wives of lower-middle-class and working-class alcoholics in an attempt to involve spouses in treatment and to increase the co-operation of the husbands. These classes, which ran for two to six weeks, over a total of eighteen months, were not psychotherapeutic. Instead they aimed to provide information on alcohol abuse and on the availability of community resources as well as to introduce wives to the self-help organisation for relatives of alcoholics, Al-Anon. This was facilitated by the presence of an Al-Anon representative at the groups.

The results highlighted the difficulty of involving the wives since the majority attended only one session, and very few referred themselves to Al-Anon. In addition the authors observed that the inclusion of the wife in some cases, far from facilitating the husband's treatment, actually aroused his antagonism, especially if his own therapy was already in progress. Examining the factors which determined the wife's response to treatment, the authors concluded:

> To ascribe the difficulties in treating wives of alcoholics to poor motivation only, grossly over-simplifies the problem. In our Clinic it appears that the marital relationship plays a more definitive role than the attitude or character of either spouse in determining treatment response. Nor can one overlook social and cultural factors.

This study illustrates clearly the barriers to involving spouses in treatment and highlights the importance of sociocultural factors in shaping the use made of services. The middle-class ethos of Al-Anon was found to deter many of this sample from participation and the clinic groups only appeared to be used by those in acute and immediate crises.

Several features merit comment in these accounts of group therapy. First, it will be apparent that difficulties in engaging clients have constituted a persistent obstacle to the implementation of group therapy. Yet despite this, there do not appear to have been any investigations into the reasons for the poor take-up rate. Secondly, all the accounts of group therapy have been confined to a discussion of treatment for wives of male alcoholics. The very occasional reference to the attempts to involve non-alcoholic male spouses is usually incidental, and, without any further exploration, indicates the failure to attract husbands into their wives' treatment (Macdonald, 1958).

Finally, it will be clear that it is not possible to draw any reliable conclusions from the studies concerning the benefits of group therapy. Nevertheless despite these limitations, group therapy has remained a popular form of treatment.

Family Casework

A major drawback to the group therapy programmes described was that they precluded access to help for relatives whose drinking spouse refused treatment. By contrast the starting point of family casework is often the relative, who might seek and receive help for a variety of problems apart from drinking without the necessity of involving the drinking spouse.

Family casework[4] is one of the main tools of social work in both Britain and the USA. Concerned with the amelioration of problems in social functioning, the distinguishing feature of family casework is the consideration it pays to the social determinants of distress, whilst neverthless still acknowledging the importance of individual factors in mediating the response to social circumstances.

It would therefore seem a particularly appropriate perspective on which to base alcohol treatment programmes with the family. Yet there are remarkably few studies reported in the literature which set out specifically to test the tenets and efficacy of family casework. One of the earliest and most widely quoted studies was carried out in the USA by Cohen and Krause (1971), whose overall aim in a four-year large-scale project was to develop an effective treatment for the male alcoholic and his non-alcoholic wife and thereby to arrest family disintegration. In particular they were concerned to compare the efficacy of two approaches to treatment, both of which were rooted in a casework framework, but differed substantially in emphasis. In the first approach alcohol abuse was regarded as 'a symptom of other problems in the alcoholic and members of his family' and treatment was thus concentrated on the alleged underlying problems. This was the customary so-called 'traditional' approach to treatment used by the agency involved in the study, the Family Service Association (FSA), which only rarely aimed specifically to modify excessive drinking or to involve the alcoholic. The second approach, which for the purposes of the study was described as 'experimental', viewed the alcohol abuse as the primary disorder and also as 'a chronic, progressive disease'. According to this view the successful treatment of alcoholism would automatically lead to a resolution of the other problems in the family.

The basic design of the study involved the random allocation of 298 new referrals to one of three groups: an experimental group (E) who were provided with treatment based on the disease model; a control group (C) who received 'traditional' family casework; and a further control group (O) who also received 'traditional' family casework, but whose caseworkers were unaware of participating in a research project. This group was included to counter any possible bias resulting from the knowledge of participation in the experiment. The allocation was carried out to secure a distribution of 146 in the experimental group and the number of cases in this group was claimed to be 'equal to the number of cases in the C and O groups combined', although six cases would therefore appear not to be accounted for. Since all these groups received treatment a fourth untreated group (P) was provided. Unfortunately its potential value was diminished both by its small size (N=23) and the manner by which it was assembled since the P clients were collected not randomly, but consecutively after the formation of the other groups was completed. As the demographic characteristics of this sample were not provided by the authors it is not clear whether they matched those of the other groups. In addition, for undeclared reasons, follow-up assessment data in respect of the P group were very limited and insufficient to provide comprehensive comparisons with the treatment groups. It was also evident that a large proportion of the outcome data was based on judgements of the caseworkers who had carried out treatment, thereby introducing a possible bias; in other instances it was derived from self-administered questionnaires whose reliability and validity were undemonstrated.

The results were based on reduced numbers: of the original 146 clients in the experimental group, only 111 were eventually treated and of these only 74 were evaluated at follow-up. The authors did not provide the actual number of clients treated in the control groups, but it has been estimated elsewhere (Fischer, 1976) that about 41 clients were seen in each of the C and O groups.

After 17 months' treatment, the findings in respect of the husbands' drinking (derived from the wives' reports) indicated a greater improvement in the experimental group (E). Here 48 per cent were recorded as having reduced their intake and a further 15 per cent had become abstinent. The figures for the control group (C) were 33 per cent and 5 per cent respectively, but it was not made clear whether these differences were significant. No equivalent figures were provided for either the O group or the untreated group. With regard to the wives, the authors concluded that 'the E treatment regimen was not shown to have helped the wives of alcoholics feel better or relate to or act towards other family members in a better adjusted manner than did the C and O regimens'.

However, what was more striking was the finding that there were no differences between the various treated groups and the untreated group in terms of the wives' self-appraisal, mood, attitudes towards alcoholism and satisfaction with family relationships. Equally important was the finding that at the end of treatment about 30 per cent of the couples in the E and C groups had separated in contrast with 4 per cent of the untreated group. (No figures were provided for the O group.) Divorces in the E group were significantly higher than those in the C group. Although the authors suggest that these figures could be interpeted as an indication of 'emancipation' on the part of the wives this view would nevertheless appear to conflict with one of the original aims of the project, namely that of averting family disintegration.

On face value these results point to the superiority of disease-oriented treatment over traditional family casework in terms of drinking outcome but suggest a failure of both approaches to ameliorate family cohesion and morale. The findings however must be evaluated in the light of the defects in data and methodology already mentioned here and criticised previously in similar vein by Fischer (1976).

Family Therapy

It has already been mentioned that one advantage of family casework is that relatives may receive treatment irrespective of the commitment of the excessive drinker. Although this makes good practical sense, it seems at odds with the interactionist perspective purported to underpin family casework, since it is hard to understand interaction between people if only one party is present. This suggests that in the final analysis family casework is concerned with the behaviour of individuals; it may extend its inquiry to other family members but as Walrond-Skinner (1976) notes 'the family is used *instrumentally* as a means of assisting change' within individuals (author's italics).

Family therapy, by contrast, reverses this process and is only interested in the functioning of individuals in so far as they shed light on the needs of the family as a whole. Thus the basic unit of analysis is the entire family.

Family therapy can be underpinned by a variety of perspectives, including psychoanalytic theory and learning theory. But in the field of alcohol abuse and the family it is the tenets of general systems theory (GST) which have predominated.

The distinguishing features of GST are its concern with the functioning of the system as a whole (which may itself be part of a larger system) and its methods of explaining the mechanisms by which systems maintain themselves and deal with change (see also Chapter 7). The original ideas sprang from the dissatisfaction of von Bertalanffy (1968) with the reductionist tradition in the natural sciences, which he claimed attempts to isolate the object of inquiry from its context in order to study it, and where explanatory theories tend to be based on cause/effect hypotheses, usually linked together in linear fashion. It is this wish to exclude all extraneous variables that GST rejects as inappropriate to the study of living organisms. Precisely because they are alive, they are dynamic, so that their relationship with their environment is constantly evolving. This in turn means that it is impossible to distinguish between the potentially relevant and the extraneous. On the other hand, as Hall *et al.* (1975) note in their discussion of systems theory, 'There is little point in looking for a pattern in a kaleidoscope whilst it is turning; the scene is changing too rapidly'. What is needed is a method of inquiry that will yield the clarity of the still photograph but with the use of a cine-camera. GST asserts that this can be done by studying the interrelationships between organisms which, it is argued, although dynamic, constitute an organised and coherent pattern.

When GST is applied to the study of the family, several principles emerge. First, the family is conceptualised as an open system, whose members, as sub-systems of the main system, occupy certain consistent relations with one another. These relations are regulated through the roles family members adopt, the styles of communication and the informal and formal rules that govern family life. None of these three areas (rules, roles and communication) has derived from GST. The bulk of work on role behaviour has been pioneered by sociologists, whilst the theories of communication originated in the field of mental health, where it was postulated that certain styles of communication predisposed to the development of schizophrenia (Bateson, 1960; Mischler and Waxler, 1968). What is unique about GST is its integration of these three areas and its postulate that the particular patterning of rules, roles and communication brings about the homeostasis of the family. This term describes the structural and emotional equilibrium the family achieves in order to ensure its survival. Whether or not the equilibrium is satisfactory is not implied by the concept of homeostasis. What it indicates, however, is that the needs of the system take precedence over those of the individual so that vulnerable individuals may be sacrificed to ensure the survival of the system. Various mechanisms exist to promote stability. Scapegoating is one option in which the family allows one member to carry blame for collective difficulties. Serving an identical function, symptom formation by one party represents another solution. Neither of these mechanisms orginated with GST; it is the way in which they are linked to the concept of homeostasis that is distinctive.

Why systems should be so resistant to change and adopt seemingly pathological solutions which would appear to push the family nearer to dissolution than stability is not explained by GST except in terms of the need for homeostasis. Yet although this mechanism can be demonstrated clearly in physical phenomena, such as, for example, in the regulation of body temperature, it is harder to extend the analogy to the realm of family functioning. For it seems to presuppose the existence of hidden, natural behavioural limits governing family interaction, which if exceeded, call into play the self-regulatory mechanism. This in turn implies the existence of identifiable norms shaping family life. But whilst there have been many attempts to locate these, so far studies have pointed to the heterogeneity of family life styles (Jordan, 1972; Moos and Moos, 1976).

One of the criticisms made of GST is that it dwells excessively on the ways in which systems resist change and tells us little about how "they can, do and should change' (Hall *et al.*, 1975). This is surprising since a central tenet of GST is that open systems are dynamic and thus have an inherent capacity for growth. Yet very little information is available to explain the mechanisms by which growth is promoted. Since the main function of treatment is change, this is a serious charge. Yet in other respects GST has proved most valuable. What it has done is to free research from its preoccupation with attempts to establish if the family is a causal agent in the development of drinking problems. Family therapy practised from a GST perspective simply by-passes the whole issue by providing a framework for understanding the interdependency of behaviour. According to GST everyone is both victim and persecutor; blame cannot be apportioned to any one partner within the family since all are concerned to ensure the survival of the system. Emphasis on inter-relationships in turn requires that alcohol be examined, not as an arbitrary phenomenon, but as an integral part of family functioning. Where previous theories have often polarised into those with an exclusive focus on drinking behaviour (e.g. disease model) or those which deal only with the resultant harm, GST unifies these two areas into aspects of each other.

A study carried out by two American social workers was one of the first to apply GST family therapy to the treatment of excessive drinking (Meeks and Kelly, 1970). Their study was limited to a sample of only five families with interactional problems. After an initial intensive phase in which patients and spouses were seen separately, a treatment plan based exclusively on family therapy which sought to include children was implemented. Therapy focused less on the roles and rules that GST suggests may determine family behaviour than on the characteristic styles of communication.

The authors claimed that after one year of treatment interaction within the five families had improved and that two of the men had achieved abstinence whilst three drank less frequently. However, apart from the limitations of a very small sample, the study has a number of methodological imperfections which limit confidence in the results.

First, any changes that occurred could not be attributed necessarily to the use of family therapy because no control group was used, and since the administration of family therapy was preceded by another form of treatment, this clearly could have influenced the outcome. Secondly, the various parameters of intrafamily behaviour and communication appeared imprecise and impressionistic. For instance, 'family interaction' was defined as 'the quality of communication and relating in problem solving efforts' without stating how any of these terms were to be measured. Thirdly, the data collection was derived from 'selected' tape recordings made during the course of treatment rather than at its end and the criteria for such selection were unspecified. Finally, it is not clear whether the assessments were carried out independently or by the therapist.

Although the study clearly fails to prove the value of family therapy, it is useful in providing a descriptive account of this style of therapeutic endeavour. It also illustrates the practical difficulties of involving children in therapy since only one of the three families with children consented to their participation.

Meeks and Kelly have expressed an interest in the concept of homeostasis, suggesting that it 'serves to minimise the threats of disruption and pain to the family' but have not developed this idea. More recently Steinglass has examined the function of alcohol in a series of observational and treatment studies, which are described in detail in Chapter 7 of this volume.

The original studies (Steinglass *et al.*, 1977; Steinglass, 1979) were carried out on a small sample which, due to recruitment difficulties, consisted of only ten couples with long-standing drinking problems in at least one of the partners. The early studies were carried out in a hospital setting that was designed to simulate the home environment, but more recently the programme has been extended to provide longitudinal observations of larger size cohorts. These have been conducted in patients' own homes thereby providing a better approximation to '*in vivo*' conditions. A further innovative feature of the studies was that no restriction on drinking was imposed in order to provide an opportunity to study interaction between couples both in states of sobriety and intoxication.

Steinglass found that certain types of behaviour and verbal exchange only occurred in sobriety, others only when intoxicated. Moreover this patterning was highly repetitive and predictable, which runs counter to the notion that the behaviour of excessive drinkers when intoxicated is often impulsive and variable. Surprisingly, however, neither partner could predict in advance his or her behaviour when intoxicated, which suggests that implicit interactional rules existed of which neither partner was aware.

These observations formed the rationale for a group-based pilot programme of family therapy lasting six weeks. The specific goal of treatment was to modify marital interaction, which it was postulated would 'lead to increased marital satisfaction, improved psychological functioning and symptom relief, including reduced drinking'. A battery of standardised tests, some of which consisted of self-completion questionnaires, were administered at intake to the ten couples who comprised the sample of whom one or both had a history of at least five years' drinking problems (only three wives had a drink problem). These tests provided quantitative data on various aspects of social interaction and on the mental state of both partners. Before therapy the wives as a group demonstrated significantly higher levels of depression and anxiety than did husbands. The authors claimed that this finding, together with self-reports by wives of difficulties in psychosocial functioning, was consistent with the GST hypothesis that disturbance is exhibited not just by the 'identified patient' but by other family members, and thereby supported the use of family-focused intervention.

However, the results of therapy based on eight couples available for follow-up at six months were disappointing since they did not indicate any consistent relationship between changes in drinking behaviour, marital interaction and psychiatric symptomatology. Among the alcoholic subjects there was little improvement in psychiatric symptoms and marked improvements in this area were recorded in only two wives. The changes in all areas of social and interactional functioning as measured by the instruments of assessment showed only slight and nonsignificant improvements. Alcohol consumption was reduced in four subjects (in two of whom the level had been reduced by a modest 20 per cent) and abstinence was reported in one instance. One subject had increased his intake and in the remainder there was no change. There were, however, reported improvements in the pattern of drinking but the criteria of improvement in this respect seem equivocal. For example, one subject who changed his pattern of drinking from a variety of beers and spirits in restaurants and bars in the company of others to drinking only distilled spirits when alone was regarded as improved.

The originality of Steinglass' work lies in his exploration of behaviour in states of intoxication. Where many clinicians have simply ignored the possibility that drunkenness may provide valuable therapeutic information, Steinglass has gone further to incorporate his clinical observations into a broader social psychological context. However, it has not been possible to demonstrate the value of these ideas in treatment since the evaluative study displayed many of the problems encountered in other reports. The study also shows how practical constraints can hamper attempts to carry out adequate evaluation. Difficulties in recruitment limited the sample to ten couples and led to the absence of any control group. Although the study had the merit of using standardised tests, measuring pre- and post-therapy functioning, it was not clear whether those assessments which were not self-administered questionnaires were made by independent observers. Finally it is possible that the results may have been affected by the variation in the location of treatment (both home and hospital were used) but this variable has not been isolated for independent study.

Although Steinglass had been unable to demonstrate a consistent relationship between improvements in drinking and marital functioning, Gacic (1978; 1980) reported a very close correlation between these two areas. His study was carried out at the Centre for Family Therapy for Alcoholism in Belgrade and was established to investigate the comparative effectiveness of family therapy with what was referred to without definition as 'traditional' or 'classical' therapy. Family therapy offered on an out-patient basis was divided into three stages. An initial prepatory phase lasted from 'one to a hundred sessions', followed by a two-month period of intensive daily treatment with a final 'stabilisation' period in which the patient and family were seen weekly for a year or more. Family therapy was also supplemented by group therapy involving friends, relatives living away from the patient's home and even employers. Despite the fact that these additional forms of treatment are a unique feature of the study their contribution to the results has not been studied separately.

An experimental sample of 50 males who were provided with family treatment, involving children and spouses, were compared with a demographically and numerically similar group who had received 'traditional' therapy at the Institute six years earlier in 1968. Each group was assessed one year and five years after the termination of treatment. The results appeared striking with significant differences reported between the two groups in relation to drinking behaviour and family functioning at one year follow-up. Thus 78 per cent of the experimental group achieved abstinence in comparison with 38 per cent of the controls and 90 per cent of the experimental sample improved in their family situation as compared with 38 per cent of the control sample. Significant between-group differences were also found in other areas, such as 'somatic conditions, mental conditions, vocational efficacy and general social adjustment' but none of these parameters was defined or measured. Nor is it made clear whether the control group was assessed by independent assessors. But it is possible that a bias was introduced into the assessment of the experimental group since some of the assessments were made by those who carried out the therapy.

These improvements in the functioning of the experimental group were also reported to be sustained at five year follow-up, but surprisingly no comparable data were provided for the control group. Finally it is disappointing that no consideration has been given to the possibility that the very extensive contact with therapists might have influenced the outcome.

Several other studies have been carried out into family therapy which all enthusiastically asserted its value in the treatment of excessive drinking. Unfortunately, many of these potentially interesting accounts (Esser, 1971; Shapiro, 1977; Forrest, 1978; Crafoord, 1980) have been confined to description and their ideas were not put forward in a way amenable to testing.

This is not merely a matter of academic nicety. Since family therapy is currently very fashionable, it is imperative to substantiate its claims. Regrettably, far more critical debate on the value of family therapy has taken place outside the alcohol field rather than within it, although the findings of the major alcohol-related studies highlight the very issues vigorously debated elsewhere.

One central issue is the relationship between symptomatology, family interaction and outcome. The evidence from other fields of inquiry has been contradictory. For example Alexander and Parsons (1973), in a comparison of two forms of family therapy in the management of delinquent teenagers, found a positive correlation between the presenting complaint and family interaction at follow-up. A decrease in reported recidivism was found only in those families who had achieved a significant increase in reciprocity and clarity of communication. However a preliminary report by Lask (1980) on family functioning and asthma in children found a less clear relationship between these two areas.

Thus some of the contradictions found by Steinglass and Gacic are also borne out in other fields of disturbance. More importantly, they re-open the whole debate on the criteria for including the family in treatment and suggest that at the present these criteria rest as much on theoretical perspective and value judgement as on evidence based on empirical study. This is clearly illustrated by Lask's (1980) discussion on the merits and drawbacks to family therapy for all types of problems:

> In defining the goals we have to decide whether we are more concerned with the presenting complaint, or the family system. The presenting complaint is usually expressed in individual rather than interactional terms, and is therefore easily identifiable, but rather simplistic . . . In contrast the family system is considered in more interactional terms, and consequently is more difficult to describe, but it does convey a more comprehensive view of the problem.

While a 'comprehensive' view may sound intrinsically superior to a 'simplistic' symptom-based categorisation, it masks the fact that at present there are no agreed typologies for classifying family disorder. Nor is there consensus as to the indications and contra-indications for family therapy. Skynner (1969) has suggested it should not be used if the family contains a member suffering from a psychosis. Others have argued against it in cases where the marital relationship is so precarious that attempts at modification could seriously jeopardise the stability of either partner (Pittman and Flomenhaft, 1970), but still others have taken precisely the opposite view (Martin, 1977). Although these contradictory viewpoints raise as many questions as they solve, they at least bring the debate into prominence. Steinglass (1976) is unusual in the alcohol field in addressing this issue. He suggests that middle- and upper-class intact families may derive benefit from a family-oriented psychosocial approach, whilst single alcoholics might be helped better by a 'biomedically-oriented approach with pharmacotherapy, behaviouristic techniques and group therapy', although he does not substantiate this proposition. Although social class membership has frequently been a determinant of access to family therapy (Mannino and Shore, 1972; Lorion, 1978; Minuchin, 1974), many practitioners outside the alcohol field have pointed to the absence of any sound therapeutic reason to account for this. It is therefore surprising that Steinglass' controversial views have failed to stimulate more debate. Finally, there is a surprising lack of discussion as to which family members should be included in family therapy for excessive drinking. Children have hardly ever participated and this appears to be unrelated to their particular age. Wilson and Orford (1978) have suggested that one reason for this may be the wish on the part of the therapists to preserve alleged childhood innocence, and this argument has some force in considering the position of very young children. Nevertheless, even in the case of toddlers, their exclusion runs counter to the tenets of family therapy (Walrond-Skinner, 1976) and also ignores the well-documented evidence on the difficulties that children of excessive drinkers encounter (Cork, 1969; Haberman, 1966) (see Chapter 8). It is also surprising that there is very little reference to the possibilities of including in treatment those relatives who do not live in the same house as the excessive drinker.

Too many important issues still remain unresolved to be able to support the use of family therapy without reservation. As yet the claims on its behalf remain at the level of theory and they still need to be substantiated by evaluative research.

Transactional Analysis (TA)

TA is a latecomer in the field of understanding and treatment of alcoholism and its followers are still fairly few. It grew out of the work of Eric Berne (1964), who analysed human behaviour from the point of view of interpersonal communication. What was new about Berne's theory was his marriage of psychodynamic psychology to communication theory. Berne suggested that the human personality is made up of three ego states, Parent − Adult − Child, which in function appear similar to the Freudian descriptions of Superego − Ego − Id. The difference however, according to TA, is that these ego states all reside within consciousness, and are readily observable to others. In addition less emphasis is placed on the importance of the first few years of life in personality formation. Although emphasising human capacity for change, none the less TA has a partially deterministic undercurrent. It suggests that individuals formulate a life-plan, called a 'script', which is usually decided upon before the age of fourteen (Steiner, 1971). Because it is conscious, it is held to be reversible and for this reason TA followers reject the accusation of determinism, arguing that: 'The patient is considered responsible for his actions because his disturbance is the result of decisions he has made' (Steiner, 1971). However, this skirts the possibility that the individual may have no control over the situation leading to his disturbance.

It is asserted that the adoption of a script has clear consequences for adult life and TA outlines a number of 'existential positions' (sic) available to the adult. These essentially concern the individual's sense of ease and comfort with himself and have been couched in popular language as "I'm OK . . . ", "I'm not OK' etc. However, unlike existentialism, the individual's sense of self is conceptualised in relation to other key figures. Thus the expression of the individual's psychology is intrinsically bound up with his view of others leading to formulations such as "I'm OK . . . You're OK . . . ", 'I'm OK . . . You're not OK' etc. These positions are best perceived by an analysis of transactions between individuals, which Berne (1964) has compared to games. As in most games, at least two people must participate, there must be a beginning and end, and the progress is guided through the formulation of rules. The defining characteristics of the TA game is that there is a psychological 'pay-off', or motive and gain to both players, which nevertheless is covert.

Steiner (1971) has elaborated on the kinds of games alcoholics are likely to play. He outlined three main variants, all of which serve to endorse the alcoholic's self view, described by Steiner as 'I'm no good and I know it, but you are no good either, and since you don't seem to be aware of it, I'm going to expose you'. The family are inevitably drawn into this game and indeed actively contribute to it. Steiner and Berne both seem to indicate that some kind of psychological assortative mating takes place whereby the partners' psychological needs dovetail, though the results of the match may be entirely destructive.

Only one example of the alcoholic game will be given as they all illustrate a common paradigm. In the 'Drunk and Proud' game Steiner (1971) quoted the example of the alcoholic player who aims to discredit the flawless self-perception of his non-alcholic spouse. He thus behaves outrageously, finally provoking his partner to lose self-control. For example, he might stay out very late and be berated on his return. The alcoholic then meekly apologises, giving the wife no option but to continue her diatribe or accept his apology, thereby providing the payoff to the alcoholic. According to TA, she has lost face in either situation. These two alternative reactions are held to represent particular roles, characteristic of the transactions between the excessive drinker and spouse. To continue the invective is to behave as a 'Persecutor', needlessly humiliating the drinker; but to withdraw is to become a

'Patsy' — an American term which suggests that the individual is made to appear foolish by allowing himself or herself to be fobbed off with inadequate excuses, instead of laying the blame where it belongs. Neither of these reactions achieves its end of making the alcoholic change, so that the alcoholic has won his game on two counts. He has undermined his partner's self-image and justified further excessive drinking. What the pay-off to the spouse is, is by no means clear and surprisingly appears not be be explained by Steiner.

Steiner claimed that these manoeuvres represent prescribed family roles in an alcoholic marriage and Albretsen and Vaglum (1971, 1973) found some empirical support for this view in a Norwegian study of twelve hospitalised wives of alcoholics, which was set up to test the tenets of TA. All of the women required hospital psychiatric in-patient treatment for depressive symptomatology and six had developed 'suicidal problems'.

The authors suggested that certain TA roles may lead to symptom formation. By a retrospective evaluation of the wives' TA roles prior to hospitalisation, it was reported that those wives who had moved from the role of Rescuer to Persecutor became ill. The authors claimed that the role of Persecutor was 'intolerable to these women' and suggested that they therefore entered the allegedly more socially acceptable role of 'Patient'.

Follow-up was carried out between two and three years later and it was found that the six women who were without symptoms and whose husbands were drinking less were those in the Rescuer role. Four with symptoms were in the role of Patient and one in the role of Persecutor.

What is missing from this account is a description of the criteria by which roles were classified, or the recognition that retrospective analyses are bound to be unreliable because the past is viewed through the lens of the present. In general, the criteria by which symptoms were assessed and measured are absent and it is not made clear how the assessment of the husband's drinking status was made. Finally, there is no discussion of the very important finding that four women had become divorced, of whom two were in the Rescuer role. For all these reasons it is not possible to draw any reliable conclusions from the treatment results. This is important because of Steiner's claims that TA 'generates specific therapeutic techniques for treatment', which come from the therapist's ability to analyse the transactional roles of the partners and develop new ones.

Steiner's book, which is the fullest description of TA treatment for alcohol abuse, carries disappointingly little information on specific techniques involving family members apart from detailing the benefits of group therapy using TA principles, and concentrating on the problems of this approach for therapists.

TA is in essence a form of psychotherapy and as such pays no attention to the sociocultural determinants of drinking or indeed to social environmental pressures. It is too early to evaluate the impact of TA, and further inquiry is needed to test the validity of its tenets before assessing its contribution to the treatment of the family with an excessive drinker.

Behavioural Treatments

If TA is a very recent development, behavioural approaches to the family can be traced back to the nineteenth century. A fascinating early example occurs in Anne Bronte's *The Tenant of Wildfell Hall* (1969 edn), which takes the unusual situation of describing the treatment offered to a child by its mother. Horrified at the way in which her estranged husband is encouraging their child, Arthur, to enjoy alcohol to excess, Mrs Huntingdon formulates her own treatment programme:

> But if I had stinted him in his usual quantity of wine, or forbidden him to taste it altogether, that would only have increased his partiality for it, and made him regard it as a greater treat than ever. I therefore gave him quite as much as his father was accustomed to allow him — as much, indeed, as he desired to have, but into every glass I surreptitiously introduced a small quantity of tartar-emetic — just enough to produce inevitable nausea and depression without positive sickness. Finding such disagreeable consequences invariably to result from this indulgence, he soon grew weary of it, but the more he shrank from the daily treat, the more I pressed it upon him, till his reluctance was strengthened to perfect abhorrence. When he was thoroughly disgusted with every kind of wine, I allowed him, at his own request, to try brandy and water, and then gin and water; for the little toper was familiar with them all, and I was determined that all should be equally hateful to him. This I have now effected; and since he declares that the taste, the smell, the sight of any one of them is sufficient to make him sick, I have given up teasing him about them, except now and then as objects of terror in cases of misbehaviour: 'Arthur, if you're not a good boy I shall give you a glass of wine', or, 'Now, Arthur, if you say that again you shall have some

brandy and water', is as good as any other threat: and, once or twice, when he was sick, I have obliged the poor child to swallow a little wine and water without the tartar-emetic, by way of medicine; and this practice I intend to continue for some time to come; not that I think it of any real service in a physical sense,but because *I am determined to enlist all the powers of association in my service:* I wish this aversion to be so deeply grounded in his nature that nothing in after life may be able to overcome it. (Author's italics.)

Although this early example relates to aversion therapy, this mode of treatment is rarely used in contemporary practice. There are of course several other types of behavioural therapy applicable to the treatment of alcohol abuse, including self-regulation training and covert sensitisation but both these and aversion therapy are directed towards the individual; only behavioural family counselling, as its name implies, specifically aims to include the family centrally in treatment.

The techniques of behavioural marital and family therapy are grounded in a social learning model of behaviour. This asserts that behaviour is learned rather than innate, with the corollary that it can be unlearned and that it is shaped by the consequences of social interaction, which themselves reflect both the influences of past life experience as well as the current situation. This perspective has been applied to the understanding of marital behaviour and, just as is true of TA, it is held that certain interactional marital patterns maintain abusive drinking.

While Billings *et al.* (1979) and Kennedy (1976) disputed the unique features of alcohol-complicated marital interaction, there is nevertheless a general consensus in the professional literature on the overall high levels of marital conflict, affecting in particular the areas of warmth and hostility, coercion and control (Jacob, *et al.*, 1978; Orford *et al.*, 1976b) for which couples require help (see Chapter 8).

The broad goal of behavioural family counselling is to bring about an alteration in the interactional patterns within the marriage which maintain excessive drinking. Whilst this approach does not differentiate behavioural treatments from any of the approaches discussed so far, the emphasis placed on the systematic use of planned social reinforcement to shape behaviour, and the overriding concern with measuring outcome by attention to observable behavioural rather than attitudinal change are its unique features.

Miller (1976) described an individual case study which illustrates very clearly the principles and practice of behavioural family counselling. A 44-year-old man who drank four to six pints of bourbon weekly complained that his wife's critical comments and looks increased his consumption. For two weeks prior to the start of treatment measures were taken to establish his daily consumption level. Meanwhile, the couple were also asked to identify the changes they would like to see in themselves and each other. This information was then used to provide the basis of a behavioural contract between the couple in which goals of therapy as well as the means to attain them were specified. It was jointly agreed by the couple that the husband would reduce his consumption from its current level of seven to eight glasses daily to between one and three. If he drank more, he agreed to pay his wife a sum of money which she would then spend frivolously — an activity thoroughly enjoyed by the wife and equally intensely disliked by her partner, and therefore held to be likely to deter abusive drinking.

If these tactics appear to emphasise the use of negative sanctions, from the standpoint of the husband at least, it should be remembered that they were jointly agreed by the couple in a form of social bartering in which one partner traded off one form of personally unacceptable behaviour for another. Moreover, the use of punishment was accompanied by the jointly agreed goal of increasing the mutual demonstration of affection, reflecting the importance behaviourists attach to the use of rewards as well as sanctions. At the end of treatment the husband was drinking moderately and the couples were reported to have improved. This progress was maintained at six-months follow-up.

Another case study by Miller and his colleagues (1976) using the same approach reported equally promising results. Although both these reports were based on single cases, the use of pre-treatment behavioural analyses and the specification of measurable concrete goals lent some weight to the findings.

Supportive evidence for the use of behavioural family counselling was found by Hedberg and Campbell (1974) in an American study of 49 alcoholics devised to compare the efficacy of four different forms of behaviour therapy (systematic desensitisation, covert sensitisation, aversion therapy and behavioural family counselling). The latter was the only approach to involve the spouse and used a mixture of behavioural learning procedures focused on improving communciation between couples. The methodology introduced a novel feature: in order to provide a facility for examining if the outcome of treatment could be influenced by the client's own commitment to a specific aim, subjects were allowed to choose between a goal of abstinence and controlled drinking. In addition, the authors sought to examine possible ante-cedent environmental determinants and consequences of drinking be-haviour by the use of a standardised questionnaire in which details of alcohol consumption were also recorded. To ensure comparability of procedure, patients in all groups received the same number (25) and sequence of treatment sessions. Follow-up evaluation was carried out at six months by the patient's therapist and was therefore subject to possible bias.

The majority of patients (N=36) selected abstinence as their goal, and of these the best results were secured by the behavioural coun-selling regime where 80 per cent achieved their selected aim, in com-parison with 60 per cent and 36 per cent in the systematic desensitisa-tion and covert desensitisation groups respectively. When those who had selected controlled drinking as their target were considered, systematic desensitisation emerged as the most successful treatment, but the num-bers within each treatment sub-sample were too small to allow reliable conclusions to be drawn about the effect of the choice of the target goal. Furthermore, the overall number of patients who consented to aversion therapy (four out of twelve patients who were initially assigned to this treatment) was too small to be meaningfully included in the analysis.

While the results lent support to the use of behavioural family counselling as a treatment tool to secure improvement in drinking, the lack of any statistical analysis in any of the data precludes any firm conclusion in this respect. Moreover since the study was confined to an exclusive concern with drinking behaviour, the differential effects of the four types of treatment on family functioning were not explored. In the end it is the needs of the individual drinker which have taken prece-dence.

This need not be the case. As the two studies by Miller indicate, the strength of a behavioural family approach lies in its capability of responding simultaneously to the needs of both or several family members. Indeed the success of the strategy depends on the notion of a mutual reciprocity of rewards, duties and responsibilities so that the needs and rights of one partner are always judged in relation to those of the other. It is this emphasis on reciprocity, coupled with the fact that clients are given a considerable degree of autonomy in order to effect changes in their lives that often makes behavioural family coun-selling a very acceptable form of treatment to clients.

Ecological Programmes

Remarkably few of the studies reviewed so far have placed the family in its wider social context. The majority of therapeutic strategies have placed a primary emphasis on the internal psychological problems of the family. This bias is surprising since in many of the models outlined there is nothing in their theoretical formulations to indicate a differential weighting to the interior psychological functioning of the family. It is also well-known that social difficulties such as housing problems and financial hardship beset all families with drinking problems irrespective of social class membership (Moss and Beresford Davies, 1967) and indeed are amongst some of the first areas of family functioning to be affected.

It was to redress this imbalance that the ecological programmes were developed, their goal being to deal with 'reality problems as an integral part of the psychological treatment process' (Mannino and Shore, 1972) and these 'reality problems' included housing,legal difficulties and unemployment. Flanzer and O'Brien (1977) described their own programme of 'family focused treatment and management', which they developed at Wisconsin University:

> Family focused management that views the family not only as an internal system, but as a system interacting with larger external systems, can concentrate on assisting family members not to be trapped in the 'alcohol system' by providing a range of carefully linked knowledgeably administered community resources . . .

The programme rested on a highly elaborate and rather mechanistic attempt to analyse the families' needs into a hierarchy, comparable to that developed by Maslow (1970) to conceptualise individual needs. The authors suggested a pyramid progressing upwards from a base of needs for physical safety, food and shelter, socioeconomic security and social interaction to the summit of 'family actualisation'. The aim is to help families progress up the needs ladder or to stabilise their position at any given level. Understanding of, and capacity to deal with, each need level requires different professional skills, and for this reason Flanzer and O'Brien argued the necessity of a multi-disciplinary approach to alcohol abuse.

Their paper is more persuasive at the level of objectives than regarding the means to attain them and few details of practical applications are provided. The emphasis on multi-disciplinary intervention for problem drinkers has become the accepted canon in the United Kingdom (DHSS, 1978) though references to its importance seem to appear less commonly in the USA. So, too, the positioning of the family in its broad social context is important, but the idea that family needs can be separated into neat discrete hierarchies is questionable. Yet this is a central pivot of the authors' thesis and the recommendation for multi-disciplinary professional involvement arises directly out of it.

Flanzer and O'Brien's model to some extent stands apart from the other community-based experiments because of its comprehensive scope, embracing all social class groups — at least at a theoretical level. Other programmes aim at much more specific target groups.

Pattison (1965) described the establishment of a scheme in Cincinnati for lower-class multi-problem families. Concerned by the persistent failure of the clinic setting to attract and retain in treatment families of this group, his unit trained public health nurses to offer treatment in the home to supplement the help of the clinic.

Over the 15-month period of treatment the sample of families received assistance in the care and management of the children, marital counselling and, where necessary, were offered referral to other community agencies to deal with legal and financial difficulties. Two of the seven families did not complete the programme: in one case the family left the area; in the second case the excessive drinker died.

The results at the end of treatment, based on nursing reports suggested that four families had improved in respect of marital harmony, social functioning and alcohol intake by the excessive drinker. In only one case was no improvement in drinking or other parameters observed.

Pattison suggested that one of the major benefits brought by the scheme was the ability of the public health nurses to maintain contact with families when they began to default from attendance at the clinic. He concluded by suggesting that the results were sufficiently encouraging to warrant the establishment of controlled clinical trials.

This case report is important because it provides a valuable insight into some of the difficulties experienced by staff in the administration of a programme of active campaigning work. Some became overwhelmed by the extent of the clients' problems and the demands that were placed on them. As a result the public health nurses themselves required staff support and guidance.

Pattison was concerned with ways of keeping in touch with families over a protracted period. By contrast, Davis and Hagood (1979) investigated the possibilities of short-term intensive help. A sample of 48 families in which the mother drank excessively took part in the study.

Of these half were single-parent families with young children and among the remainder there were instances in which both parents abused alcohol. Over three-quarters had previously received treatment for excessive drinking.

A six-week period of intensive treatment was given by specially trained paraprofessionals called family rehabilitation co-ordinators (FRCs) to all family members living in the same household in the immediate period following the mother's most recent hospitalisation. Using a behavioural task-oriented approach, the FRCs provided guidance in household management, the care and discipline of the children, discussed interpersonal problems and, where appropriate, referred families to welfare agencies. The project ran for three years and follow-up data were presented on the first 36 of the original cohort and an unspecified number of children aged twelve or above.

Although the authors purported at six-month follow-up to find improvements in abstinence rates (23 out of 36), family communication and household management, serious methodological weaknesses cast doubt on the conclusions. The basis for sample selection was 'mutual agreement' between clients and staff but the criteria underlying this process were not specified. No control group was used and the assessment, based on an unstructured interview, did not indicate how the outcome criteria were to be measured. Nor was it clear who undertook the post-treatment assessment. Finally, no pre-treatment measures of functioning were available so that it is impossible to determine which factors were prepotent in outcome.

This is unfortunate since it means that the innovative features of the study were lost. First, some careful thought had been put into the timing of treatment so that it coincided with the immediate post-hospitalisation period, which is known to be associated with relapse. Secondly, the sample was unusual since the problems of female excessive drinkers, dual-drinking families and single parents are under-reported in the literature.

Another experiment by Hunt and Azrin (1973) gives us more indication of the active ingredients in treatment. It took a small sample of eight males who were offered a 'community reinforcement approach' (CRA) to treatment. This model is based on the operant-reinforcement approach of Skinner and suggests that excessive alcohol intake prevents the person from gaining rewards in any areas of his life other than alcohol. Indeed, through neglect, these areas gradually become increasingly problem-ridden, thereby increasing the attractiveness of alcohol. The main thrust of the experiment was therefore to increase the client's vocational, social, recreational and familial satisfactions. Since the source of these are located within the community, the experiment gained its title, though the first part of the programme began in hospital, but was subsequently continued in the home.

The study was very well designed, using a control sample matched in all important respects, who were followed up for six months. From the first day the CRA group were given help with legal problems, financial and employment difficulties. They were put into contact with lawyers, given advice about ways of job-seeking or performance in interviews. Help was also offered in the marital sphere using behavioural techniques. Clients who did not have a natural family, where possible, were 'fostered' with a 'synthetic' family consisting of employers, relatives, or the clergy. Six months after treatment had ended, statistically significant differences emerged in the outcome of the two groups. The CRA group spent more time with their families, drank less and spent much less time in hospital. They had found better jobs and indeed were earning twice as much as the controls. Marital satisfaction also differentiated the groups. Prior to the start of the experiment, all five married couples had considered divorce and two had already separated. At six months follow-up all were still together whereas two of the four controls had separated.

These results are impressive and several features of the programme merit comment. First, they were achieved by paraprofessional staff. Secondly, it is a very good example of a broad-spectrum approach to therapy with a genuine psychological focus. Indeed it is ironic that poverty and unemployment has been tackled so enthusiastically not by family therapists but by behavioural psychologists, whose detractors would accuse them of a narrow mechanistic view of human nature. Here certainly they appeared to demonstrate a rather greater appreciation of the complexity of factors which make for human fulfilment than the claustrophobic focus on internal family dynamics. Finally, the imaginative use of 'synthetic' families for single problem drinkers is unique in this field. The only, but major, problem the experiment poses is its applicability to large numbers. Its implementation in times of economic recession would be difficult and the possibility of securing good jobs and rapid results, essential to the philosophy of Hunt and Azrin, is uncertain.

Several features stand out in these studies. They tend to involve socially and economically deprived groups, to make use of paraprofessional staff, and are more practical in their approach to the resolution of psychological as well as social problems. It would be tempting to posit a 'two nations' view of treatment indicating a schism between models, methods and aims, on the basis of social class membership. It is the view taken by Mannino and Shore (1972):

> It has become clear that we can less and less separate the person's environment from his personal functioning, regardless of his social class. With the poor there is clearly a lack of balance between help with reality issues and intrapsychic issues due to a disproportionate emphasis on the former. With other groups likewise a lack of balance occurs, but the distribution of weight is reversed. Many therapists attempt to treat families giving no consideration to the many reality problems the family must face in its day-to-day living.

However, it is important to acknowledge that different social groups may have different needs and the variety of programmes that exist may at least in part reflect these. None the less, whether it can also explain the greater use of paraprofessional staff in ecological programmes is debatable.

Treatment or Advice

All the case studies reported so far have been established to investigate the impact of one or more particular type of treatment. With one exception (Cohen and Krause, 1971) none has examined the possibilities of spontaneous remission through the provision of a no-treatment control group, even though studies (Cahalan *et al.*, 1969; Saunders and Kershaw, 1979) have suggested that excessive drinkers may overcome problems without seeking help. Nor have the reports attempted to examine the effects on outcome of varying the quantity of treatment provided to families. There is however, one important British study which sheds light on this question (Edwards *et al.*, 1977). It suggests that minimal intervention may be no less effective than 'a therapeutic regime which might fairly represent the average package of help which a well supported centre anywhere in the western world would today offer the alcoholic who enters its doors'.

In their carefully designed study, 100 male alcoholics and their wives who had been referred to the Alcoholism Family Clinic at the Maudsley Hospital in London, were randomly allocated to one of two different treatment groups called 'Advice' and 'Treatment' after a comprehensive psychological, social and physical assessment. Couples from the advice group were given approximately half an hour's guidance in which it was stated that the 'responsibility for attainment of the stated goal (total abstinence) lay in their own hands, rather than being anything which could be taken on by others'. In contrast, the treatment group was provided with a comprehensive programme of out-patient care, and where necessary, in-patient treatment. Each patient in this group was allocated for therapy to a psychiatrist and his wife to a social worker. The psychiatric approach was focused on the development of strategies for abstinence and for handling reality problems, interpersonal relationships, particularly marital difficulties; where indicated a limited psychotherapeutic approach was also used. The patients were also encouraged to attend AA and offered drink deterrent medication (calcium cyanamide). The social worker provided counselling on reality problems and marital problems, and if indicated, practical advice regarding employment.

Monthly structured information from the wives of both groups was collected by social workers at four weekly intervals during the twelve months between intake and follow-up. Final assessments were also made of the patients and wives by psychologists and social workers respectively at twelve months on anniversary of intake.

The study achieved a very good follow-up response since only four patients from the advice group and two from the treatment group were lost at the end of treatment. The overall results were striking; no statistical differences in outcome were found between the two groups in respect of drinking behaviour and a range of defined indices of social adjustment which included time off work due to sickness or unemployment, perception of the marital situation based on separate reports from the husband and wife and evidence of financial hardship.

Moreover, the authors were able to demonstrate that the crucial distinctions between both the quantity and type of treatment received by the two groups were well maintained. The advice group did not seek compensatory help from other agencies and the treatment group did not reject the treatment provided by the family clinic, although it should be noted that no information was sought about attendance at social service departments. A further possible weakness in what is a well-conceived and conducted study, and one which is duly acknowledged by the authors, is the absence of double blind procedures and the possible influence of observer bias since some of the data were collected by the social workers who had conducted treatment. Furthermore it seems surprising that in a facility in which psychiatrists contributed to both assessment and treatment, no specific assessment of psychiatric status was recorded.

However in general this study stands out for its rigorous approach and its findings, which are of central relevance to any discussion of family treatments, merit serious consideration. It is however also important to bear in mind that the overall result may hide an inter-action effect between types of treatment and type of problem so that some couples may improve under an intensive regime and others do better with brief advice. Indeed, in a further analysis of two year follow-up data the same team produced evidence of such an inter-action (Orford *et al.*, 1976a) although the numbers in the latter analysis were reduced. Nevertheless it is the conclusions of the initial study which have caused considerable debate because they carry major policy implications:

> Until further information is available as to the efficacy of costly and intensive interventions, services should primarily be developed in terms of economic and rather low-key programmes. This would provide the basic network for 'first aid' and counselling, and the base for later planned development when it is known what sort of services ought to be developed.

Before considering the extent to which these views have been incorpor-ated into policy guidelines, one final approach to family treatment will be discussed which differs from all the other strategies under review in several important respects — this is the self-help movement, Al-Anon.

Al-Anon

All the treatment strategies described so far have been run by profes-sional or paraprofessional helpers. Al-Anon stands in sharp contrast to these. It is a self-help programme run by and for people whose lives are affected by the excessive consumption of alcohol of a close relation and can be joined irrespective of whether the alcoholic is still drinking or has attained sobriety.

Al-Anon was first set up in the late 1930s and soon established groups internationally, and today there are more than 16,500 in 70 countries, with over 600 in the UK and Eire.

Although there is a headquarters in each country, groups are admini-stered locally and are entirely self-governing. What is often not realised is the unique character of each local group. Although all share a common philosophy and apply the same running procedures, the particular social background of the members and the style and content of discussion will vary enormously from area to area.

In many ways Al-Anon is an extremely complex organisation to understand. It has often been called a way of life rather than a specific therapy for alcohol abuse, because its tenets transcend the specifics of the alcoholic marriage and represent a particular philosophical view of man, which is essentially spiritual. The programme contains many contradictions. As with its twin organisation, Alcoholics Anonymous, it subscribes to the belief that alcohol abuse is a disease, so that a sober alcoholic is none the less forever an alcoholic. If this seems to assert an essentially pessimistic view of both human endeavour and the disease process, Al-Anon at the same time derives its chief organising principle from its emphasis on individual capacity to change. Indeed the whole Al-Anon programme turns on the didactic lesson that whilst the individual is powerless over the behaviour of others, he can change his own. One might ask why the wife should need to change her own behaviour if the alcoholic is suffering from an incurable disease. Here again the contradictions of Al-Anon emerge. For although Al-Anon quite clearly rejects an interactional view of the causation of alcohol abuse, it places considerable weight on the wife's capacity (albeit unintentionally) to perpetuate the process through her own behaviour. Thus it is not just the alcoholic, but frequently the spouse too, who is described as 'sick'.

These contradictions cannot be resolved rationally. Their 'truth' is to be found more at the level of faith and here Al-Anon offers a coherence and comfort which has no counterpart in the secular treatment programmes described earlier. Al-Anon asks its members to hold to a belief in the freedom to choose for oneself, thus offering hope, whilst at the same time acknowledging the constraints and limitations on the individual. It teaches acceptance but not resignation. Thus Al-Anon is religious in the sense that it believes in a higher power beyond the individual, but this is left unnamed and unattached to any specific religion.

The concrete expression of this philosophy is articulated most clearly through Al-Anon's operational principles. Members of Al-Anon are taught to 'detach with love'. The catchphrase has often been misunderstood and taken to mean that the non-alcoholic spouse selfishly cuts him/herself off from the suffering of the alcoholic and proceeds to organise life exclusively around his/her own needs and pleasures. But what the phrase really suggests is that the individual must try to unravel the tight knot of symbiosis, whereby the spouse's entire life revolves around futile attempts to change the alcoholic. Instead the partner is encouraged to achieve some measures of personal fulfilment so that the need to control the alcohol abuser is reduced and so that some pleasure is introduced into an otherwise unhappy situation. This approach is eminently sensible. First, it acknowledges the need for individuals to receive rewards as well as punishments in life and is thus in close sympathy with a learning theory view of behaviour. Secondly, empirical studies have repeatedly shown that whilst the natural reaction to the stress of living with an alcoholic is to make attempts to control his/her behaviour, these rarely achieve their desired ends (Orford *et al.*, 1975). Thus the spouses need to be explicitly taught to lessen their hold.

A recent study in the USA set out to test Al-Anon's success in this respect (Gorman and Rooney, 1979). Questionnaires were sent out to 168 wives of alcoholics attending a sample of twelve Al-Anon groups in the Washington area. The majority of members were middle- and upper-class and white. The study achieved a 73 per cent response rate and found clear support for Al-Anon's tenets. According to the wives' self-reports, the longer the wife had been a member of Al-Anon, the less likely she was to use 'negative coping strategies'. (These refer to behaviours such as coaxing, nagging, pleading, covering up, pouring drink away, etc.) Moreover, this decrease was noted even when the husband continued drinking, though the attainment of sobriety also led to a reduction in negative coping but this outcome correlated less with abstinence than with Al-Anon membership. This study is important not only for its conclusions, but because it is literally the only one of its kind.

Ablon (1974) has analysed the impact of Al-Anon from a different perspective. She did an 18-month participant observation study of a variety of West Coast, Californian Al-Anon groups. As in Gorman and Rooney's study, the typical Al-Anon member was white, middle-class and aged between 30 and 50. She found two key sets of factors accounted for Al-Anon's popularity. The first derived from the educational approach which has already been discussed and the second related to the particular medium of helping, based on group discussion and support. Albon laid particular emphasis on the warm, supportive atmosphere of the groups where hostility and confrontation were rare, and suggested that this is one of the main reasons why wives do not 'resist' scrutiny of their own behaviour, as is so frequently experienced at the hands of professional helpers. The purpose of the group meeting is not advice-giving, but to help the individuals find their own solution by the sharing of a common problem. She suggested that although self awareness is emphasised, the chief goal is 'pragmatic action'. Finally, one of the most important aspects of Al-Anon is the opportunity it gives the individual for restitution. As the spouse gradually overcomes problems he/she is given the opportunity to help others via activities such as manning the switchboard and welcoming new members. In this way the spouse can act as a model, asserting the possibility of recovery to newcomers, and thereby reinforcing self confidence. As a result the gulf between helper and helped is bridged.

It is not known how well Al-Anon works for non-middle-class individuals. Ablon has suggested that it may be particuarly well suited to people who believe in the power of discussion to overcome difficulties and who are sufficiently committed to their marriages to invest considerable energy in Al-Anon. But often even these individuals do not join Al-Anon until their spouse's drinking has become severely uncontrolled. Far too little is known about its impact and there is an urgent need for further study into its membership, programme and effects.

What Al-Anon illustrates very clearly is its capacity to foster pride in its members and thus, as Robinson has pointed out in his study of AA, to 'transform a stigmatised feature into something positive' (1979). Precisely for this reason it challenges the common view that non-specialist services are the best means of destigmatising unattractive conditions. For as Jones (1972) has argued in a discussion of services for the mentally ill, there is a danger of simplistically exaggerating the benefits of a non-specialist response, which in some cases may lead to the neglect of the needs of particular groups.

Discussion

Over the 30-year period under review there has been a steady growth of interest in developing family-focused intervention. The form of that involvement is widely varied both in terms of the ways in which the family is included and the type of strategies available. However, it is hard to identify any clear historical trends which might have determined the usage of different approaches. It seems that the repertoire of family-focused help has simply widened over the years as new forms of intervention have been introduced and these have tended to supplement rather than replace older established strategies such as group therapy.

Undoubtedly one important factor in stimulating experimentation with new forms of treatment has been the use of theory. Indeed, one can discern a very clear relationship between the development of new theoretical concepts and the growth of new treatments. In part the literature on treatment has made use of theories which specifically relate to the investigation of alcohol abuse, so that, for example, psychological theories of 'the alcoholic marriage'have been pivotal in shaping the form and content of group therapy. But investigations into treatment have also reflected a readiness to cross over into other related fields of study, seen most clearly in the borrowing of general systems theory to inform family therapy. Indeed this cross-fertilisation is in sharp contrast to the insularity noted by Orford (1975) in his discussion of the theoretical literature on alcohol and marriage. Thus in many ways interest in theory has had a liberating effect: at a practical level it has helped to extend the range of available treatment options, and because theories drawn from other disciplines have been found relevant to the treatment of families with an excessive drinker they have helped start to break down the barriers which have hitherto kept separate the treatment of alcohol-related disorders from other forms of disturbance. Nevertheless this process appears to be still at an early stage, since no accounts could be found in the literature which discussed the possible benefits of combining in treatment excessive drinkers and their families with others suffering from different problems.

In general this cross-fertilisation appears to have operated very selectively. There has been a greater readiness to draw on theories concerned with the study of the internal functioning of the family than those which place it in its broader social context, despite evidence to indicate that a key determinant of drinking problems is the sociocultural context (Royal College of Psychiatrists, 1979). Yet the impact of environmental pressures such as poverty, unemployment, poor housing and social isolation has been little studied, though in other fields of morbidity, such as depression, these factors have been shown to be very important (Brown and Harris, 1978). This suggests that although the literature on family treatment of excessive drinking reflects a move away from a purely symptom-based model to one incorporating the family environment, a schism still exists between the understanding of the multi-factorial causation of alcohol abuse and the models of treatment on which practice is based.

It would be wrong to attribute this bias exclusively to the choice of theoretical stance. For indeed, as already noted, many of the theories which have underpinned practice claim to emphasise the relationship between family functioning and environmental resources. It seems likely therefore, that the differential weighting given to psychological functioning may be due to the context in which treatment is carried out. For example, the fact that many programmes are conducted in hospital and clinic settings may create difficulties in responding to social distress within the community. This in turn may be influenced by the emphasis placed upon psychological functioning in the training of psychiatrists and psychologists who have played a major part in service provision for excessive drinkers and their families.

In general the literature on treatment presents some important biases. Most notable among these is the term 'family treatment'. In fact, the majority of studies are confined to reports of couples. When children are included, lower age limits are usually set and the part they play in therapy often seems peripheral. Little information is provided as to the extent of their participation and the results tend to be restricted to reports from the children themselves. Thus the term 'family treatment' seems a misnomer which is better regarded as a statement of intent than a reflection of current practice.

The type of family involved in treatment seems equally narrowly drawn. With a few notable exceptions (Davis and Hagood, 1979; Pattison, 1965) there is remarkably little information on any departure from the white nuclear family in which the excessive drinker is male. It is particularly surprising that with a few exceptions (Tamerin, 1978; Dinaberg *et al.*, 1977) the topic of family-focused help for women alcoholics has been largely neglected despite evidence documenting the substantial increase in female excessive drinking (Camberwell Council on Alcoholism, 1980). Although of smaller proportions, there has also been a growth in the number of families headed by a lone or divorced mother in the United Kingdom in the 1970s (OPCS, 1980), but accounts of the treatment of single parent families are scarce, as is the subject of the needs of ethnic minorities.

Most important of all, there is still a need for satisfactory evaluation of family-based treatment. Problem drinkers are characteristically reluctant to disclose their problem and accept treatment, but notwithstanding these particular difficulties many of the studies described suffer from a variety of methodological flaws and fail to demonstrate convincingly the efficacy of family focused intervention.

The samples have often been small and unrepresentative, and the findings based on assessments of doubtful reliability and validity. The inclusion of control groups receiving other forms of treatment is infrequent and in only one instance was a no-treatment group provided for comparison. Treatment measures have sometimes varied within the experimental samples and claims for success have been improperly ascribed to one model where several have been used. Follow-up periods have been short and sometimes varied within the samples. Finally, since many of the studies were carried out in the USA and a few in other countries it cannot be taken for granted that the findings apply to populations with drinking problems in the UK.

Implications for Policy

This chapter began by outlining the growth of concern among policy-makers to find ways of providing care for the families of excessive drinkers. Yet it will be clear by now that although there is considerable evidence to show that these families experience a variety of hardship there is very little reliable information to demonstrate the value of family-focused treatment. While policy-makers and their advisers have often deplored this deficit of knowledge they have nevertheless argued that it should not be allowed to stifle attempts to improve service provision. For example the most recent guidelines from the Advisory Committee on Alcoholism (1978) state:

> We know that in some measure what we are proposing goes ahead of research evaluation . . . We are all in favour of a great deal more research evaluation of treatment systems and only regret that there is at the moment so little to go on. It would be wrong, however, not to move towards the better development of services on this account.

While the justification for the final point in this argument is questionable, the overall outlook is not without its precedents. In 1968 the Seebohm Committee (HMSO, 1968) recommended a comprehensive reorganisation of the social services in the absence of any sound research evidence to demonstrate the efficacy of the social treatments that constituted the central justification for the proposed redeployment of personnel (Hall, 1976).

It would of course be naive to expect the formulation of policy to be determined primarily by evidence from research findings by experts in the field. In an illuminating discussion on criminological policy, Radzinowicz (1974) has highlighted the diversity of factors that help shape policy formation:

> Criminologists must be aware that the specific solution of many legal and penal problems cannot be determined exclusively or even

predominantly by the factual criminological evidence which they can provide. There are deep-rooted and far reaching issues of public morality, of social expediency, of the subtle and vital balance between the rights of the individual and the protection of the community, which underly decisions of penal policy, and must often override the conclusions of experts.

It seems likely that these considerations apply with equal force in the substantive field of alcohol abuse. In the end humanitarian concerns and political pressures place demands on policy-makers to develop services for a group that can be described as both 'deprived and depraved' (Packman, 1975) in terms of the hardship they experience personally and cause to society at large.

Faced by these dilemmas, policy-makers have tried to ensure a variety of treatment measures by placing a major emphasis on the importance of 'flexible' service provision. This has been a feature of all guidelines since they first appeared in 1962, and is forcibly expressed in a memorandum to hospital authorities in 1968 (Ministry of Health HM (68) 37); 'Finally, the absence of a reliable cure for alcoholism requires that treatment facilities should be organised so as to permit flexibility, experiment and research'. Ten years later, the Advisory Committee argued in similar vein, 'Moreover, what we are proposing is no more than a well coordinated flexible system of medical, social and voluntary services within which there will be scope for both individual variation and the introduction of new ideas'.

However, if the goal of policy has been to achieve variety in treatment approaches, it has not always succeeded in practice because some agencies, in particular the community-based statutory agencies, have not played as full a part in the treatment of excessive drinkers and their families as intended (Shaw *et al.*, 1978). For example, although the 1968 hospital memorandum and circular 21/73 emphasised the importance of social work support, two years later (DHSS, 1975) the DHSS was forced to urge social workers not to 'shrink away' from dealing with alcohol abuse.

The repercussions of the failure of community agencies to put policy recommendations into operation became more evident when recognition of drinking problems in the population began to increase in the 1970s (DHSS, 1978). This factor undoubtedly contributed to the decision to carry out a full reappraisal of the function and organisation of services for excessive drinkers and their families and in 1975 an expert Advisory Committee was appointed which reported three years later (DHSS, 1978). (See also Chapter 10.)

As its central recommendation it proposed that the main responsibility for excessive drinkers and their families should be carried by the primary care team, consisting of social workers, general practitioners and probation officers, as well by a wide range of non-statutory agencies such as the Samaritans and Marriage Guidance Council.

Whether the recommendations of the Advisory Committee, if they are accepted, will succeed where previous guidelines have failed remains to be seen. What seems certain is that if the Report is implemented it will severely restrict the scope for those intensive forms of treatment discussed in this review, since they are likely to be costly in both time and money. Even if the efficacy of these forms of treatment were to be demonstrated, logistical factors are likely to make them impractical since no substantial increase in manpower or resources in the near future is envisaged by the Committee. Indeed there is likely to be an even greater pressure on existent services because the overall goal of service provision has become very ambitious. Thus in a phrase redolent of Beveridge, the Committee declared, 'We intend every person with a drinking problem should be able to find the help he needs'.

It cannot be assumed that a shift to less intensive forms of treatment will be harmful. Indeed the results of the study by Edwards and his colleagues (Edwards *et al.*, 1977) discussed earlier (which surprisingly is not referred to in the Report) would indicate that this need not be the case.

In general, from the perspective of the family and its needs, there are clear gains to be made by a generic response. For it is the family who has been particularly penalised by specialist treatment. As stated at the outset of this chapter, relatives have frequently been left on the periphery, despite the fact that their own sufferings may be as intense as those of the problem drinker. Indeed the current organisational context has in particular excluded children and only magnified their isolation. It is also true that the characteristic problems experienced by families, such as depression in the wife, behavioural disturbance in the children, social isolation and financial hardship, are the fundamental concerns of many generic workers such as general practitioners and social workers. They are extensively shared by other groups who live with a partner suffering from a social or psychological disorder (Rutter, 1966; Tizard and Grad, 1951; Shepherd *et al.*, 1966, 1979) and they respond in similar ways. Indeed the continual utilisation of theories from other fields is a clear indication that the family of the problem drinker can be dealt with under the much broader framework of disturbed family functioning. This is not to deny that alcohol abuse does pose some special and specific strains, but these should not override the commonality of disturbance it shares with other areas.

What is very clear is that an even greater pressure now rests on the advocates of the intensive forms of treatment to demontrate their superiority over simpler, less esoteric programmes. This will entail not only a greater methodological rigour, but a more fundamental shift in outlook, which will pay due regard to the diversity of individual and family experience. For although it has been shown in this review that several treatment models exist alongside one another, at present they merely seem to compete for pre-eminence. While it is naive to assume that any system of care could cater fully for the variety of individual and family need, the evidence from this review seems to suggest that the heterogeneity of family life styles and aspirations recognised in sociological studies (Jordan, 1972; Moos and Moos, 1976) and in creative literature, has been largely ignored. Tolstoy realised the enormous variation in human suffering and he documented this in the opening lines of *Anna Karenina* when he wrote ' . . . each family is unhappy in its own way' (Tolstoy, 1877). The alcohol family treatment literature has as yet to take this into account.

Notes

1. This was based on the Cornell Medical Index which was not designed to measure changes in psychiatric symptomatology but as a screening agent to detect psychiatric cases and even in this respect can be markedly inefficient (Goldberg, 1972).
2. Some of the items on the 'social ineffectiveness scale' appear to describe personality traits unrelated to social functioning (e.g. overdependent, intrapunitive, hyperactive, overly systematic).
3. Marital satisfaction was assessed by means of an adjective checklist devised specifically for the study.
4. The more general and commonly used term is 'social casework' which covers both individual and family casework. The core features of each form are the emphasis on psychosocial functioning and the use of a 'warm, supportive . . . yet disciplined relationship' (Yelloly, 1980) with the caseworker to effect change.

12 THE PREVENTION OF DRINKING PROBLEMS IN THE FAMILY

Jim Orford

Introduction

Talking about prevention is in vogue. We are frequently reminded that modern medicine's most spectacular triumphs, over infectious diseases, have been in the sphere of prevention rather than that of treatment. When psychological problems are the focus of concern, the argument in favour of prevention may be still stronger. Our treatment techniques are of unproven potency and when a large number of studies and clients are grouped together, demonstrable gains in comparison with leaving problems untreated are slight (Smith and Glass, 1977). Besides which, the shortage of professional manpower to deliver psychological treatment services is such that it has been described as a 'crisis' (Hawks, 1973; Cowen, 1980). Non-professionally trained workers and volunteers can undoubtedly relieve this crisis to some extent, particularly in view of the evidence that they are at least as effective as, if not slightly more so, than the professionals in treating many psychological problems (Durlak, 1979). But the disparity between potential demand for and availability of services is great and will remain.

The mental health professions have been criticised for adopting a 'passive-waiting' style of work which enables them to respond only to casualties once they have occurred, and in many cases to respond only selectively to those casualties who obtain access to their services. Clinical psychology, the discipline with which I am most familiar, can be roundly criticised on this score at the present time. A few lone voices, principally from the US, such as Cowen's (1980), are raised in protest at this exclusive preoccupation with the repair of casualty. Cowen and others of his persuasion argue for a move towards 'community psychology' with its emphasis upon positive health, a 'reaching out' mode of work, and prevention. Other disciplines have engaged in the same heart-searching.

Preventive action in mental health is less evident, sadly, than talking about it. There are probably theoretical, practical and ethical reasons for this state of affairs. At a theoretical level, sound understanding of environmental factors which promote or detract from mental health is sparse. There has been much recent work linking stressful life events (including family stressors such as bereavement, births, separation, infidelity, new roles, etc.) with the occurrence of both physical and psychological symptoms. Although this is a consistent finding, it has been pointed out that life events account for only a small percentage (around 10-30 per cent) of the variance in symptom rates (Cochrane and Sobol, 1980). Studies such as that of Brown and Harris (1978) are beginning to fill in the gaps in our understanding of the way the link between stress and disorder is mediated. Social integration in the family (cohesiveness, including the possibility of an intimate, confiding relationship with another adult in the family being part of the picture), extended family, neighbourhood, work place, and wider community has the strongest claim on our attention. Social integration is, however, a vague notion and lacks the immediacy and tangibility of, say, uncontaminated water supply when it comes to developing a preventive strategy around these factors.

Nor is it so clear how society can prescribe improvements in mental health, since the practical problems are so formidable. At a very pragmatic level the funding required for pilot preventive projects is far greater than for treatment projects, on account of the large numbers of people at which preventive campaigns need to be aimed and the length of follow-up required to judge effectiveness. Notable amongst the very few projects that have overcome these difficulties in the areas of psychological health and handicap is the Milwaukee project (Heber, 1978) which successfully showed how borderline mental handicap could be prevented by providing educational and social stimulation for low-IQ mothers and their children. A further example is the Stanford Heart Disease project (Farquhar *et al.*, 1977) which demonstrated the effectiveness of mass-media persuasion (with an extra increment in effectiveness added on top by additional face-to-face persuasive communication) in reducing behaviour likely to increase the risk of cardiac failure (smoking, weight, stress, low physical activity, non-nutritious diet).

Those who would prevent, rather than treat casualty, must also face daunting ethical questions (McGuire, 1980). For one thing preventive work may achieve a desired goal but may produce undesired side effects, some of which could not easily be anticipated at the outset. In the case of drug use and abuse (including alcohol) a strong case can be made (e.g. Westermeyer, 1978) that restrictiveness (brought about by law, social climate, or economic forces that restrict availability and increase cost) is associated with a relatively high rate of abstinence, and a reduced rate of certain drug-related problems (medical complications and consequences perhaps), but an increased amount of certain kinds of social harm associated with the use of the drug (particularly criminal activities). The US and alcohol before, during and after prohibition, and Laos and opiates before, during, and after the recent ravages of war (Westermeyer, 1978) provide good examples of dramatic changes over short periods of time, the results of which may be used to support this thesis. Quite apart from the problems of reconciling intended and unintended effects of prevention, there is the basic issue of loss of individual freedom to contend with. Opposition to the compulsory use of car seat belts and crash helmets for motorcycle users, fluoridation of water supply, and restrictions on smoking in public all testify to the quite widespread feelings of resentment which arise particularly when it appears that one section of the population is restricting the freedom of behaviour of another for the latter's 'own good'.

Primary Prevention of Drinking Problems in the Family

Barriers in the way of doing good preventive work are such that the imbalance between treatment and prevention work in the field of alcohol problems is almost total. Perusal of the abstract editions of the *Journal of Studies on Alcohol* confirms the impression that our collective style is currently one of casualty responding. Furthermore, a family perspective is even more difficult to discern in the preventive area than in areas such as epidemiology, diagnosis and treatment. Regrettably it is not possible to review work that has been done in the area of prevention of alcohol problems in the family, because to this writer's knowledge no work directly on this topic exists. The purpose of this chapter must rather be to suggest and hint at possibilities in the hope that this may contribute to a climate of opinion which promotes preventive action.

Contagion and Drinking

The lack of a family perspective on alcohol problem prevention is surprising in view of the emphasis given to the availability of alcohol in much recent writing on the subject (e.g. Royal College of Psychiatrists, 1979), and the evidence reviewed by Davies in his chapter in this volume that the family is a key agency through which alcohol is made available to the individual. The alcohol field is fortunate, in comparison with many others, in the impetus given to thinking about prevention by the 'discovery' that some indices of alcohol-related problems in the population (particuarly cirrhosis death rates) are strongly positively correlated with rates of total alcohol consumption for the population as a whole (de Lint, 1977). In particular Ledermann (1956) speculated that this and other findings could be explained by a process of social contagion —his 'boule de neige' — whereby increments or decrements in amounts of drinking accumulated in size like a rolling snowball as a result of social inducement, pressure and availability from colleague to colleague, neighbour to neighbour, friend to friend, and family member to family member. The social contagion theory of the generation of drinking and drinking problems seems to this writer to be the nearest we can come at present to a general explanatory theory which could form a background to the design of preventive efforts. It is not incompatible with the evidence that there is a partial genetic component, nor with the view that some personalities are more at risk than others.

As a widely available, recreational drug, largely consumed in the company of other people, it would be surprising indeed if a person's drinking was not highly responsive to the example and reactions of his or her associates. This is recognised by many of those who treat problem drinkers, as witness the insistence of Hunt and Azrin (1973) and others that people undergoing treatment seek the company of 'buddies' who set an example of moderate drinking, and by the work of Foy *et al.* (1976) who have gone so far as to teach problem drinkers the 'skill' of resisting pressure from others to drink.

Social contagion contains a number of elements which are separable in theory but usually inextricably intertwined in reality. One of these is sheer availability: if parents do not drink wine with dinner regularly, it is not available for the children to taste at least in that setting. A second is social pressure which may range from absent to coercive, and from encouraging of drinking to discouraging of drinking. A third is social reinforcement or punishment for drinking. Here it is important to bear in mind that the reinforcing or punishing properties of social behaviour may be by no means obvious: is laughter at a child's intoxication at the Christmas party rewarding because of the child's pleasure at causing mirth and being the focus of attention, or punishing because of the pain of embarrassment and ridicule?

The fourth element, and arguably the most important, is that of observational learning or modelling. It is now generally accepted that one of the most powerful processes involved in the acquisition of behaviour involves a person adopting behaviour that has been witnessed in others. Adoption is more likely if the behaviour is observed repeatedly, if the 'model' is liked or respected or is important, and if the model's behaviour appears to meet with rewarding consequences. There is perhaps a fifth element not completely covered by the first four, which we may wish to call 'pure contagion', whereby people simply tend to do what other people around them are doing. Some combination of these elements must be at work in the experiments, of which a number have now been conducted, showing the potent influence upon drinking rate of one's drinking companions. An experiment by de Ricco (1978) is an example of studies of this kind. Subjects drank with three companions (all strangers and confederates of the experimenter). At first the latter drank at a rate determined by the natural drinking rate of the subject. During later parts of the experiment two of the three companions deliberately drank faster and one slower, and at other times the reverse. All subjects increased and decreased their drinking rate with the behaviour of the majority of their drinking companions.

Family Training about Drinking

If most people begin drinking in the family setting (see the evidence reviewed by Davies in this volume), then it seems likely that the family provides a major context in which very specific social contagion takes place. Rate of drinking is only one parameter involved, although it may be counted a most important one in view of the link between drinking rate and peak blood alcohol level, and the finding that excessive drinkers drink at a significantly faster rate than social drinkers (Schaefer *et al.*, 1971). Other aspects of drinking which discriminated excessive drinkers and social drinkers in the Schaefer study, and which may be contagious within a family setting, are size of sip or gulp, and types of alcoholic drink preferred (straight spirits versus diluted spirits or weaker beverages). Equally, and perhaps more important than these micro-aspects of drinking 'topography', may be factors such as time of day, occasion or reason for drinking. By observing adult members of the household (not forgetting the usually neglected influence of siblings, especially older siblings) drinking in a way which is limited to certain occasions and which is serving limited social functions, a youngster may be most likely to pick up a pattern of usage of alcohol, and acquire a concept of the value or meaning of alcohol, which is discriminating and restrained.

We do not have the evidence to know whether such a detailed formulation of drinking training at home is correct. It is, however, consistent with what is known about the conditions for learning new behaviour, and with survey evidence suggesting a consistent and moderately strong correlation between the drinking habits of parents and their children. If it can be assumed that there is enough truth in this view to base preventive action upon it, what actions should follow? I would argue that this view makes the currently fashionable style of health education, based on the provision of information in schools, look sadly misdirected. In one sense schools may be the very last places in which to try and influence the drinking attitudes and practices of young people, because schools are one of the few types of setting which are virtually alcohol-free and which therefore provide no opportunities whatsoever for the contagious transmission of drinking behaviour, good or bad. They are, however, the source of much new learning and it is upon the argument that health education can be woven into the regular curriculum that much present-day health education practice in Britain is based.

Even so, this approach would seem to have little chance of success if the major influence is the home. Here we have to strike up the oft-sung lament about lack of close home-school relations in education. Despite the fact that the home constitutes a major influence upon all aspects of education or achievement (although Rutter *et al.*, 1979, recently produced evidence that quality of school is also correlated with achievement), parents are not treated as full partners in the educational process. It seems particularly short-sighted to provide education at school with little reference to the family when dealing with a topic such as alcohol use. Teachers can lay no claim to special knowledge or freedom from bias or maladaptive attitudes about alcohol, and the family meanwhile has all the ingredients for effective interpersonal influence (powerful authority figures, long-term intensive contact, opportunities for observational learning, opportunities for practice and feedback on performance). There seems little chance of a conventional health education approach being successful whilst education is defined as education in a school setting, and where home-school relations continue to be distant. If I am right in my diagnosis then the treatment must lie in prevention *in the family*. There are obvious difficulties in achieving such an aim. The challenge is not a new one, however, to those concerned with prevention: reaching the intended target population is one of the main and most difficult tasks of any preventive work. For a start those concerned with the drinking of youngsters and their families might try approaching the Parent-Teacher Association first. Whatever the setting, and the means of bringing the participants to it, the aim should be to impart information and to suggest drinking practices to parents and their children jointly.

Drinking in Broader Context

The view of the learning of drinking behaviour which has been adopted so far in this chapter is over-simple on at least two counts. Both of the complications which I shall introduce take us further away from a specific examination of drinking and further towards a less focused view of drinking within a broader context of socialisation and psychological adjustment. This move from the particular to the general is comforting in so far as it allows us to view individuals as whole people. On the other hand this move is discomforting since the prescriptions for primary prevention are consequently more global, even grandiose, and far less precise.

First, we should perhaps recognise that alcohol-related problems and disabilities are multiple and include such aspects as drunken driving and alcohol-related violence. The use of alcohol provides a link between such disparate problems but each has its specific elements which may be as important if not more so. The prevention of drunken driving, for example, may have as much to do with the establishment of safe driving habits as with the acquisition of safe drinking practices. Similarly it may be short-sighted to lay the blame for drink-related violence at the door of faulty drinking socialisation rather than at the roots of violence itself. Violent behaviour is probably transmitted within the family in much the same way as drinking behaviour, in particular by modelling by adults and by admired figures depicted on television (Belson, 1979).

Attitudes towards the media at home, towards advertising, towards consumption pressure, and towards the use of public houses, all may be as influential as specific attitudes towards drinking *per se*. It also needs to be asked whether the aim of prevention should be the specific alteration of alcohol-use attitudes and behaviour or, more generally, the non-problem use of drugs with dependence potential. There is evidence of positive correlations between alcohol use, smoking, and the use of other drugs (Jessor and Jessor, 1977), and evidence of a correlation between the overall drug-using habits of children and their parents (Smart and Fejer, 1972).

The second major way in which the perspective can be broadened is by paying due heed to the warning, with which we are now so familiar, that the determinants of social behaviour are many and are interrelated in a complex fashion. This multi-factorial view has been pursued most systematically by Richard and Shirley Jessor in their longitudinal studies of drinking problems, drug use and other forms of youthful 'deviance' (e.g. Jessor and Jessor, 1977). They attempt to account for individual differences amongst young people in high school and college, and for changes in behaviour during school and college years. Their theory is a complex one, taking into account aspects of the perceived *environment* (such as family and peer group support for alcohol use), personality (e.g. values placed upon achievement and independence), and *behaviour* (including other forms of conventional or unconventional, conforming or deviant behaviour). The influence of a person's family of origin has an important place in their scheme but only as one element amongst a number. Amongst others, upon which family life may have an important bearing, are values, attitudes towards deviance generally, and the complementarity of family and peer group influences.

Under the heading of values, the Jessors' consistent finding is that valuing academic achievement is associated with deviant behaviour negatively, and that valuing independence is associated positively. Hence those young people who place high value upon independence and low value upon academic achievement are particularly likely to report excessive drinking and other forms of deviance. In so far as these are values which may be transmitted in the family, it can be argued that imparting values and behaviours which are incompatible with excessive drinking may be as effective a route to preventing drinking problems as a frontal attack on drinking itself (see the chapter by Davies for a related argument).

Further complexity is a⎡ded by Jessor and Jessor when they consider parental and peer group influence and the 'fit' between them. Their studies confirm the repeated finding that the drinking of friends is the strongest correlate of drinking behaviour amongst older teenagers and young adults (e.g. Orford *et al.*, 1974). They argue, however, that the influence of the peer group will depend to a large extent upon the similarity of this influence and that of the home. Where the values and attitudes espoused, and behaviours modelled by the peer group, are markedly different from those of the home, then it must be supposed that the company of the peer group is being sought for certain personality-linked reasons such as rebellion, or independence, or at least that the individual concerned will be subject to conflict.

Similar views to do with different sources of social influence on a person's drinking and the way in which they articulate together have been put forward by others. Wilkinson (1970) reviewed evidence which seemed to support his argument that negative or repressive parental controls on drinking, particularly when associated with making an emotional issue out of drinking, were likely to lead to initiation into relatively unrestrained drinking practices *outside* the family. Persuaded by this line of evidence, Wilkinson proposed that young people should be permitted to drink at an early age in a non-coercive climate within the family. His proposals have not found universal favour in recent years. For one thing, there is a firm body of opinion now that the encouragement of moderate drinking behaviour in one context adds to rather than replaces harmful drinking behaviour in other settings (the 'aggregation' hypothesis — see the chapter by Shaw in this volume). Furthermore, we have lived through a time in recent years during which young people have increasingly been introduced to drinking at earlier ages within the home, and yet the trends have been towards increased national consumption in almost all countries and as far as we can tell increasing rates of alcohol-related problems.

Building Resistance

Alcohol and alcohol problems as a field of study has developed into a specialism and can be criticised for being too focused and narrow in its outlook (Orford, 1975). This blinkered approach, focusing exclusively on alcohol use to the virtual exclusion of other and wider aspects of individual and social functioning, has certainly been true of the alcoholism treatment field and of the 'alcoholism in the family' field. There is a real danger that it will become true with prevention also. Much of the discussion in this chapter so far has proceeded on the assumption that the best way to prepare people to resist excessive or harmful drinking is to provide them with appropriate alcohol-specific socialisation experiences or training. It is possible to conceive, however, of a totally different approach which might turn out to be equally, if not more, effective. The abilities, skills or traits which provide the greater part of the resistance to excessive or harmful drinking may well be general in nature, acquired in a multitude of contexts other than those involving the use of alcohol, and providing resistance not only to harmful alcohol use but perhaps to psychological problems and mental ill-health of a variety of kinds.

Lay views of the factors conferring such resistance will include references to such general factors, or so I would anticipate. Notions of 'common sense', 'stability', 'security', 'strength of will' and 'conformity' would be invoked I suspect. Although such views may underestimate the factors of social pressure and influence for which there is so much evidence (to give just one example, see Plant, 1979, on occupational influence), and neglect altogether the possibility of genetically transmitted physiological influences which may confer resistance (as suggested, for example, by Goodwin, 1976), there is no sound evidence to allow us to reject them out of hand.

The very generality of such constructs, however, makes them uninviting as goals for alcohol problems prevention. Although many would doubt the quality of the research upon which the conclusion is based, to date it has to be concluded that the evidence for personality determinants of alcohol problems is slight. Furthermore, if traits concerned with emotional or cognitive functioning are implicated in the development of drinking problems, these may be as much genetically inherited as environmentally transmitted via the family or in some other way.

Nevertheless, general preventive approaches to building mental health and preventing psychological problems are in existence and it is important that those of us who specialise in alcohol problems should be aware of them and should consider their relevance to our speciality. Most of these approaches have been pioneered in the USA, have been reported by American community psychologists (e.g. Zax and Specter, 1974; Cowen, 1980), and are less well-known in Europe. One approach, for example, has been to train children in 'interpersonal cognitive problem solving (ICPS) skills'. These include abilities to detect problems, to generate alternative solutions, to set realistic goals, to plan ahead, to make decisions, and to evaluate the consequences of solutions to problems. There is evidence that the existence of these skills differentiates between well-adjusted and relatively poorly-adjusted people at various ages, that these skills can be taught, and that when acquired increased competence in cognitive problem solving 'radiates' to aspects of general adjustment. Elements of this approach are contained within the social skills and personal problem solving approach to therapy advocated in Britain by Priestley et al. (1978).

A second approach, based on work at the University of Iowa, has focused on the way in which children learn to perceive and interpret human behaviour. Central to this approach is the distinction between causal thinking, in which behaviour is viewed as having reasons or causes in the form of motives or situational determinants, and non-causal or punitive thinking, where reasons and motives are disregarded. The pioneers of this approach argued that the latter perspective led to unsatisfactory human relationships and often to psychological problems, and furthermore that adults such as teachers frequently modelled this approach, for example by punishing pupils for misbehaviour without questioning pupils' motives or reasons. Work within this framework has demonstrated that teachers can be trained to give children a causal orientation, and there is evidence that when this is done children are less authoritarian, less anxious and feel more secure.

The 'social skills' approach originating with Argyle (e.g. 1980) and his colleagues in Oxford is a British variant of this general approch to building resistance to psychological problems. Probably for very much the same reasons as were discussed when considering the school-based nature of much focused alcohol preventive education, these general approaches to building competence have been principally concerned with teachers and schools and scarcely at all with parents and families. Once again this seems short-sighted. Although it has to be admitted that psychological theories of personality development have over-emphasised the family and under-emphasised other spheres of socialisation influence such as the school, the reverse is surely an even more fundamental error. Although its focus was intellectual development and its relevance to our present concern therefore tangential, the Milwaukee project for mildly mentally handicapped mothers and their young children (Heber, 1978; Falender and Heber, 1975) is exemplary in its long-term persistence in improving the mothers' child care and employment skills and in its concern with evaluation. Here was a project which not only provided an enriched educational programme for the children but also was concerned to improve the general nature of the environment provided for the children by their mothers and which demonstrated an effect (children showed an advantage of 20-30 IQ points over control children) which had persisted several years after the project finished.

Socialisation or Control?

Preventive approaches hinted at so far in this chapter share what Staulcup *et al.* (1979), in their review of alcoholism prevention projects funded by the US National Institute on Alcohol Abuse and Alcoholism, call the socialisation theory view. These authors note that all the prevention programmes they review adopt this theory despite the existence of an alternative, namely 'control theory'. More and more in recent years, associated with the 'discovery' of the log normal or skewed frequency distribution curve for alcohol consumption in a population (de Lint, 1977), a direct relationship has been posited between levels of alcohol consumption in society and rates of alcohol-related problems. Hence the prescription for prevention is the reducing of societal levels of consumpton as a key factor. Unlike socialisation theory, within which it can be argued much of this chapter has been written:

Control theory places little emphasis on the individual drinker's atti-

tudes, knowledge, values and beliefs about drinking, or on the
major socialization forces (e.g. family, peer group, school, community) that may affect individual drinking. Rather, emphasis is
placed on methods of regulating the supply of alcohol such as taxation, limited advertising and limited numbers of distribution points,
or on establishment of a fixed level of per capita consumption . . .
(Staulcup *et al.*, 1979, p. 944).

Classic public health prevention theory advocates that attention be
paid to the agent (in this case alcohol) as well as to the host (the
drinker) and to the environment in which they interact. Two facets of
the availability of the agent, alcohol, immediately suggest themselves
as being of relevance to the family although there are undoubtedly
many others. The first concerns the role of the public house in Britain
as an institution which governs the availability of alcohol in the family
setting. Barker's (1978) comparison of 'behaviour settings' in 'Mid
West', USA and 'Yoredale' in England, found that children were
excluded from a significantly higher proportion of settings in the
English town than the American. Although children may be excluded
from settings where liquor is sold in either country, the public house
probably has far greater significance as a social centre in Britain than
does its counterpart in other parts of the world (see the chapter by
Shaw in this volume). The exclusion of young people from such an important social behaviour setting, one in which the consumption of
alcoholic beverages figures so prominently, must have significance for
the prevention of alcohol problems, although it is difficult to be sure
what the significance is. It could be argued that an uneasy balance has
been struck, as a result of the historical development of the public
house and the evolution of licensing legislation, between the needs of
families for socialising and for entertainment on the one hand, and the
need to protect the young from over-exposure to drinking settings on
the other. The social needs of whole families are complex and include
the needs of parents to survey the behaviour of young children, and the
increasing needs of both parents and children to be separate from one
another for increasing periods of time as children increase in age. The
provision of opportunities for entertainment and socialising which met
these needs would upset the balance, and the way in which use of alcoholic beverages was permitted or restricted in any new settings so
created would have an important bearing on the prevention of drinking
problems.
   A second matter of undoubted relevance is that of increasing home

production of alcoholic drinks, although once again the degree to which this will affect rates of new drinking problems is not at all clear. A simple interpretation of social control theory would argue that the increasing availability of alcoholic drinks at moderate cost would be bound to increase overall consumption and hence rates of alcohol-related problems. The effect of home production of beer and wine is almost a test case of socialisation versus control theory. Whilst the latter would predict increased problems, the former would counter-argue that this moderate home influence would protect young people against immoderate influences elsewhere. That no confident prediction about the effects of home production can be made is an indication of the continuing, unresolved dispute between the socialisation and control positions.

Preventive Work with Children of Problem Drinkers

One of the problems of preventive work in any health-related field is that, in the natural course of events, only a minorty of the population would be expected to suffer the type of ill-health or experience the type of problem against which prevention is aimed. In one sense a lot of the work is therefore wasted, particularly if there exists any tendency for those who are prone to the disorder or problem concerned to be missed by the method designed to deliver the preventive campaign. This might be the case, for example, if prevention work is carried out in schools and if those most likely to suffer later ill-health are particularly likely to be frequent truanters from school. In theory at least, one of the best ways of economising effort is to concentrate attention on sub-populations known to be at particularly high risk. In the case of alcohol problems such a sub-population appears to be one consisting of people who have had a parent with a drinking problem. Goodwin (1976) has reviewed many studies which have reported a raised incidence of parental problem-drinking amongst clinical samples of alcoholics or problem drinkers and concluded that alcoholism definitely 'runs in families'. More recently, Cotton (1979) has similarly concluded from his review of the literature that there is a raised incidence of alcohol problems in first-degree relatives of people identified as having a clinic-ally significant alcohol problem themselves.

The conclusion must surely be that children with problem-drinking parents should be the target of work designed to prevent the high rate of later drinking problems which we can expect this group to show.

Furthermore, in view of the adverse environmental conditions to which some children of problem drinkers are exposed and the increased rate of psychological problems which they already demonstrate in childhood and adolescence (see the chapter by Wilson in this volume), we can be fairly sure that drinking problems do not constitute the only problems against which prevention work might be aimed with this group.

Knowing that a group is at high risk is only part of the background required to begin to design effective preventive intervention. We need in addition to know why the group is at high risk. Here we have some leads and suggestions which make theoretical sense, but few sound facts. Each of the following possible explanations of the link between excessive drinking in one generation and the next is credible, but we need to start to choose between them if we are to intervene effectively:

(1)　The child positively *identifies* with a parent who presents a model of excessive or harmful drinking.

(2)　No-one in the family offers a satisfactory *model* of non-deviant moderate drinking, or else the child fails to identify with the parent who does offer such a model because of a breakdown in family relationships. For either reason the child is at risk of modelling his/her drinking upon that of heavy drinkers outside the family.

(3)　Because of *unsatisfactory relationships* in the family of upbringing, the child experiences frequent depression, anxiety or low self-esteem or self-confidence, and these traits put the person at risk for excessive or harmful drinking.

(4)　Living with a problem-drinking parent in some cases involves interference with the normal process of *friendship formation*. Lack of skill or confidence in making friends leads to social isolation which puts the person at risk of harmful excessive drinking.

(5)　Children of problem-drinking parents have a genetically raised *predisposition* of some kind, mediated physiologically or psychologically, and lack information about the inheritance of drinking problems and how they can be avoided.

Whatever the mechanisms, the fact remains that opportunities are wasted at present for acting upon the knowledge of this link between the generations. Efforts are often made by therapists to involve the spouses of problem drinkers in the latters' treatment, although this is usually in order to improve the chances of successful treatment for the problem drinker rather than in recognition of the risks to the spouse's health and well-being. As Wilson points out in her chapter in this book, steps are very rarely made to involve the excessive drinker's children, whether they be 'children', adolescents or adults themselves.

Increasingly, members of the mental health professions are acquiring training and building confidence in conducting family therapy, and it is becoming increasingly likely that members of new generations of workers will possess the inclination and confidence to undertake such work in units and agencies where problem drinkers are treated. Although there is little sound evidence to date that family therapy is effective in achieving greater positive changes in family life than occur without it (Gurman and Kniskern, 1978), the treatment of families which contain young members and which are complicated by alcohol problems in one or other parent constitutes a highly important testing ground for family therapy approaches (Steinglass, 1976).

One of the few family therapy approaches for which positive gains have been well documented is the behavioural family treatment approach of Alexander and his colleagues (e.g. Klein *et al.*, 1980). This approach has concentrated upon increasing the rate of positive family interactions, such as time spent together talking. Families were included which contained a delinquent youngster, and evidence has been presented that the approach can prevent future delinquency in the case of the identified problem members of the families, and can also prevent future delinquency in the case of siblings (Klein *et al.*, 1980). To my knowledge the application of such an approach to families complicated by drinking problems has not been considered directly. This approach might be particularly useful during the phase of reintegration of a former problem drinker in the family – a phase recognised long ago by Jackson (1954) to be problematic. In view of the known moderate rate of short-term improvement in drinking problems (Emrick, 1975), it might have particular application for non-problem-drinking spouses and their children in cases where the co-operation of the drinking parent could not be obtained, although ideally the latter would be included.

The children of problem drinkers are particularly likely to be 'fatherless', and may also be more frequently 'motherless' than the average, both literally because of family breakdown, and also on account of the father's or mother's preoccupation with drinking. If deprivation of parental affection, attention and stimulus is an important mediating factor in the intergenerational transmission of drinking problems, then approaches become relevant which attempt to prevent by making good the parental deficiency. One such approach, which again to my know-ledge has not been employed within the alcohol specialty, is that of Companionship Therapy. The approach has been described and evalu-ated in full by Goodman (1972) and a replication study has been pub-lished by Dicken *et al.* (1977). The approach consists of recruiting and supporting the work of young adults, often students, who act as indivi-dual companions for youngsters who are creating problems at home or at school. Companions are instructed quite carefully about the minimum contact with the youngster in question (usually one meeting a week as a minimum) and their approach to the family (often single parent families). Activities are varied but usually include trips, sports and games, and sometimes just meeting at home. There appear to be grounds for cautious optimism at least about its effects on young prob-lem teenagers in the short term. At least the scheme is well-received by youngsters and parents and the latter rate their children as less disturbed. The evidence so far suggests that 'outgoing' companions (as rated by other volunteers during an initial selection task involving role-playing) achieve most gains with their youngsters.

Companionship therapy is perhaps just one of a number of innovative approaches which might profitably be attempted with young people at high risk of developing alcohol problems as the target group. Intermediate treatment (e.g. Waterhouse, 1978) is a related, British approach, for example. An alternative, of relevance to older teenagers or young adults, is Azrin *et al.*'s (1975) 'job finding club'. Unemployed young people who had been in trouble with the law received training in job finding and selection interview skills and as a group pooled their knowledge about available employment. Significantly more were in employment at follow-up than was the case for a control group.

The point here is not that we should adopt wholesale programmes that have been employed with other groups; rather that we should recognise that children of problem drinkers are at high risk and that we should be bold and imaginative in designing responses to their needs as others have begun to do with other groups.

Although children of problem drinkers constitute the most clear-cut case of a group of people at relatively high risk of developing drink-ing problems, there are probably others. These might include people who are recently divorced (Bloom *et al.*, 1978, have recently summar-ised the evidence that rates of psychological problems of many sorts are high in this group), the recently widowed, particularly perhaps the elderly widowed, and immigrant groups from abstinent or ambivalent cultures of origin who in their new countries are exposed to relatively permissive drinking norms (O'Connor, 1978). Some such groups may be recognised as having special needs — witness the growth of self-help groups for widows, such as Cruse in the UK and the Widow-to-Widow programmes in the USA (Caplan and Killilea, 1976) — but the idea of a specific proneness to drinking problems remains uncertain and the prescriptions for alcohol-problems prevention work are not at all clear. Pregnant mothers-to-be constitute a special case on account of the apparent existence of the foetal alcohol syndrome (see the chapters by Davies and Wilson in this volume) and the fact that this group is more readily available as a target for prevention than are most.

This opportunity for preventive work is full of dangers however and raises many of the salient questions about public health campaigns. The temptation is to rush in with fear-arousing appeals to pregnant women to stop or curtail their drinking. The literature on persuasion by fear arousal is very complex and inconsistent in its conclusions however (Janis and Rodin, 1979), and should be studied in detail by those proposing work in this area. It appears that under some circumstances high fear-arousing appeals are more effective than others, whilst the reverse is the case under other circumstances. The relevant circumstances appear to include the anxiety level of the person on the receiving end of the persuasive appeal, and the degree of personal involvement of the person in the issue involved. It seems unlikely that women who are anxious, both in general and about pregnancy and future parenthood in particular, and who have any degree of dependence upon drinking, would respond at all well to preventive attempts which involved the arousal of fear on account of the foetal alcohol syndrome.

Secondary Prevention

This chapter has been largely concerned with primary prevention, or the prevention of the occurrence of the development of problems. However, the three categories of prevention outlined by Caplan (1964) — primary, secondary and tertiary — are not totally distinct. Primary and secondary prevention in particular begin to merge when we consider high-risk groups who may already be showing early problems.

Less space will be devoted in this chapter to secondary prevention, the early identification and treatment of problems at an incipient or formative stage before help is normally sought, as these topics have been dealt with more fully by Harwin and Ritson in their chapters. I would however like to draw attention to the work which suggests that spontaneous remission of drinking problems occurs (e.g. Roizen *et al.*, 1978), and particularly to the recent work in Scotland by Saunders and Kershaw (1979). The latter workers identified, by means of a social survey, people who considered they had had a drinking problem in the past but no longer had this problem. They confirmed, in so far as this is possible by means of careful interview, that this was indeed the case and tried to establish possible reasons for the remission of these problems. The major reasons to which remission was attributed by the people concerned consisted of positive changes in life circumstances. Obtaining work or improvements in work conditions were amongst these reasons, but the most frequently stated reason was 'marriage'. Getting married — many of those concerned reported remission of problems in their twenties — was cited by many as the cause of remission. Although it is difficult to prescribe marriage for those with early drinking problems, an understanding of what it is about the married state which may confer resistance to drinking problems might go a long way towards suggesting useful approaches for secondary prevention within the family. Saunders and Kershaw's findings are, in a very general sense, in keeping with the conclusions of those such as Cochrane and Sobol (1980) and Janis and Rodin (1979) who have written about the importance of social support in the prevention of psychological problems generally. Janis and Rodin's notion of social support is particularly apposite because it contains as ingredients both close, accepting, affectional ties, as well as the imposition of norms and obligations. Arguably, it is this combination of social bonding and social control which imparts to marriage its preventive potential.

Prescriptions for deliberate preventive interventions are still not clear, however. In the search for such prescriptions, the reader will perhaps forgive me at this point if I leap to a quite different area of research on alcohol and the family. As a result of analyses of questionnaire data about the coping behaviour of wives of treated alcoholics, we suggested that effective coping behaviour might consist of reactions which were 'engaged' (as opposed to those that involved avoidance of, or withdrawal from, the drinker) but 'discriminatory' (directed against drinking but not the drinker him/herself) (Orford *et al.*, 1975). The evidence in support of this contention was flimsy, and furthermore it is unknown whether the coping reactions which work for wives of identified problem drinkers would work for the husbands or wives of early non-identified problem drinkers. It may at least be hypothesised that it is 'coping' behaviour of this kind which nips incipient drinking problems in the bud early in the history of some marriages, and which might with profit be adopted by others who live with people who start to develop alcohol dependence. Such behaviour might at least stand the best chance of avoiding coercion or withdrawal, two forms of behaviour which some family therapists believe in general terms to be most characteristic of troubled families (Patterson *et al.*, 1975).

Evaluation

Reference has already been made in the introduction to the difficulty of assessing the effectiveness of preventive work. Of those preventive projects reviewed by Staulcup *et al.* (1979), a few had adopted an experimental design and some others had employed a quasi-experimental design. Only three of the projects they reviewed were carried out within a family framework, and one fell within the group that had been subject to satisfactory evalutive procedures. Tempting though it is to mount preventive effort with good intentions, treating evaluation as a hoped-for luxury to be added later if possible, we should know better. McGuire (1980) has outlined a seven-step plan for designing preventive communication campaigns in social problem areas. Evaluation is listed as an integral part of any such campaign and one that should run parallel with other steps in the plan. For example, the very first step involves establishing a priority list of targets, and McGuire stresses that this should be submitted to various experts for their comments. A final evaluation should occur at the end of the campaign and this:

> should be undertaken by outsiders who did not participate in the preceding six steps of designing and carrying out the social influence campaign, and so have more objectivity. The purpose of the final evaluation is to determine the cost of the campaign and its intended and unintended effects, both good and bad, along with an analysis of its strong and weak points and suggestions for how subsequent campaigns might be improved (p. 360).

McGuire points out that although the evaluation phase of social action campaigns has been neglected, there is in fact now a great deal of advice available in handbooks and other texts on programme evaluation (e.g. Riecken and Boruch, 1974).

13 OVERVIEW: PROBLEMS IN ESTABLISHING A FAMILY PERSPECTIVE

Judith Harwin and Jim Orford

At many points in this book the importance of adopting a family perspective on drinking problems has been emphasised, both for understanding the origins of behaviour as well as for understanding its effects. The term 'family perspective' is a loose one and it has been used in different ways by different authors. However, common to all is a belief in the interdependency of behaviour between family members. This interdependency operates in both subtle and obvious ways to shape attitudes as well as behaviour. But while a family perspective emphasises the notion of reciprocity, writers differ in the way in which they wish to use the concept. For some it may simply mean that recognition needs to be paid to the individuals who surround the drinker, by acknowledging both the resources they may bring to the resolution of difficulties as well as the stresses they personally undergo. Others go further and argue that the unit of analysis should be the family rather than the individual person. They suggest that any singling out of one family member as the identified patient may be counter-productive and may serve only to avoid a proper assessment of events occurring at the level of the family as a whole.

It seems to us as editors that the evidence in support of some kind of family perspective is strong, and that less and less can an approach which isolates the individual from his or her family context be regarded as sufficient. But we are equally aware that at the present time the centrality of the family is emphasised far more in theory than in practice.

Resistance to Taking a Family Perspective

Although we had been aware of some resistance to taking a family perspective upon psychological problems in general, and on drinking problems in particular, the compiling of this book has left us in no doubt that such resistance is both subtle and widespread. Despite the trends, noted by both Shaw and Longmate in their chapters, towards an increasing location of drinking practices within the family group,

260

alcohol consumption and alcohol problems in particular are still treated predominantly as individual affairs.

Those authors who have written about treatment for problem drinkers and their families (the chapters by Ritson and Harwin) have told us that it has been, and continues to be, a struggle to establish a family view and to engage family members in the treatment process. The barriers lie in structural aspects of treatment services, as well as in attitudes held both by the public and the professionals. Steinglass has pointed out in his chapter that analysis at the family level has been largely missing from the previous literature, and that the family life cycle approach, a dominant perspective in the general literature on the sociology of the family for more than a decade, is still largely missing from the literature on alcohol problems in the family. There is a fascinating parallel between this neglect of the family and the reluctance of the English legal system, as described by Johns in her chapter, to deal with marital problems where excessive drinking plays a major part.When children are not directly involved, the law is reluctant to intervene in family matters and there is no English equivalent of the Family Court system to be found in some other countries. Provision within the health and social services is similarly structured in a way that makes simultaneous treatment of several family members difficult.

Other contributors have told us of their difficulties in finding sufficient reference to the family within the literature on the specific topic which we asked them to address in their chapter. Despite its clear implications for family functioning, Leland has demonstrated that the literature on sex roles and alcohol use refers little to family life. Longmate's chapter has shown how little of the historical material on the subject refers to families and, hoist by his own petard, one of us was unsuccessful in his search for work on the prevention of drinking problems which was based within families. It seems that most of us have adopted the view of alcohol use and problems which Ghinger and Grant find to be more characteristic of the English or American novel than of English language plays.

Over-specialisation on Alcohol

Working on this book has only reinforced the view felt by both of us, and expressed by one of us some years ago (Orford, 1975), that the accumulated body of theory, knowledge, and practice in the field of alcohol studies has been weaker than it could have been, had it borrowed more from outside the confines of its own specialty. A number of our contributors have through their writings persuaded us to return to this theme in this final chapter.

We consider the chapters that concern children to be particularly persuasive in this regard. Davies has argued that our ideas of how drinking behaviour is transmitted environmentally within the family (he reviews the evidence showing that genetic transmission cannot be ignored either) must be more complex than hitherto. The evidence suggests that the development of drinking attitudes and behaviours cannot be separated from general value orientations and styles of living. This important point adds in our view to the argument for cross-fertilisation between the alcohol studies literature and the far wider and richer literatures on child and adolescent development.

The same could be said of Wilson's chapter on children of excessively drinking parents, and of that section of Orford's chapter which deals with possibilities for prevention amongst such children. The short- and long-term problems faced by such children are hardly unique to them and it seems unlikely that the solutions will be special to this group alone. The themes which Wilson highlights, such as family violence, marital conflict and breakdown in normal parent-child relationships are all general, and raise the question whether there is indeed *anything* special about the family complicated by excessive drinking in a parent. Friendship formation is picked out as being a developmental task which may be interfered with by parental problem drinking. Once again this argues for the establishment of links with other fields, in this case the larger literature in social psychology on friendship choice and the acquaintance process. Orford's plea in his chapter is that we borrow from the now well-established field of community psychology, with its emphasis upon the evaluation of new preventive programmes with high-risk groups.

Our contributors have also brought home to us the need to establish sound links with the ever-growing women's studies literature. Shaw points out the increased importance of women as purchasers and consumers of alcoholic beverages (although Longmate shows that they were special targets for marketing of certain alcoholic drinks in the eighteenth century). Despite this recent trend and the increasing proportion of women amongst problem drinkers, many of our authors (Wilson, Harwin, Jacob and Seilhamer) state that women drinkers and their families have been given proportionately very scant attention in research and writings on alcohol and the family. Although, like Jacob and Seilhamer, Leland concludes that the heterogeneity to be found amongst research subjects is such that generalisable conclusions are difficult to draw, the evidence she reviews on women's sex roles and the effects of drinking convinces us that a full account of women's drinking (and we believe of men's also) cannot be given without some reference to sex roles. If this is the case, then the literature on this subject, which has become enormous in recent years, becomes a must for inspection by the student of alcohol and the family.

Limitations of a Family Perspective

The most important limitation on the use of a family perspective upon drinking problems is the very obvious one that not all excessive drinkers live within families. Indeed, we know that one of the hazards of alcohol abuse is the very high risk it carries of family break-up. Equally, there is a small but important group of drinkers who have never married and who have formed only the loosest of social bonds. For these groups a family perspective can offer little.

There is also a danger of exaggerating the centrality of the family to the neglect of the wider social determinants of behaviour. Shaw has shown how family drinking habits are inextricably bound up with political and economic pressures, reflecting the vagaries of market forces, the changing role of women in society, and policies which restrict or encourage access to alcohol. It is in the sphere of treatment that this broad social perspective has often been neglected; practitioners have accorded primacy to familial interpersonal relationships, forgetting that hostility and conflict may stem as much from financial hardship, employment and housing difficulties as from any clashes of personality or drinking disputes.

Furthermore, one of the most important perspectives advocated by several authors in this book, systems theory, despite its evident advantages, has some particular weaknesses. Steinglass makes clear early in his chapter that the emphasis of the family systems approach is upon stability, maintenance and resistance to change. Although we believe the approach can accommodate change as well as maintenance (morphogenesis as well as morphostasis), we agree that its particular strengths lie in the understanding it affords of *stability*, which is certainly not the whole picture. We know that families complicated by excessive drinking very frequently break up, rather than remain together (as Jacob reminds us in his chapter), and that the involvement of family members in treatment is associated with better outcomes even when the treatment is not aimed at changing the family (Harwin). The theoretical position which Steinglass develops in his chapter places particular emphasis upon the cyclical, on-off nature of intoxication and sobriety. This ignores the fact that amongst those who seek help many have a pattern of continuous, daily heavy drinking.

In her chapter, Harwin recommends a critical examination of general systems theory, looking at both its advantages and disadvantages. We are at least now in the position of being able to choose between two models of alcohol problems and the family, each of which commands widespread support. The general systems theory model is one. The other is a model which views alcohol dependence as a recognisable condition (albeit one which has multiple psychological, social and physiological determinants, and which is more often seen in various shades of grey than as black or white), which causes stress to those in the family who come into close contact with it, and which provokes them into coping in ways which are more or less adaptive and which either serve to maintain or to curtail the excessive drinking of the family's problem drinker. At the present time we think it unlikely that either one of these two models will prove clearly superior to the other in explaining known facts and in eliciting research which produces new findings. Harwin's account of Al-Anon is important in this regard. She describes an organisation which eschews a family systems view but which may nevertheless succeed sometimes in producing changes in family systems in ways that are associated with good outcomes for family members. Both of these models are welcomed, but we would particularly support further experimentation with a systems perspective since our knowledge of this approach still lags behind our understanding of the dependence-stress-coping model.

The Positive Side of Alcohol in the Family

By editing a book on *alcohol* in the family, rather than on alcoholism or problem drinking and the family, we hoped to avoid the exclusively negative view of alcohol in the family which is imparted by a clinical or pathological perspective. To a degree this has been successful. A number of our authors have pointed out that the effects of drinking, even of drinking which is apparently excessive, need not have a negative influence on other family members or upon the family as a whole. Steinglass points out that the findings of his research show that family life is not always disturbed by drinking, even when a family member has been identified as having a drinking problem, and Wilson argues that drinking *per se*, as opposed to such factors as violence and distortion of family relationships which sometimes accompany excessive drinking, need not have negative effects. Longmate warns us against assuming that unhappy states of affairs, such as poverty, are necessarily the effects of over-drinking: indeed historically he believes that the relationship has been the other way around, with poverty the *cause* of heavy drinking. Ghinger and Grant conclude their chapter by stressing that novelists and playwrights have largely seen alcohol as a recreational, celebratory and largely non-problematic accompaniment of other activities. Perhaps, however, we should allow Longmate the last, and controversial, word. He concludes by rejoicing in what he sees as 'the fact that, compared with a hundred or more years ago, alcohol is 'at last coming to occupy its proper place in family life, as a valued companion and friend', and that alcoholic beverages can now be bought in nearly every major supermarket with 'no more moral obloquy attaching to it than to beefburgers or fish fingers'. If deliberately provocative, this nevertheless is intended as a corrective to a view of alcohol as an unmitigated evil.

REFERENCES

Ablon, J. (1974) Al-Anon family groups: impetus for learning and change through the presentation of alternatives. *American Journal of Psychotherapy, 28, 1,* 30-45
—— (1976) Family structure and behaviour in alcoholism: a review of the literature. In: Kissin, B. and Begleiter, H. (eds), *The Biology of Alcoholism, Vol. 4, Social Aspects of Alcoholism,* Plenum Press, New York
ACCEPT (1977) *Second Annual Report,* ACCEPT, London
Aitken, P.P. (1978) *Ten to Fourteen-year-olds and Alcohol,* HMSO, Edinburgh
Albee, Edward (1962) *Who's Afraid of Virgina Woolf?* Atheneum Press, New York
Albretsen, C.S. and Vaglum, P. (1971) The alcoholic's wife and her conflicting roles – a cause for hospitalization. *Acta Sociomedica Scandinavica, 1,* 41-50
—— (1973) The alcholic's wife and her conflicting roles II – a follow-up study. *Scandinavian Journal of the Society of Medicine, 1,* 7-12
Alexander, J. and Parsons, B. (1973) Short-term intervention with delinquent families. *Journal of Abnormal Psychology, 81,* 219-25
Alliance News (1976) Women drink more wine, less tea. Temperance Alliance, Ltd, Nov./Dec., London
Annual Abstract of Statistics (1979), HMSO, London
Argyle, M. (1980) Interactions, skills and social competence. In: Feldman, P. and Orford, J. (eds), *Psychological Problems: The Social Context,* Wiley, Chichester.
Azrin, N.H., Flores, T. and Kaplan, S.J. (1975) Job finding club: a group assisted programme for obtaining employment. *Behaviour Research and Therapy, 13,* 17-28
Bacon, M. (1974) The dependency-conflict hypothesis and the frequency of drunkenness. Further evidence from a cross-cultural study. *Quarterly Journal of Studies on Alcohol, 35,* 863-76
—— (1976) Alcohol use in tribal societies. In: Kissin, B. and Begleiter, H. (eds), *The Biology of Alcoholism, Vol. 4, Social Aspects of Alcoholism,* Plenum Press, New York
Bacon, S.D. (1945) Excessive drinking and the institution of the

of the Family. In: Jellinek, E.M. (ed.), *Alcohol, Science and Society*, Yale Centre of Alcohol Studies, New Haven, Connecticut (reprinted in 1972 by Greenwood, Connecticut)

Bailey, M. (1961) Alcoholism and marriage: a review of research and professional literature. *Quarterly Journal of Studies on Alcohol, 22,* 81-97

Bailey, M., Haberman, P. and Alksne, H. (1962) Outcomes of alcoholic marriages: endurance, termination or recovery. *Quarterly Journal of Studies on Alcohol, 23, 4,* 610-23

Bailey, M.B. (1965) Al-Anon family groups as aids to wives of alcoholics. *Social Work, 10,* 68-74

Bard, M. (1974) The study and modification of intra familial violence. In: Steinmetz, S.K. and Strauss, M.A. (eds.), *Violence in the Family*, Dodd, Mead, New York

Barker, R.G. *et al.* (1978) *Habitats, Environments, and Human Behaviour*, Jossey-Bass, San Francisco

Barry, H. (1976) Cross-cultural evidence that dependency conflict motivates drunkenness. In: Everett, M.W., Waddell, J.O. and Health, D.W. (eds), *Cross-Cultural Approaches to the Study of Alcohol*, Mouton Publishers, The Hague

Barry, H. and Blane, H.T. (1977) Birth positions of alcoholics. *Journal of Individual Psychology, 33 (1),* 62-9

Bastide, M. (1954) Une enquête sur l'opinion publique à l'égarde de l'alcoolisme. *Population, 9,* 13

Bateson, G. (1960) Minimal requirements for a theory of schizophrenia. *Archives of General Psychiatry, 2,* 477-91

Baudelaire, C. (1857) *Les Fleurs du Mal*, Poulet-Malassis et de Broise, Paris

Beckman, L.J. (1975) Women alcoholics: a review of social and psychological studies. *Journal of Studies on Alcohol, 36,* 797-824

—— (1978a) Sex-role conflict in alcoholic women: myth or reality. *Journal of Abnormal Psychology, 87, 4,* 408-17

—— (1978b) Psychosocial aspects of alcoholism in women. In: Seixas, F.A. (ed.), *Currents in Alcoholism, Vol. 4, Psychiatric, Psychological, Social and Epidemiological Studies*, Grune and Stratton, New York

Bedford College Survey (1966) Reported in: McGregor, O.R. Blom-Cooper, L. and Gibson, C. (eds) (1970) *Separated Spouses*, Duckworth, London

Beels, C. and Ferber, A. (1969) Family therapy – a view. *Family Process, 8,* 2

Belsky, J. (1978) Three theoretical models of child abuse: a critical review. *Child Abuse and Neglect, 2*, 37-50

Belson, W. (1979) *Television Violence and the Adolescent Boy*, Saxon House, Farnborough, England

Berman, K.K. (1968) Multiple conjoint family groups in the treatment of alcoholism, *Journal of the Medical Society of New Jersey, 65*, 6-8

Bermann, E. (1973) *Scapegoat*, University of Michigan Press, Ann Arbor

Berne, E. (1961) *Transactional Analysis in Psychotherapy*, Grove Press, New York

—— (1964) *Games People Play*, Grove Press, New York

von Bertalanffy, L. (1968) *General System Theory*, Braziller, New York

Billings, A., Kessler, M., Gomberg, C. and Weiner, S. (1979) Marital conflict resolution of alcoholic and nonalcoholic couples during drinking and nondrinking sessions. *Journal of Studies on Alcohol, 40, 3*, 183-95

Blacker, E. (1966) Sociocultural factors in alcoholism. *International Psychiatry Clinics, 3*, 51

Blane, H.T. (1968) *The Personality of the Alcoholic*, Harper and Row, New York

Blane, H.T. and Chafetz, M.E. (1971) Dependency conflict and sex-role identity in drinking delinquents. *Quarterly Journal of Studies on Alcohol, 32 (4)*, 1025-39

Bloom, B.L., Asher, S.J. and White, S.W. (1978) Marital disruption as a stressor: a review and analysis. *Psychological Bulletin, 85*, 867-94

Booz-Allen and Hamiton, Inc. (1974) *An Assessment of the Needs and Resources for Children of Alcoholic Parents*. Prepared for the US National Institute on Alcohol Abuse and Alcoholism (Rep. No. PB 241-19), National Technical Information Service, Springfield, Va

Boyatzis, R.E. (1976) Drinking as a manifestation of power concerns. in: Everett, M.W., Waddell, J.O. and Heath, D.W. (eds), *Cross-Cultural Approaches to the Study of Alcohol*, Mouton Publishers, The Hague

Brewers' Society (1979) *UK Statistical Handbook*, Brewing Publications Ltd, London

Bronte, A. (1969 edn) *The Tenant of Wildfell Hall*, Panther, London

Brown, G.W. and Harris, T. (1978) *Social Origins of Depression: A Study of Psychiatric Disorder in Women*, Tavistock, London

Bruun, K., Edwards, G., Lumio, M., Makela, K., Pan, L., Popham, R.E., Room, R., Schmidt, W., Skog, O.J., Sulkunen, P. and Osterberg, E. (1975) *Alcohol Control Policies in Public Health Perspective*, Finnish

Foundation for Alcohol Studies, Publication No. 25, Helsinki

Buckley, W. (1967) *Sociology and Modern Systems Theory*, Prentice Hall Inc., Englewood Cliffs, New Jersey

Burton, G. (1962) Group counselling with alcoholic husbands and their non-alcoholic wives. *Marriage and Family Living, 24*, 56-61

Burton, G. and Kaplan, H.M. (1968a) Group counselling in conflicted marriages where alcoholism is present: clients' evaluation of effectiveness. *Journal of Marriage and the Family, 30*, 74-9

—— (1968b) Marriage counselling with alcoholics and their spouses. II. The correlation of excessive drinking behaviour with family pathology and social deterioration. *British Journal of Addiction, 63*, 161-70

Burton, G., Kaplan, H.M. and Hudd, E.H. (1968) Marriage counselling with alcoholics and their spouses. I. A critique of the methodology of a follow-up study. *British Journal of Addiction, 63*, 151-60

Burton, M. (1974) *An Alcoholic in the Family*, Faber and Faber, London

Busch, H. and Feuerlein, W. (1975) Sozialpsychologische aspekte in ehen von alkoholikerinnen (Social-psychological aspects in marriages of alcoholic women). *Schweizer Archiv für Neurologie, Neuroschirurgie und Psychiatrie, 116*, 329-41

Busch, H., Kormendy, E. and Feuerlein, W. (1973) Partners of female alcoholics. *British Journal of Addiction, 68*, 179-84

Bynner, J.M. (1969) *The Young Smoker*, HMSO, London

Cadogan, D.A. (1973) Marital group therapy in the treatment of alcoholism. *Quarterly Journal of Studies on Alcohol, 34*, 1187-94

Cahalan, D. (1970) *Problem Drinkers*, Jossey-Bass, San Francisco

Cahalan, D., Cisin, I.H. and Crossley, H.M. (1969) *American Drinking Practices: A National Study of Drinking Behaviour and Attitudes*, Monograph No. 6, Rutgers Center for Alcohol Studies, New Brunswick

Camberwell Council on Alcoholism (1980) *Women and Alcohol*, Tavistock, London

Caplan, G. (1964) *Principles of Preventive Psychiatry*, Basic Books, New York and Tavistock Publications, London

Caplan, G. and Killilea, M. (eds) (1976) *Support Systems and Mutual Help: Multidisciplinary Explanations*, Grune and Stratton, New York

Cartwright, A.K.J., Shaw, S. and Spratley, T.A. (1975) *Designing a Comprehensive Community Response to Problems of Alcohol Abuse*, Report to the Department of Health and Social Security by the Maudsley Alcohol Pilot Project

Chafetz, M.E., Blane, H.T. and Hill, M.J. (1971) Children of alcoholics: observations in the child guidance clinic. *Quarterly Journal of Studies on Alcohol, 32*, 687-98

Clark, W.B. (1964) *Sex Roles and Alcohol Beverage Usage*, Working Paper No. 16, Social Research Group, School of Public Health, University of California at Berkeley

Clayton, R.R. (1975) *The Family, Marriage and Social Change*, D.C. Heath, Lexington, Mass.

Clifford, B. (1960) A study of the wives of rehabilitated and unrehabilitated alcoholics. *Social Casework, 41*, 457-60

Cochrane, R. and Sobol, M. (1980) Life stresses and psychological consequences. In: Feldman, P. and Orford, J. (eds), *Psychological Problems: The Social Context*, Wiley, Chichester, England

Cohen, P.C. and Krause, M.D. (1971) *Casework with the Wives of Alcoholics*, Family Service Association of America, New York

Coote, A. and Gill, T. (1977) *Battered Women and the New law*, Inter-Action Imprint, 54-90 Prince of Wales Road, London NW5 and National Council for Civil Liberties, London

Corder, B.F., Corder, R.F. and Laidlaw, N.D. (1972) An intensive treatment program for alcoholics and their wives. *Quarterly Journal of Studies on Alcohol, 33*, 1144-6

Cork, R.M. (1969) *The Forgotten Children: A Study of Children with Alcoholic Parents*, Alcoholism and Drug Research Foundation of Ontario, Toronto

Costello, R.M. (1973) Alcoholism treatment and evaluation in search of methods II. *International Journal of Addiction, 10, 5*, 857-76

Cotton, N.S. (1979) The familial incidence of alcoholism: a review. *Journal of Studies on Alcohol, 40*, 89-116

Cowen, E.L. (1980) The community context. In: Feldman, P. and Orford, J. (eds), *Psychological Problems: The Social Context*, Wiley, Chichester, England

Crafoord, C. (1980) Put the booze on the table: some thoughts about family therapy and alcoholism. *Journal of Family Therapy, 2*, 71-81

Davies, J.B. (1981) Drinking and alcohol related problems in five industries. In: Hore, B. and Plant, M. (eds), *Alcohol Problems in Employment*, Croom Helm, London

Davies, J.B. and Stacey, B. (1972) *Teenagers and Alcohol*, HMSO, London

Davies, P. (1979) *Some Comparative Observations on Alcohol Consumption, Alcohol-related Problems and Alcohol Control Policies in the United Kingdom and Other Countries of Europe*, MRC Institute of Medical Sociology, Aberdeen

Davis, D.I., Berenson, D., Steinglass, P. and Davis, D. (1974) The adaptive consequences of drinking. *Psychiatry, 37*, 209-15

Davis, T.S. and Hagood, L. (1979) In-home support for recovering alcoholic mothers and their families: the Family Rehabilitation Co-ordination Project. *Journal of Studies on Alcohol, 40, 3*, 313-17

Demone, H.W. Jr. and Wechsler, H. (1976) Changing drinking patterns of adolescents during the last decade. In: Greenblatt, M. and Schuckit, M.A. (eds), *Alcoholism Problems in Women and Children*, Grune and Stratton, New York

Deniker, P., Saugy, D. and Ropert, M. (1964) The alcoholic and his wife. *Comprehensive Psychiatry, 5*, 374-83

Department of Health and Social Security (1973) *Community Services for Alcoholics*, Circular 21/73, London

―― (1975) *Better Services for the Mentally Ill*, Command no. 6233, HMSO, London

―― (1978) *The Pattern and Range of Services for Problem Drinkers*, Report by the Advisory Committee on Alcoholism, HMSO, London

Departmental Committee on Liquor Licensing (1972) *Report*, Command no. 5154, HMSO, London

Departmental Committee on Scottish Licensing Law (1973) *Report*, Command no. 5354, HMSO, Edinburgh

Dicken, C., Bryson, R. and Kiss, N. (1977) Companionship therapy: a replication in experimental community psychology. *Journal of Consulting and Clinical Psychology, 45*, 637-46

Dight, S. (1976) *Scottish Drinking Habits*, HMSO, London

Dinaberg, D., Glick, I.D. and Feigenbaum, E. (1977) Marital therapy of women alcoholics. *Journal of Studies on Alcohol, 38* 1247-57

Drewery, J. and Rae, J. (1969) A group comparison of alcoholic and non-alcoholic marriages using the interpersonal perception technique. *British Journal of Psychiatry, 115*, 287-300

Dukes, C. (1891) *Alcohol and Childhood*

Durlak, J.A. (1979) *Comparative effectiveness of para-professional and professional helpers.* Psychological Bulletin, *86*, 80-92

Edwards, G.(1971) Public health implications of liquor control. *Lancet, 21*, 424-5

Edwards, G. and Guthrie, S. (1967) A controlled trial of in-patient and out-patient treatment of alcohol dependency. *Lancet, 1*, 555-9

Edwards, G., Chandler, J. and Hensman, C. (1972) Drinking in a London suburb: I. Correlates of normal drinking. *Quarterly Journal of Studies on Alcohol, 6,* 69-93

Edwards, G., Hensman, C. and Peto, J. (1972) Drinking in a London suburb: III. Comparisons of drinking troubles among men and women. In: *Surveys of Drinking and Abstaining: Urban, Suburban and National Studies. Quarterly Journal of Studies on Alcohol,* Supplement No. 6, 120-8

Edwards, G., Orford, J., Egert, S., Guthrie, S., Hawker, A., Hensman, C. Mitcheson, M., Oppenheimer, E. and Taylor, C. (1977) Alcoholism: a controlled trial of 'treatment' and 'advice'. *Journal of Studies on Alcohol, 38 (5),* 1004-31

Edwards, P., Harvey, C. and Whitehead, P. (1973) Wives of alcoholics, a critical review and analysis. *Quarterly Journal of Studies on Alcohol,* 34, 112-32

el-Guebaly, N. and Offord, D.R. (1977) The offspring of alcoholics: a critical review. *American Journal of Psychiatry, 134,* 357-65

Emrick, C.D. (1975) A review of psychologically oriented treatment of alcoholism. II. The relative effectiveness of different treatment approaches and the effectiveness of treatment versus no treatment. *Journal of Studies on Alcohol, 36,* 88-108

Eriksson, K. (1968) Genetic selection for volunary alcohol consumption in albino rats. *Science, 159,* 739

Esser, P.H. (1971) Evaluation of family therapy with alcoholics. *British Journal of Addiction, 66,* 251-5

Ewing, J.A. and Fox, R.E. (1968) Family therapy of alcoholism. In: Masserman, J. (ed.), *Current Psychiatric Therapies,* No. 18, Grune and Stratton, New York, pp. 86-91

Ewing, J.A., Long, V. and Wenzel, G.G. (1961) Concurrent group psychotherapy of alcoholic patients and their wives. *International Journal of Group Psychotherapy, 11, 3,* 329-38

Falender, C.A. and Heber, R. (1975) Mother-child interaction and participation in a longitudinal intervention program. *Developmental Psychology, 11,* 830-6

FARE (1979) *Information on Alcohol and Alcoholism Services Now,* FARE, London

Farquhar, W.J., Maccoby, N. *et al.* (1977) Community education for cardiovascular health. *Lancet, 1,* 1192-5

Finlay, D.G. (1974) Alcoholism: illness or problem in interaction. *Social Work, 19,* 398-405

Fischer, J. (1976) The *Effectiveness of Social Casework,* Charles C. Thomas, Springfield, Illinois

Fitch, M.J. *et al.* (1975) Prospective study on child abuse. Paper presented at the American Public Health Association Convention, Chicago

Flanzer, J.P. and O'Brien, G.M. St. L. (1977) Family focused treatment and management: a multi-discipline training approach. In: Madden, J.S., Walker, R. and Kenyon, W.H. (eds) *Alcoholism and Drug Dependence: A Multidisciplinary Approach*, Plenum, New York

Flintoff, W.P. (1972) As cited in Glatt, M., *The Alcoholic and the Help He Needs*, Priori Press, London

Forrest, G.G. (1978) *The Diagnosis and Treatment of Alcoholism*, Charles C. Thomas, Springfield, Illinois

Foulkes, S.H. and Anthony, E.J. (1965) *Group Psychotherapy*, 2nd edn, Penguin Books, Harmondsworth

Fox, R. (1956) The alcoholic spouse In: Eisenstein, V. (ed.), *Neurotic Interaction in Marriage*, Basic Books, New York

Foy, D.W., Miller, P.M., Eisler, R.M. and O'Toole, D.H. (1976) Social skills training to teach alcoholics to refuse drinks effectively. *Journal of Studies on Alcohol, 37*, 1340-5

Freeman, M.D.A. (1979) *Violence in the Home*, Saxon House, Farnborough, Hants.

French, R.V. (1884) *Nineteen Centuries of Drink in England*, 2nd edn, National Temperance Publications Depot, London

Futterman, S. (1953) Personality trends in wives of alcoholics. *Journal of Psychiatric Social Work, 23*, 37-41

Gacic, B. (1978) Family therapy and alcoholism: research results (paper resulting from research published in Gacic, B. (1978) *Family Therapy of Alcoholism)*

—— (1980) Experiences in evaluation of the family therapy of alcoholism — the Institute for Mental Health in Belgrade. Paper presented at 26th International Institute on the Prevention and Treatment of Alcoholism, Cardiff, 1980

Gayford, J.J. (1975) Wife battering: a preliminary study of 100 cases. British Medical Journal, 1, 194-7

Gelles, R. and Straus, M.A. (1979) Determinants of violence in the family: toward a theoretical integration. In: Burr, W.R., Hill, R., Nye, F.I. and Reiss, I.L.(eds), *Contemporary Theories About the Family, Vol. 1*, Free Press, New York

George, M.D. (1966) *London Life in the Eighteenth Century*, Penguin, Harmondsworth

Gerard, D.L. and Saenger, G. (1966) *Outpatient Treatment of Alcoholism: A Study of Outcome and its Determinants*, University of Toronto Press, Toronto

Gliedman, L.H., Rosenthal, D., Frank, J.D. and Nash, H.T. (1956) Group therapy of alcoholics with concurrent group meetings of their wives. *Quarterly Journal of Studies on Alcohol, 17*, 655-70

Goldberg, D.P. (1972) *The Detection of Psychiatric Illness by Questionnaire*, Oxford University Press, London

Gomberg, E. (1979) Problems with alcohol and other drugs. In: Gomberg, E. and Franks, V. (eds), *Gender and Disordered Behaviour: Sex Differences in Psychopathology*, Brunner/Mazel, New York

Goodman, G. (1972) *Companionship Therapy*, Jossey Bass, San Francisco

Goodwin, D.W. (1976) *Is Alcoholism Hereditary?* Oxford University Press, New York

Goodwin, D.W. and Guze, S.B. (1974) Heredity and alcoholism. In: Kissin, B. and Begleiter, H. (eds), *The Biology of Alcoholism, Vol. 3*, Plenum, New York

Gorman, J.M. and Rooney, J.F. (1979) The influence of Al-Anon on the coping behaviour of wives of alcoholics. *Journal of Studies on Alcohol, 40(11)*, 1030-8

Gray, W., Duhl, F.J. and Rizzo, N.D. (1969) *General Systems Theory and Psychiatry*, Little, Brown, Boston

Gurman, A.S. and Kniskern, D.P. (1978) Research on marital and family therapy: progress, perspective and prospect. In: Garfield, S. and Bergin, A. (eds), *Handbook of Psychotherapy and Behaviour Change*, Wiley, New York

Haberman, P.W. (1964) Psychological test score changes for wives of alcoholics during periods of drinking and sobriety. *Journal of Clinical Psychology, 20*, 230-2

——— (1966) Childhood symptoms in children of alcoholics and comparison group parents. *Journal of Marriage and Family, 28*, 152-4

Hall, P. (1976) *Reforming the Welfare*, Heinemann Educational Books, London

Hall, P., Land, H., Parker, R. and Webb, A. (1975) *Change, Choice and Conflict in Social Policy*, Heinemann Educational Books, London

Hall Williams, E. (1971) The neglect of incest: a criminologist's view. In: Drapkin, I. and Viano, E. (eds), *Victimology: A New Focus, Vol. 4*, Lexington, Massachussets

Hansard (1908) House of Lords, 25 November

Hanson, P., Sands, P. and Sheldon, R. (1968) Patterns of communication in alcoholic marital couples. *Psychiatric Quarterly, 42*, 538-47

Hardy, T. (1886) *The Life and the Death of the Mayor of Caster-*

bridge, Macmillan, London

Harford, T.C. (1978) Contextual drinking patterns among men and women. In: Seixas, F.A. (ed), *Currents in Alcoholism, Vol. 4, Psychiatric, Psychological, Social and Epidemiological Studies*, Grune and Stratton, New York

Hawker, A. (1978) *Adolescents and Alcohol*, Edsall and Co., London

Hawks, D. (1973) Conceptual models and manpower requirements in clinical psychology. *Bulletin of the British Psychological Society, 26*, 207-9

Heber, F.R. (1978) Research in the prevention of sociocultural mental retardation. In: Forgays, D.C. (ed.), *Primary Prevention of Psychopathology, Vol. 2*, University Press of New England, Hanover

Hedberg, A.G. and Campbell, L. (1974) A comparison of four behavioural treatments of alcoholism. *Journal of Behaviour Therapy and Experimental Psychiatry, 5*, 251-6

Hellman, L. (1939) *The Little Foxes*, Viking Press, New York

Hindman, M. (1975) Children of Alcoholic Parents. *Alcohol Health and Research World* (Winter 1975-6), 2-6

Howard, D.P. and Howard, N.T. (1978) The treatment of significant others. In: Zimberg, S., Wallace, J. and Blume, S.B. (eds), *Practical Approaches to Alcoholism Psychotherapy*, Plenum, New York

Hunt, G.M. and Azrin, N.H. (1973) A community reinforcement approach to alcoholism. *Behaviour Research and Therapy, 11*, 91-104

Information Division of the Treasury (1974) *Progress Report*, no. 56, November, London

Jackson, C. (1945) *The Lost Weekend*, Bodley Head, London

Jackson, D.D. (1965) The study of the family. *Family Process, 4*, 1-20

—— (1967) The question of family homeostasis. *Psychiatric Quarterly Supplement, 31*, 79-90

Jackson, J.K. (1954) The adjustment of the family to the crisis of alcoholism. *Quarterly Journal of Studies on Alcohol, 15*, 562-86

Jacob, T. (1975) Family interaction in disturbed and normal families: a methodological and substantive review. *Psychological Bulletin, 82*, 33-65

Jacob, T., Favorini, A., Meisel, A. and Anderson, C. (1978) The alcoholic's spouse, children and family interactions: substantive findings and methodological issues. *Journal of Studies on Alcohol, 39 (7)*, 1231-51

Jahoda, G. and Crammond, J. (1972) *Children and Alcohol*, HMSO,

London

Jahoda, G., Davies, J.B. and Tagg, S. (1980) Parents' alcohol consumption and children's knowledge of drinks and usage patterns. *British Journal of Addiction, 75*, 297-303

James, J. and Goldman, M. (1971) Behaviour trends of wives of alcoholics. *Quarterly Journal of Studies on Alcohol, 32*, 373-81

Janis, I. and Rodin, J. (1979) Attribution, control, and decision-making: social psychology and health care. In: Stove, J.C. and Cohen, F., Adler, N.E. and associates (eds), *Health Psychology: A Handbook*, Jossey-Bass, San Francisco

Jellinek, E.M. (1945) The problems of alcohol in Yale University Center of Alcohol Studies. *Alcohol, Science and Society*, rep. 1972, Greenwood, Connecticut

—— (1960) *The Disease Concept of Alcoholism*, Hillhouse, New Jersey

Jessor, R. and Jessor, S. (1977) *Problem Behaviour and Psychosocial Development: A Longitudinal Study of Youth*, Academic Press, New York

Jessor, R., Graves, T.D., Hanson, R.C. and Jessor, S.L.(1968) *Society, Personality and Deviant Behaviour*, Holt, Rinehart and Winston, New York

Jones, K. (1972) *The History of the Mental Health Services*, Routledge and Kegan Paul, London

Jordan, W. (1972) *The Social Worker in Family Situations*, Routledge and Kegan Paul, London

Kalashian, M. (1959) Working with wives of alcoholics in an outpatient clinic setting. *Marriage and Family, 21*, 130-3

Kammeier, M.L. (1971) Adolescents from families with and without alcohol problems. *Quarterly Journal of Studies on Alcohol, 32*, 364-72

Keane, A. and Roche, D. (1974) Developmental disorders in the children of male alcoholics. Proc. 20th International Institute on the Prevention and Treatment of Alcoholism, Manchester, ICAA Lausanne

Kennedy, D.L. (1976) Behaviour of alcoholics and spouses in a simulation game situation. *Journal of Nervous and Mental Disease, 162*, 23-34

King, R. (1979) Drinking and drunkenness in Crossroads and Coronation Street. In: Cook, J. and Lewington, M. (eds), *Images of Alcoholism*, British Film Institute, London

Klein, N.C., Barton, C. and Alexander, J.F. (1980) Intervention and evaluation in family settings. In: Price, R.H. and Politser, P.E. (eds),

Evaluation and Action in the Social Environment, Academic Press, New York

Knupfer, G. (1964) Female drinking patterns. In: *Selected Papers Presented at the 15th Annual Meeting of the North American Association of Alcoholism Programs, Washington, D.C.*

Lask, B. (1980) Evaluation – why and how (a guide for clinicians). *Journal of Family Therapy, 2*, 110-21

Law Commission (1973) Matrimonial proceedings in magistrates courts. Law Commission Published Working Paper, no. 53

—— (1976) Matrimonial proceedings in magistrates courts. Law Commission Report no. 77

Ledermann, S. (1956) *Alcool, Alcoolisme, Alcoolisation*, Presses Universitaires de France, Paris

Lees, F.R. and Burns, D. (1894) *The Temperance Bible Commentary*, 6th edn, National Temperance Depot, London

Lemert, E. (1960) The occurrence and sequence of events in adjustment of families to alcoholism. *Quarterly Journal of Studies on Alcohol, 21* 679-97

—— (1962) Dependency in married alcoholics. *Quarterly Journal of Studies on Alcohol, 23 (4)*, 590-609

Lewis, M. (1937) Alcoholism and family casework. *Family, 18*, 39-44

de Lint, J. (1977) The frequency distribution of alcohol consumption: an overview. In: *The Ledermann Curve: Report of a Symposium*, Alcohol Education Centre, London

Longmate, N. (1968) *The Waterdrinkers – A History of Temperance*, Hamish Hamilton, London

Lorion, R.P. (1978) Research on psychotherapy and behaviour change with the disadvantaged. In: Garfield, S.L. and Bergin, A.E. (eds), *Handbook of Psychotherapy and Behaviour Change*, 2nd edn, Wiley, New York

Lowry, M. (1947) *Under the Volcano*, Jonathan Cape, London

MacAndrew, C. and Geertsma, R.H. (1963) An analysis of responses of alcoholics to Scale 4 of the MMPI. *Quarterly Journal of Studies on Alcohol, 24 (1)*, 23-38

Macdonald, D.E. (1958) Group psychotherapy with wives of alcoholics. *Quarterly Journal of Studies on Alcohol, 19*, 125-32

Maisch, H. (1973) *Incest*, Andre Deutsch, London

Mäkelä, K. (1970) The frequency of drinking occasions according to consumed beverages and qualities before and after the new liquor laws. *Alkoholipolitukka, 35*, 246

—— (1975) Consumption level and cultural drinking patterns as determinants of alcohol problems. *Journal of Drug Issues, 5*, 344

Mandelbaum, D.G. (1967) Alcohol and culture. *Current Anthropology, 6 (3)*, 281

Mannino, F.V. and Shore, M.F. (1972) Ecologically oriented family intervention. *Family Process, 11*, 499-505

Martin, F.E. (1977) Some implications from the theory and practice of family therapy and individual therapy. *British Journal of Medical Psychology, 50*, 53-64

Maslow, A.H. (1970) *Motivation and Personality*, Harper and Row, New York

Mayer, J. and Black, R. (1977) The relationship between alcoholism and child abuse and neglect. In: Seixas, F.A. (ed.), *Currents in Alcoholism, Vol. 2, Psychiatric, Social and Epidemiological Studies*, Grune and Stratton, New York

McClelland, D.C., Davis, W.N., Kalin, R. and Wanner, E. (1972) *The Drinking Man*, Free Press, New York

McCord, W. and McCord, J. (1960) *Origins of Alcholism*, Stanford University Press, Stanford, California

McGuire, W.J. (1980) Communication and social influence processes. in: Feldman, P. and Orford, J. (eds), *Psychological Problems: The Social Context*, Wiley, Chichester, England

McLachlan, J.F.C., Walderman, R.L. and Thomas, S. (1973) *A Study of teenagers with Alcoholic Parents*, Donwood Institute Research Monograph, no. 3, Toronto

Meeks, D.E. and Kelly, C. (1970) Family therapy with the families of recovering alcoholics. *Quarterly Journal of Studies on Acohol, 31*, 339-413

Ministry of Health (1968) Memorandum HM (68) 37, *The Treatment of Alcoholism*, London

Miller, P.M. (1976) *Behavioural Treatments of Alcoholism*, Pergamon, Oxford

Minuchin, S. (1974) *Families and Family Therapy*, Tavistock Publications, London

Minuchin, S., Montalvo, B., Guerney, B.G., Rosman, B.L. and Shumer, F. (1967) *Families of the Slums: An Exploration of their Structure and Treatment*, Basic Books, New York

Mischler, E. and Waxler, N. (eds) (1968) *Family Process and Schizophrenia*, Science House, New York

Moos, R. and Moos, B. (1976) A typology of family social environments. *Family Process, 15*, 357-71

Morewood, S. (1824) *An Essay on the Inventions and Customs of Both*

Ancient and Moderns in the Use of Intoxicating Liquors, printed for Longman, Hurst, Rees, Orme, Brown and Green, London

Moss, M.C. and Beresford Davies, E. (1967) *A Survey of Alcoholism in an English County*, Cambridge (private publisher)

Murray, R. (1977) The alcoholic doctor. *British Journal of Hospital Medicine, 18*, 144-9

Myerson, D.J. (1966) A therapeutic appraisal of certain married alcoholic women. *International Psychiatry Clinics, 3*, 143-57

O'Connor, J. (1975) Cultural influences and drinking behaviour: drinking in Ireland and England: a tri-ethnic study of drinking among young people and their parents. *Journal on Alcoholism, 10*, 94-121

—— (1978) *The Young Drinkers: A Cross-national Study of Social and Cultural Influences*, Tavistock, London

O'Neill, E. (1941) *Long Day's Journey into Night*, Jonathan Cape, London

Office of Population Censuses and Surveys (1970) *Classification of Occupations*, HMSO, London

—— (1980) *General Household Survey 1979 (GHS 80/1) Government Statistical Service*, HMSO, London

Orford, J. (1975) Alcoholism and marriage: the argument against specialism. *Journal of Studies on Alcohol, 36, 11*, 1537-63

—— (1976) A study of the personalities of excessive drinkers and their wives, using the approaches of Leary and Eysenck. *Journal of Consulting and Clinical Psychology, 44* 534-45

—— (1977) Alcohol and the family. In: Grant, M. and Gwinner, P. (eds), *Alcoholism in Perspective*, Croom Helm, London

Orford, J. and Edwards, G. (1977) *Alcoholism: A Comparison of Treatment and Advice with a Study of the Influence of Marriage*, Oxford University Press, London

Orford, J. and Guthrie, S. (1976) Coping behaviour used by wives of alcoholics: a preliminary investigation. In: Edward, G., Russell, M.A.H., Hawks, D. and MacCafferty, M. (eds), *Alcohol Dependence and Smoking Behaviour*, Saxon House, Westmead, Hants

Orford, J., Guthrie, S., Nicholls, P., Oppenheimer, E., Egert, S. and Hensman, C. (1975) Self-reported coping behaviour of wives of alcoholics and its association with drinking outcome. *Journal of Studies on Alcohol, 36*, 1254-67

Orford, J., Oppenheimer, E. and Edwards, G. (1976a) Abstinence or Control: The Outcome for Excessive Drinkers Two Years after Consultation. *Behaviour Research and Therapy, 14*, 409-18

Orford, J., Oppenheimer, E., Egert, S., Hensman, C. and Guthrie, S.

(1976b) The cohesiveness of alcoholism-complicated marriages and its influence on treatment outcome. *British Journal of Psychiatry, 128*, 318-39

Orford, J., Waller, S. and Peto, J. (1974) Drinking behaviour and attitudes and their correlates amongst English university students. *Quarterly Journal of Studies on Alcohol, 35*, 1316-74

Otto, S. (1977) Women, alcohol and work. In: Grant, M. and Kenyon, W.H. (eds), *Alcoholism and Industry*, Alcohol Education Centre, London

Packman, J. (1975) *The Child's Generation*, Blackwell, Oxford

Paolino, T.J. and McGrady, B.S. (1977) *The Alcoholic Marriage: Alternative Perspectives*, Grune and Stratton, New York

Paolino, T., McGrady, B., Diamond, S. and Longabaugh, R. (1976) Psychological disturbances in spouses of alcoholics. *Journal of Studies on Alcohol, 37*, 1600-8

Park, P. (1967) Dimensions of drinking among male college students. *Social Problems, 14*, 472-82

Parker, F.B. (1972) Sex-role adjustment in women alcoholics. *Quarterly Journal of Studies on Alcohol, 33 (3)*, 647-57

—— (1975) Sex-role adjustment and drinking disposition of women college students. *Journal of Studies on Alcohol, 36 (11)*, 1570-3

Patterson, G.R., Hops, H. and Weiss, R.L. (1975) Interpersonal skills training for couples in early stages of conflict. *Journal of Marriage and the Family, 37*, 295-303

Pattison, E.M. (1965) Treatment of alcoholic families with nurse home visits. *Family Process, 4, 1*, 75-94

Pattision, E.M., Courlas, P.G., Patti, R., Mann, B. and Mullen, D. (1965) Diagnostic-therapeutic intake groups for wives of alcoholics. *Quarterly Journal of Studies on Alcohol, 26*, 605-16

Pearson, H. (1948) *The Smith of Smiths, being the Life, Wit and Humour of Sydney Smith, etc.*, Penguin Books in Association with Hamish Hamilton, London

Penrose, G.B. (1978) Perceptions of 5 and 6-year-old children concerning cultural drinking norms. Unpublished PhD thesis, University of California, Berkeley

Pittman, F.S. and Flomenhaft, K.(1970) Treating the doll's house marriage. *Family Process, 9*, 143-55

Pixley, J.M. and Stiefel, J.R. (1963) Group therapy designed to meet the needs of the alcoholic's wife. *Quarterly Journal of Studies on Alcohol, 24*, 304-13

Plant, M. (1979) *Drinking Careers*, Tavistock, London

Price, G. (1945) A study of the wives of twenty alcoholics. *Quarterly Journal of Studies on Alcohol, 5*, 620-7

Priestley, P., McGuire, J., Flegg, D., Hemsley, V. and Welham, D. (1978) *Social Skills and Personal Problem Solving: A Handbook of Methods*, Tavistock, London

Rabalais, F. (1962) *Garguantua et Pantagruel*, Edition Gérard, Verviers

Radzinowicz, L. (1974) Preface. In: Hood, R., *Crime, Criminology and Public Policy*. Heinemann Educational Books, London

Rae, J.B. and Forbes, A.R. (1966) Clinical and psychometric characteristics of the wives of alcoholics. *British Journal of Psychiatry, 112*, 197-200

Ratcliffe, M. (1979) Catch a woman customer. Supermarketing, 30 March

Report of Select Committee on Violence in Marriage (1975) Cmnd 533

Reports to the Secretary of State for the Home Department on the State of the Law relating to Brutal Assaults (1875) (C 1138) LX 129

Rhys, J. (1930) *After Leaving Mr Mackenzie*, Jonathan Cape, London
—— (1939) *Good Morning Midnight*, Constable, London

de Ricco, D.A. (1978) Effects of peer majority on drinking rate. *Addictive Behaviours, 3*, 29-34

Ridge, J.J. (1894) *The Band of Hope Catechism*, United Kingdom Band of Hope, London

Riecken, H.W. and Boruch, R.F. (eds) (1974) *Social Experimentation: A Method for Planning and Evaluating Social Intervention*, Academic Press, New York

Rieth, E. (1974) Die personalichkeit des alkolikers. *Fursorger, 42*, 1-13

Rimmer, J. (1974) Psychiatric illness in husbands of alcoholics. *Quarterly Journal of Studies on Alcohol, 35*, 281-3

Rimmer, J. and Winokur, G. (1972) The spouses of alcoholics: an example of assortative mating. *Diseases of the Nervous System, 33*, 509-11

Ritson, B. (1968) Th prognosis of alcohol addicts treated by specialised units. *British Journal of Psychiatry, 114*, 1019-29

Ritson, B. and Hassall, C. (1970) *The Management of Alcoholism*, Livingstone, Edinburgh

Robinson, D. (1979) *Talking Out of Alcoholism*, Croom Helm, London and University Park Press, Baltimore

Roizen, R., Cahalan, D. and Shanks, P. (1978) Spontaneous remission among untreated problem drinkers. In: Kandel, D.D. (ed), *Longitudinal Research on Drug Use: Emprical Findings and Methodological Issues*, Wiley, New York

Room, R. (1972) Comment on the alcohologist's addiction. *Quarterly Journal of Studies on Alcohol, 33*, 953

Royal College of Psychiatrists (1979) *Alcohol and Alcoholism: The Report of a Special Committee*, Tavistock, London

Royal Commission on Divorce and Matrimonial Causes (1909-1912) Command no. 6478

Royal Commission on Marriage and Divorce (1951-1955) Command no. 9678

Rutter, M. (1966) *Children of Sick Parents*, Maudsley Monograph, no. 16, Oxford University Press, London

Rutter, M., Maughan, B., Mortimore, P. and Ouston, J. (1979) *Fifteen Thousand Hours: Secondary Schools and Their Effects on Children*, Open Books, London

Sadoun, R., Lolli, G. and Silverman, M. (1965) *Drinking in French Culture*, Rutgers Centre for Alcohol Studies, Mongraph 5, New Brunswick, New Jersey

Sartre, J.P. (1946) *Two Plays*, Hamish Hamilton, London

Saunders, W. and Kershaw, P. (1979) Spontaneous remission from alcoholism — a community study. *British Journal of Addiction, 74*, 251-66

Schaefer, H.H., Sobell, M.B. and Mills, K.C. (1971) Baseline drinking in alcoholics and social drinkers: kinds of drink and sip magnitude. *Behaviour Research and Therapy, 9*, 23-7

Schuckit, M., Goodwin, D.W. and Winokur, G. (1972) A study of alcoholism in half-siblings. *American Journal of Psychiatry, 128*, 1132-6

Schuckit, M.A. and Morrissey, E.R. (1976) Alcoholism in women: some clinical and social perspectives with an emphasis on possible subtypes. In: Greenblatt, M. and Schuckit, M.A. (eds), *Alcoholism Problems in Women and Children*, Grune and Stratton, New York

Scida, J. and Vannicelli, M. (1979) Sex-role conflict and women's drinking. *Journal of Studies on Alcohol, 40 (1)*, 28-44

Scott, P.D. (1966) Compulsion in the treatment of alcoholism *British Medical Journal, 1*, 291

Seebohm Report (1968) *The Report of the Committee on Local Authority and Allied Personal Social Services*, Command no. 3303, HMSO, London

Shapiro, R.J. (1977) A family therapy approach to alcoholism. *Journal of Marriage and Family Counselling, 3 (4)*, 71-8

Shaw, S. (1980) The causes of increasing drinking problems amongst women. In: Camberwell Council on Alcoholism, *Women and Alcohol*, Tavistock, London

Shaw, S., Cartwright, A., Spratley, T. and Harwin, J. (1978) *Responding to Drinking Problems*, Croom Helm, London

Shepherd, M., Cooper, B., Brown, A.C. and Kalton, G.W. (1966) *Psychiatric Illness in General Practice*, Oxford University Press, London

Shepherd, M., Harwin, B.G., Depla, C. and Kairns, V. (1979) Social work and the primary care of mental disorder. *Psychological Medicine, 9,* 661-9

Shields, J. (1977) Genetics and alcoholism. In: Edwards, G. and Grant, M. (eds), *Alcoholism: New Knowledge and New Responses*, Croom Helm, London

Simboli, P. (1976) Acculturated drinking practices and problem drinking among three generations of Italians in America. PhD dissertation, School of Public Health, University of California, Berkeley

Skynner, A.C.R. (1969) Indications and contra-indications for conjoint family therapy. *International Journal of Social Psychiatry, 15,* no. 4, 245-9

Skynner, R.A. (1976) *One Flesh, Separate Persons,* Constable and Constable, London

Smart, R. and Fejer, D. (1972) Drug use among adolescents and their parents: closing the generation gap in mood modification. *Journal of Abnormal Psychology, 79,* 153-60

Smith, C.G. (1969) Alcoholics: their treatment and their wives. *British Journal of Psychiatry, 115,* 1039-42

Smith, M.L. and Glass, G.V. (1977) Meta-analysis of psychotherapy outcome studies. *American Psychologist, 32,* 752-60

Smollett, T. (1758) *A Complete History of England from the Descent of Julius Caesar to the Treaty of Aix la Chapelle,* 2nd edn, Rivington, J. and Fletcher, J., London

Snyder, C. (1962) *Alcohol and the Jews,* Free Press, Glencoe, Illinois

Speer, D.D. (1970) Family systems: morphostasis and morphogenisis or is homeostasis enough? *Family Process, 9,* 259-79

Spender, S. (1967) Introduction. In: Lowry, M., *Under the Volcano,* Jonathan Cape, London

Spring, J.A. and Buss, D.H. (1977) Three centuries of alcohol in Britain. *Nature, 270,* 567

Stacey, B. and Davies, J. (1970) Drinking behaviour in childhood and adolescence. *British Journal of Addiction, 65,* 203-12

Stafford, R.A. and Petway, J.M. (1977) Stigmatization of men and women problem drinkers and their spouses:differential perception and leveling of sex differences. *Journal of Studies on Alcohol, 38 (11)*, 2109-21

Staulcup, H., Kenwood, K. and Frigo, D. (1979) A review of federal primary alcoholism prevention projects. *Journal of Studies on Alcohol, 40*, 943-68

Steiner, C.M. (1969) The alcoholic game. *Quarterly Journal of Studies on Alcohol, 30*, 920-38

—— (1971) *Games Alcoholics Play*, Ballantine Books, New York

Steinglass,P. (1976) Experimenting with family treatment approaches to alcoholism, 1950-1975: a review. *Family Process, 15*, 97-123

—— (1979) An experimental treatment program for alcoholic couples. *Journal of Studies on Alcohol, 40 (3)*, 149-182

—— (1980) A life history model of the alcoholic family. *Family Process, 19*, 211-26

—— (1981) The alcoholic family at home: patterns of interaction in dry, wet, and transitional stages of alcoholism. *Archives of General Psychiatry, 38*, 578-84

Steinglass, P., Davis, D.I. and Berenson, D. (1977) Observations of conjoint hospitalised alcoholic couples during sobriety and intoxication: implications for theory and therapy. *Family Process, 16*, 1-16

Steinglass, P., Weiner, S. and Mendelson, J.H. (1971) A systems approach to alcoholism: a model and its clinical application. *Archives of General Psychiatry, 24*, 401-8

Streissguth, A.P. (1976) Maternal alcoholism and the outcome of pregnancy: a review of the fetal alcohol syndrome. In: Greenblatt, M. and Shuckit, M.A. (eds), *Alcohol Problems in Women and Children*, Grune and Stratton, New York

Sulkunen, P. (1976) Drinking patterns and the level of alcohol consumption: an international overview. In: Gibbins, R.J., Israel, Y., Kalant, H., Popham, R.E., Schmidt, W. and Smart, R.G. (eds), *Research Advances in Alcohol and Drug Problems, Vol 3*, Wiley, New York

Tamerin, J.S. (1978) The psychotherapy of alcoholic women. In: Zimberg, S., Wallace, J. and Blume, S.B. (eds), *Practical Approaches to Alcoholism Therapy*, Plenum Press, New York

Tamerin, J., Weiner, S. and Mendelson, J.H. (1970) Acoholics' expectancies and recall of experiences during intoxication. *American Journal of Psychiatry, 126*, 1697-704

Tizard, J. and Grad, J.C. (1961) *The Mentally Handicapped and their Families: A Social Survey*, Maudsley Monograph, no. 7, Oxford University Press, London

Tolstoy, L. (1877) *Anna Karenina*, Oxford University Press (1965 edn), London

Turner, E.S. (1950) *Roads to Ruin*, Michael Joseph, London and Collins, Toronto

Ullman, A. (1958) Sociocultural backgrounds of alcoholism. *Annals of the American Academy of Political and Social Science, 315*, 48

Walrond-Skinner, S. (1976) *Family Therapy, the Treatment of Natural Systems*, Routledge and Kegan Paul, London

Waterhouse, J. (1978) Group work in intermediate treatment. *British Journal of Social Work, 8*, 127-44

Weiner, S., Tamerin, J., Steinglass, P. and Mendelson, J.H. (1971) Familial patterns in chronic alcoholism: a study of a father and son during experimental intoxication. *American Journal of Psychiatry, 127*, 1646-51

Wells, R., Dilkes, T. and Trivelli, N. (1972) The results of family therapy: a critical review of the literature. *Family Process, 11*, 189-207

Wesson, J. (1979) Personal communication

Westermeyer, J. (1978) Social events and narcotic addiction: the influence of war and law on opium use in Laos. *Addictive Behaviours, 3*, 57-62

Wilkins, R.H. (1974) *The Hidden Alcoholic in General Practice*, Elek Scientific Books, London

Wilkinson, R. (1970) *The Prevention of Drinking Problems: Alcohol Control and Cultural Influences*, Oxford University Press, New York

Williams, A.F. (1976) The alcoholic personality. In: Kissin, B. and Begleiter, H. (eds), *Social Aspects of Alcoholism*, Plenum Press, New York

Wilsnack, R.W. and Wilsnack, S.C. (1978) Sex roles and drinking among adolescent girls. *Journal of Studies on Alcohol, 39 (11)*, 1855-74

Wilsnack, S.C. (1973) Sex role identity in female alcoholism. *Journal of Abnormal Psychology, 82 (2)*, 253-61

—— (1974) The effects of social drinking on women's fantasy. *Journal of Personality, 42 (1)*, 43-61

—— (1976) The impact of sex roles and women's alcohol use and abuse. In: Greenblatt, M. and Schuckit, M.A. (eds), *Alcoholism Problems in Women and Children*, Grune and Stratton, New York

Wilsnack, S.C. and Wilsnack, R.W. (in press) Sex roles and adolescent drinking. In: Chafetz, M.E. and Blane, H.T. (eds), *Youth, Alcohol and Social Policy,* Plenum Press, New York

Wilson, C. and Orford, J. (1978) Children of alcoholics: report of a preliminary study and comments on the literature. *Journal of Studies on Alcohol, 39,* 121-42

Wilson, C.A. (1973) *Food and Drink in Britain,* Constable, London

Wilson, P. (1980) *Drinking in England and Wales,* HMSO, London

Winch, R. (1967) Another look at the theory of complementary needs in mate-selection. *Journal of Marriage and the Family, 29,* 756-62

Winokur, G. (1976) Alcoholism in adoptees raised apart from biologic alcoholic parents. In: Greenblatt, M. and Schuckit, M.A. (eds), *Alcoholism Problems in Women and Children,* Grune and Stratton, New York

Winskill, T. (1881) *The Comprehensive History of the Rise and Progress of the Temperance Reformation from the Earliest Period to September 1881,* Privately printed and sold by the author, Warrington

Wolff, P.H. (1972) Ethnic differences in alcohol sensitivity. *Science, 175,* 449-50

Wolin, S.J. Bennett, L.A. and Noonan, D.L. (1979) Family rituals and the recurrence of alcoholism over generations. *American Journal of Psychiatry, 136, (4b),* April, 589-93

Wood, H.P. and Duffy, E.L. (1966) Psychological factors in alcoholic women. *American Journal of Psychiatry, 123,* 341-5

Yalom, I.O. (1974) Group therapy and alcoholism. In: Seixas, F.A., Cadoret, R. and Eggleston, S. (eds), *The Person with Alcoholism, Annals of the New York Academy of Science, 233,* 85-103

Yelloly, M.A. (1980) *Social Work Theory and Psychoanalysis,* Van Nostrand Reinhold Company, Wokingham, Berkshire

Zacune, J. and Hensman, C. (1971) *Drugs, Alcohol and Tobacco in Britain,* Heinemann, London

Zax, M. and Specter, G.A. (1974) *An Introduction to Community Psychology,* Wiley, New York

Zucker, R.A. (1976) Parental influences on the drinking patterns of their children. In: Greenblatt, M. and Shuckit, M.A. (eds), *Alcoholism Problems in Women and Children,* Grune and Stratton, New York

NOTES ON CONTRIBUTORS

John B. Davies, PhD, Senior Lecturer in Psychology, University of Strathclyde, Scotland

Marcus Grant, MA, Director, Alcohol Education Centre, The Maudsley Hospital, London, England

Carol Ghinger, Research Fellow, Social Research Group, School of Public Health, University of California, Berkeley, USA

Judith Harwin, BA, Lecturer in Social Work, London School of Economics, England

Theodore Jacob, PhD, Associate Professor of Psychology and Psychiatry, Department of Psychology, University of Pittsburgh, Pittsburgh, Pennsylvania, USA

Heather Johns, LLB, Solicitor and Research Student, London School of Economics, England

Joy Leland, PhD, Research Professor, Social Sciences Center, Desert Research Institute, University of Nevada System, Reno, Nevada, USA

Norman Longmate, MA, freelance writer, working in the Secretariat of the BBC, Broadcasting House, London, England

Jim Orford, PhD, Senior Lecturer in Clinical Psychology, University of Exeter and Principal Clinical Psychologist, Exeter Health Care District, Devon, England

E. Bruce Ritson, MD, Consultant Psychiatrist and Senior Lecturer, University Department of Psychiatry, Royal Edinburgh Hospital, Edinburgh, Scotland

Ruth Ann Seilhamer, BS, Department of Psychology, University of Pittsburgh, Pittsburgh, Pennsylvania, USA

Stan Shaw, MSc, Research Sociologist, Detoxification Evaluation Project, The Maudsley Hospital, London, England

Peter Steinglass, MD, Professor of Psychiatry and Behavioural Sciences, Center for Family Research, George Washington University School of Medicine, Washington DC, USA

Clare Wilson, BSc, Research Psychologist, Addiction Research Unit, Institute of Psychiatry, London, England

AUTHOR INDEX

SUBJECT INDEX

advertising 71
Al-Anon 117, 145, 191, 196, 231-4;
  effectiveness 233-4; organisation
  231; philosophy and practice
  232-3
Al-Ateen 145, 163, 191
Alcoholics Anonymous 145, 190-1
attitudinal change 87

behavioural treatment 221-4;
  aversion therapy 222;
  effectiveness of 223-4; goal,
  principles, practice 222-3
beverages: beer 13, Beer Act 16-17;
  gin 14-15; whiskey 12; wine
  12-13; alcohol free 19

children: alcoholic 9, 24; knowledge
  of alcoholic drinks 78-80, social
  learning of 81-2; see also young
  persons
children of alcoholics 151-66; abuse,
  neglect of 14-15, 21-2, 153-4,
  see also legislation; additional
  roles undertaken 159-60; antisocial behaviour 161-2; emotional
  problems 162; family structure
  156-8, only child 157, separation
  from parents 156-7, sibling
  relationships 157; family therapy
  with 165-6, 198-9, 218; learning
  difficulties 162; parental conflict
  152-3; parental drinking patterns
  158; parent-child relationship
  154-6, social distance 155, with
  non-drinking parent 156;
  prevention for 253-6; research
  into 151-2; risk of alcoholism in
  162; services for 163-5, see also
  Al-Ateen; social isolation 160-1;
  see also foetal alcohol syndrome
  and transmission

deviancy theory 83-4, 103-4
drinking practices: aggregation
  theory 67; class differences 15-16,
  62, see also working class
  drunkeness; in history 9-24,
  ancient times 9-11, Middle Ages

11-12, modern times 13-24;
  modern British 61-72, rising consumption in 67-8; social
  influences on 56-72, American
  Jewish and -Irish 56-7, reduction
  in national differences 60, viticultural and non-viticultural
  57-61

ecological programmes 225-9; community reinforcement approach
  227-8; family rehabilitation
  coordinators 227; significant
  features of 228

family casework 207-10
family perspective 260-5; limitations
  of 263-5; overspecialisation,
  effects of 261-3; positive view of
  alcohol 264-5; resistance to 260-1
family systems theory 127-50, 159;
  alcohol in systems maintenance
  139-41; bargain, quid quo pro
  134; basic principles 128-32,
  boundaries 132, communication
  patterns 132, family as system
  132, homeostasis 130-1, identified patient 131; comparison
  with other models 137, 141;
  distinctive features of alcoholic
  family 133-4; life-cycle model
  142-50, and interactive pattern
  146-50, and social stress theory
  143, phases 143-6; patterns of
  interaction 134-9; see also family
  therapy, spouses
family therapy 194-200, 210-18; and
  general systems theory 210-12;
  community education about 197;
  comparative effectiveness 215-17;
  disadvantages 217; first
  assessment interview 198; group
  therapy 196; in US health care
  system 197; involving children in
  165-6, 198-9, 218; logistical
  problems 194-5; origins of 197-8;
  studies of treatment by GST
  family therapy 212-15; therapist
  styles 199

293